# The Stolen Light

Yitzchak (Izo) Leibowitz

The stories in this book are all based on true stories, and were told personally to the author. The names of those involved have been changed to maintain their privacy.

The Stolen Light
by: Yitzchak (Izo) Leibowitz
Translated by: Rivka Levy and Joshua Genuth

NaNach Nation, Inc.
www.nanachnation.org
nanachnation@gmail.com

Ordering Information:
Quantity sales. Special discounts are available on quantity purchases by corporations, associations, Meifitzim and others. For details, contact the publisher at the address above.

The Stolen Light

ISBN 978-1-943726-14-1

10 9 8 7 6 5 4 3 2 1

Second Edition

Printed in Israel

# Table of Contents

With Hashem's Help and Loving Kindness

# The Stolen Light

### Translator's Foreword

The following accounts are all based on true stories, and were told personally to the author. The names of those involved have been changed to maintain their privacy. In order to maintain the flavor of the original narratives, I retained many of the original Hebrew terms (*in italics*), particularly those referring to Jewish ideas and concepts. You can find detailed explanations of these terms in The Glossary at the back of the book.

I'd like to thank Sarah Prais for her help with the translation; G-d for all of His kindnesses and for keeping me alive every day; my husband and kids for being them; and Rebbe Nachman for giving me the merit of working on this book.

B.R.L.

# The Stolen Light

**Prologue**

ROSH HASHANA EVE. It's the dawn of the New Year, and I'm in the city of Uman, in the country of Ukraine, on 5 Pushkina Street, Apartment 9.

I'm sitting in the small apartment, studying the weird people on all sides of me, and wondering to myself, *'what on earth am I doing here?'*

It occurs to me that if my friends could see me now in this absurd situation, they'd be laughing harder than they'd ever laughed before.

And do you know why? Because I'm known amongst my *chevra*, my group of friends, for being a fanatical atheist. I'm vehemently opposed to anything religious - especially anything religiously Jewish - and that's why it's so hysterically funny that on Erev Rosh Hashana I'm sitting here in this room, surrounded by a motley bunch of *baalei teshuva* and uber-orthodox guys from Meah Shearim, Bnei Brak, Elad, Bet Shemesh and Tzfat. As the night goes on, I'm discovering that each guy's story is more bizarre than the next.

What's going on here? It's like being stuck in some surrealist play or *film noir* that gets more and more absurdly unreal and unbelievable with each passing minute. The only difference is, this is no cinema - these guys are passing their stories off as completely true.

It's just before 10:30pm. Not much longer till we're supposed to be eating our evening meal. I'm squashed around a table with 30 other guys, some of whom I already know, but most of whom I've never seen before. We're packed into a small, stinky room on the ninth floor of an awful concrete building in Uman, in the Ukraine. I'm looking at all the salads, fish and meat that are piled on the table and feeling ravenously hungry. At least the food looks like it belongs in the 21st century.

# The Stolen Light

The man who made all the food is Pinchas Bardogo, a really scary, funny character that you'll hear more about a little later. Bardogo is the group's cook. When a few of us got to the apartment a couple of days before the holiday started, Bardogo enlisted us in his intensive training program for junior cooks, and together, we cooked up enough food to feed a whole army battalion for a month.

So there's me, and thirty other people who don't stop smiling and laughing, which is kind of surprising to me - I was sure that hanging out with all these *charedim* was going to be one of the most boring, annoying and miserable experiences of my life. Naturally, bizarre religious topics are their main conversational content – but inexplicably, they're having a great time about it. Even though I look like I'm part of their group, I don't buy a word of what they're saying; but I'm smiling and nodding along with everyone else despite the fact that really, I'm not one of them. I don't think like they do, or believe like they do, or have the slightest interest in believing like they do.

I am starving and desperately waiting to eat, but I'm even more desperately waiting for when the meal is actually going to be over, for reasons that I'll tell you about in a minute. But these people seem to have all the time in the world. They aren't in any rush to eat, and it looks like none of them are even planning to go to sleep tonight.

I have no idea when these people actually *do* sleep, or if they even sleep at all. They're completely energized all the time, praying, learning, talking, eating - sorry, they're not actually *eating;* they're just 'raising up the holy sparks' - that's how they explain away the fact that they need to eat. They have 'holy' reasons for everything. They can't just admit that they're really hungry and they feel like packing in a juicy steak or something. No, they have to explain to each other that really, they're just rectifying the soul of some poor guy who somehow got stuck in the pot roast.

I'm not arguing with them about all their crazy ideas, even though it should be clear that I don't agree with them, or believe a word they're saying. Instead, I'm joining in with all their bizarre little ceremonies and rituals, because, you know, when in Uman... So when they start singing, I sing along with them; when they stand up to do *Kiddush*, I stand up with them; when they start dancing like lunatics - I run off to the bathroom, because I haven't got the energy to dance around for 10 hours straight like they do.

There are other times when I disappear too, like when they want to go to the local forest for hours, to 'talk to *Hashem*'. Initially, I went along with them - I like trees - but personally, I don't have anything to say to G-d, so instead I went and talked to the Russian peasants who were trying to sell me some dodgy shapeless thing, hand-carved from wood.

Back to the meal: I don't care so much that they want to do all the weird things that they want to do, but it's really upsetting me that they're doing it on *my* time. It's nearly midnight, and we should have been eating hours ago! When I'm hungry, I can get really annoyed, and I can feel that my temper is starting to fray. If we were dealing with normal people, we would have finished eating ages ago and already be tucked up in bed. But I'm learning frustratingly that these people are anything but normal.

We came back from the synagogue two hours ago already, and that whole experience was also incredibly traumatic. I really thought I was going to go crazy. The last time I was in shul was for my own circumcision, and ever since then, I've given all synagogues a wide berth. My flatmates all told me, "What's the problem?! We're just going to the *Kedusha* Factory!" I told them: "No problem! But in every real factory, you get at least a 10 minute coffee break once in a while." But I was talking to the wall, just as much as they were.

Ok, I grudgingly decided, at least I'll take a look at what Jewish praying is all about. That didn't happen either, at least not in the way I envisioned, because as if on cue, everyone around me started screaming their heads off and jumping around. And it's not because everyone there was the athletic type, because they really weren't. There were fat people there who I'd bet anything had never, ever, seen the inside of a gym - but now? They were jumping around all over the place like they had springs screwed into their feet. The floor was literally shaking.

I couldn't believe my eyes. I stood outside the synagogue watching it all without going in, because they were packed in there like hot-wired sardines at some enormous holy rave.

It was amusing for five minutes, but then my patience ran out, and I really wanted all the praying to finish already and get back to our apartment at #5 Pushkina Street. Not that the apartment was really all that great, but I'd had enough of the jumping sardine show. All I wanted to do was eat some food and then go to sleep at a reasonable time, like a normal human being. That's what you're meant to do on religious holidays, isn't it? Eat yourself stupid and then fall zombie-like into bed? After all, it's not like I came to Uman to pray; I was there to do something much more *important.*

My brother was sitting across from me at the table. I caught his eye and whispered to him, "I'm dying from hunger, here. I barely ate anything since breakfast. When are we going to eat already?" He merely smiled at me and motioned that it would be just a little while longer, but I knew that his 'little while' could easily last another two hours. If they weren't all talking so much Torah, they'd be able to hear my stomach rumbling from across the room, and they'd know that they were dealing with a medical emergency that required a

3

massive plateful of food, immediately! But they weren't paying the slightest bit of attention to me, or to any of my basic, natural, material needs. These guys were all 'spiritual'; they'd spent hours excitedly praying and shouting, and getting all lit up with holy enthusiasm. But when I was in *shul*, I barely had the strength to open the *siddur* to see what they were reading that was making them all so happy.

I was hoping that by the end of my trip I'd discover the secret of why they'd all put in so much effort into getting to Uman in the first place. Before I got here myself, I thought that maybe people came to Uman for the amazing scenery, or the fascinating day trips, or the delightful five star luxury accommodations. But Uman is the opposite of a real holiday. You stand up all day, you barely sleep, you work like a dog just to have something edible in the fridge - and you pay a bucket load of money for the privilege. And really, none of it makes sense - it costs more to fly from Israel to backwards, remote, primitive Uman than it does to get to the USA. But year after year, these people knock themselves out financially and physically to get here and share a small room with seven other people they've never met before. And, to my great bewilderment, the greatest irony of all is that they look like they're enjoying themselves much more than the people who go on holiday to places with proper hotels, good restaurants and interesting things to do in the evenings.

When I used to go on 'real' holidays with my parents, I often noticed that most of the people around us were miserable, stressed and annoyed. They looked like they couldn't wait for their 'relaxing break' to be over, because the kids were driving them crazy all the time to buy them something, or take them somewhere, or to shell out a whole bunch of cash to go surfing, diving, or jeeping in the desert. Most people ended up working much harder and having much less fun on holiday than they did when they were back at their desks. They couldn't wait to pack up and leave. But these *frummies*? They look like they're loving every second of it.

## Chapter 1

*Let me tell you about the passenger who showed up at the very last minute.*

As I was saying, I really don't understand the way it works with these religious fanatics. Let me share some examples, so you can get a flavor of just how weird these charedi people really are, and the lengths they went to just to get to Uman. Personally, I couldn't understand what the big attraction was in Uman, or why so many apparently sane people could be crazy enough to go through the whole traumatic experience again and again, year after year.

There in the synagogue Erev Rosh Hashana, I began wondering what I was doing, because really, I would have preferred to stay back in the apartment. That way I could have eaten whatever and whenever I wanted without having to wait for anyone to say *Kiddush*, because like I said, I hadn't eaten anything since 3pm. But these strange people have even stranger rules, and one of them is that you're forbidden to eat before you've heard *Kiddush*.

So anyway, I see that I'm not going to be able to sneak some food without blowing my cover, so I decide I may as well go to shul with my brother and a few of the guys from the apartment. Of course, I don't tell *them* all this, I just feign enthusiasm for wanting to go pray. I'm so convincing that my brother even heads off to a little kiosk and comes back with a prayer book for me that he bought for a dollar. I kissed that *siddur* like it was the long-lost love of my life, and pretended it was the happiest day of my life.

A few minutes before the Rosh Hashana holiday starts, I'm standing quite a distance away from all the *chassidim* around me (especially my brother) trying to smoke my last cigarette for a while. This year, Rosh Hashana falls out on *Shabbat*, and it's REALLY forbidden to smoke on *Shabbat*. If it wasn't *Shabbat*, it would have been OK, but just my luck, I got a bunch of additional restrictions to keep this year when I'm play-acting being religious. Each new law I learn seems to be even more strange and random than the last, and I can't help wondering which idiot came up with all these stupid ideas in the first place, and for what purpose?

Anyway, I'm feeling so happy to be smoking that cigarette, but also painfully aware that it's going to be at least another 24 hours before I can do this again, so I'm really trying to enjoy every drag I take. All of a sudden, I see some crazy *chassid* come running in my direction from the drop-off point for those just arriving in Uman from Kiev. I'm sure he's about to grab the cigarette out of my hand and stone me for desecrating the Sabbath or something, so I immediately toss it away and make like I'm just about to go into shul to pray.

The *chassid* slows down, and I see he looks exhausted and worn, like he's been travelling for days. As soon as he sets eyes on me, he says, "Can you watch my stuff for a few minutes? I just need to go and dunk in the *mikveh*, and then I'll be back." Not waiting for an answer, he just plunks his backpack down in front of me and disappears.

I think to myself: "This guy is so naïve to be leaving all of his valuables with me, of all people. If he had any idea what I was planning to do in Uman over Rosh Hashana, he never would have done that in a million years..." While I'm waiting for him to come back, I wonder what planet he's from, showing up in Uman like that, less than five minutes before the *Chag* starts. I mean, where is the guy going to sleep? What's he going to eat? All the lodging and meals were booked solid a long time ago.

Three minutes later, he's back, and I don't even recognise him initially, because now he's dressed like a prince, in a white *kippa* and white *kittel*, like a lot of the other people around here. Even for a cynic like me, it's amazing to see how one minute the streets are full of people dressed in their depressing, dreary, black clothes, and the next, they are suddenly overflowing with holy looking 'white people'. It's surreal, like watching a massive game of Reversi, and even I have to grudgingly admit that it's a sight to behold.

Now that's he's freshened up and changed into his white clothes for the holiday, this *chassid* in front of me looks like he's been transformed into someone else entirely. He thanks me for watching his stuff, then looks at his watch and says, "I think the *Chag* already came in. I can't touch my stuff now because it's *muktzeh*."

I thought I misheard him, so I asked him, "Do you want me to take your stuff back to my apartment for you?"

He looks at me with this shocked expression on his face, and he tells me: "I can't ask my fellow Jew to do something that's forbidden for me to do! G-d is going to help me. I'm going to leave my stuff here, and I'm sure G-d is going to look after it all just fine until I can come back and get it after the *Chag*. Although, maybe I will try and ask a *posek* if I could use a *shinui* to move it somewhere a bit less out in the open."

The guy is clearly bonkers! Otherwise, he wouldn't even think about leaving all his valuables here, in the middle of the street, in the middle of Uman, just so that he wouldn't touch *muktzeh*. I tell him in an offhand way, so he'll really believe me, "I already asked a *posek*, and he told me it's fine to move it."

"Really? Who'd you ask?"

Uh-oh. Now I'm in trouble. I didn't bank on him asking me that. I tell him, "I asked Nachman." What else can I say? Firstly, I don't know any other rabbis, and secondly, pretty much every other person I've met here is named Nachman so the chances must be good that at least one of them is a rabbi. Seriously, you call out 'Nachman' here, and fifty kids come running up to you and ask you what you want. I think they must give them a name AND a number, to keep the confusion to a minimum. "Nachman 5, your dad is waiting for you in the parking lot; Nachman 45, sit down and stop talking so much; Nachman 100, why aren't you praying?"

"Which Nachman did you ask?" the *chassid* asks me, then answers his own question: "Was it Nachman Burstyn? I didn't even know that he'd made it to Uman this year!"

"Yeah, that's the one. Nachman Burstyn. Of course he's here this year! How did you know who I asked???"

Now, he's looking at me like he just won the lottery. After all, he guessed the correct rabbi, and Nachman Burstyn is here this year. Life just doesn't get any sweeter. I didn't wait for him to answer me; I just picked up his bag and told him over my shoulder, as I headed off down the street, "I'm taking your stuff to my apartment. We're staying at Pushkina 5, the ninth floor." I had no idea what just came over me. Why, all of a sudden, did I care if this complete stranger left his stuff in the middle of the street in Uman, to the point that I made up a whole story just so I could take his stuff back to my apartment? After all, he really didn't look like he had anything worth stealing, but I guess you can't always tell. Sometimes, the sketchiest looking dudes are the ones packing the most cash.

But then, if I were going to take his stuff, why'd I tell him where I was staying? And why'd I tell him to come and get his stuff once the holiday was over? While I'm thinking all this, he starts thanking me profusely and giving me all these blessings, like everyone does to everyone else around here.

Back on the street, I get away from him as fast as I can, and sprint off back to the apartment, making it look like I'm running to do a *mitzvah*, which of course I am:

# The Stolen Light

as soon as I get into the empty apartment, I light up a big, fat cigarette, and then another one, and boy, do I enjoy them. When I'm done, I lock up and head back down in the direction of the synagogue. As I already told you, I can't really get into all the praying. I try a couple of times to open the *siddur* and follow along with the service, but my head is all fuzzy from lack of food, and I can't read anything. Every time I try, I just get side-tracked trying to figure out what I'm actually doing here, in this place where everything is so bizarre and surreal.

After what seems like a million years, *shul* is finally over. I thought we'd finish up and then everyone would run back to their apartments to eat as fast as they could. I'm wrong. No one is running anywhere. Not only are they not running, they're all strolling along at a snail's pace, as though they just finished a five course meal and just needed a leisurely walk to work it all off.

They're all complimenting each other, blessing each other, shaking hands with each other, praising how nicely the *chazzan* sang the service, asking each other if they know who the *chazzan* was going to be following morning... I'm watching all these pleasantries, and I'm going crazy. I'm shifting from foot to foot; my mouth is twitching (and it's going to continue doing that until I put something in it) - and then far off in right field, I spot the *chassid* I met just when the holiday was beginning.

I catch his eye, and I motion to him to come over to me. I'm not a prophet, or a *tzaddik*, like a lot of the people around here like to refer to each other by default, but I can see that he hasn't got anywhere to go. He's not in a rush, and he's scanning the crowd, trying to spot any familiar faces, so I call him over.

He gives me a big smile, and he's really happy to see me. He's got that 'fired up with holiness' look and he walks over to me, and he immediately starts giving me blessings:

"May you be signed and sealed for a good year, and may you be written in the Book of Life immediately, and written in the book of the *tzaddikim*, and in particular, in the book of Rebbe Nachman," he tells me.

"Yeah, same to you," I reply, and then head off towards my apartment. But 'head off' isn't really the right way of describing what's happening, because I'm averaging about two meters an hour. Why? Because all 30,000 people who were praying at the synagogue left at exactly the same time, and the street looks like it got hit by a blizzard of holy white people everywhere you looked, five meters deep. It's taking an incredibly long time to get anywhere near my building, and even longer to actually make it up to the ninth floor.

So while I'm standing desperately just trying to move, I ask the mysterious *chassid*, "How come you only got here at the very last second? What happened to you?"

As you'll come to understand over the following pages, if you ever give a Breslever *chassid* the chance to tell you even a little bit about themselves, you are just going to hear one story after another about all the 'unbelievable miracles' that '*Rabbeinu*' did for them.

"My brother, you wouldn't believe the amazing miracles I've been sent just to get to Uman this year." Mmhm. Just as I thought. But I nod at him like I'm really interested. I need something to pass the time until I manage to move another couple of feet.

"As you probably know, every year when you want to come to Uman for Rosh Hashana, you get sent *miniot*, really big obstacles and problems from Heaven, to try and stop you. One year, you don't have enough cash for the ticket, another year your wife doesn't want you to go, but *Rabbeinu* tells us that all these *miniot*, all these obstacles, they're really just in our head. *Gut yom tov!*" As he's telling me his story, he's also giving loads of people in the crowd blessings and good wishes. By the time we get to my apartment, he's blessed at least fifty of his buddies, and at least another fifty people that he most likely never saw before in his life.

I'm also getting blessed all over the place by people who don't know me from Adam, and I have to admit that the warmth and camaraderie of the people here is really something else. Of course, that doesn't mean I'm going to lose my marbles and make *teshuva*, but I can appreciate how unusually nice it is, from a purely human and social viewpoint. Anyway, this is the mysterious *chassid*'s story:

*"Listen, every single year for the past seven years that I've come to Uman to be by Rabbeinu, I've had crazy stuff happen, but the stuff that happened this year is hardly to be believed.*

*"Really, everything that was going on this year started last Rosh Hashana. Every year, you come away from Uman Rosh Hashana on fire, ready for any of the tikkunim, or spiritual rectifications, that G-d is going to send you. And you really are ready for it! Whatever difficulties you need to be sent to fix your soul, you're up for it! So really all the problems I encountered this year were already saved up from last Rosh Hashana.*

*Baruch Hashem, my family lives in Tzfat and I'm not one of those people who brings home 10,000 shekels every month. If I'm lucky, I manage to earn around 6,000 a month, maybe 7,000 if I get a bit of a bonus. Baruch Hashem, I have lots of expenses and lots of kids - eight, may they be healthy and well, and grow up to be G-d-fearing whole-hearted Breslev chassidim, Amen Sela. Anyway, as I was saying, if I'm having a good week, I put 50 shekels in my kupat Uman, and if I'm having a great week, I put 100 shekels in there, because this year I decided I'm going to get to Uman without going into debt to pay for the ticket. I say that every year, and every year, I have to borrow the money, but this year is going to be different.*

*Baruch Hashem, I managed to save 600 shekels, when I realized that I needed to buy those glass olive oil things for the menorah because Chanuka was around the corner - and at the same time, I realized that we'd also run out of diapers, which even I can see we need. There isn't any money in my bank account, I don't have anyone I can ask to lend me some cash, and my wife is having a nervous breakdown (we really need the diapers...). Man, am I going through some real tikkunim here! My wife has reached the end of her rope, so I take 200 shekels out of my kupat Uman and I write myself an I.O.U. for the money.*

*Another month goes by, and all of a sudden, my kupat Uman is full only with notes from me, saying that I owe it 600 shekels. Once again, I get to the month of Elul just before Rosh Hashana, with no money to pay for a ticket. Once again, I also get hit with a bunch of other big bills and expenses at exactly the same time: the phone bill, the electric bill, the water bill, the municipality tax bill - they all land on my doorstep together. How can I fly to Uman this year, if it means leaving my wife and family without water, electricity or a phone? What are they going to eat for the holiday? And if that's not enough, as soon as I get back from Uman, how am I supposed to pay for Sukkot, and all the things you need to celebrate the festival properly, like a kosher lulav and etrog? I realize I'm going to need a massive suitcase full of cash to pay for everything I need.*

*I wish it was different, but I don't have a job that gives me a fixed income, and the demand for my services really drops off just before the holidays. Usually, my brother and sister-in-law help me out by letting me pay my bills on their visa card, and then I write them checks over the coming months to pay off what I owe them. Baruch Hashem, they're still letting me do it - which is a big miracle all by itself, because I still owe them so much money from previous months, and it's not like they have a surplus of money themselves - although they definitely aren't on the bread line, the holy tzaddikim that they are, may G-d bless them and preserve them and help them to make complete teshuva and come back to Him very quickly, Amen. But let's say that between them, they're bringing home between ten and twelve thousand a month, which sounds like a lot, but their standard of living is completely different from ours.*

*We get by, even when things are extremely tight. We're used to making do without many luxuries, while they have two kids and a dog, and the kids go to lots of extra-curricular activities, and every room in the house has a computer and a plasma TV, and everyone has a new bike, and they go on holidays - not that I'm criticizing them, G-d forbid, may they be healthy, Amen. You can see what sort of amazing people they are by the fact that they've never asked me to pay back all the money I owe them. But I hate being in debt to them, all the same.*

*Anyway, I'm wondering where I'm going to find the money I need when an old friend from the kibbutz I grew up on calls me up to see if he can come and say hello. I haven't seen him for seven years, because he moved to the U.S. and he's making a good living moving furniture around, but he also works like a dog, and he's only here in Israel now because his wife gave birth, so he took a bit of time off work to be with her and the baby. I have to tell you, this guy is brilliant. If he made teshuva, I have no doubt that he would quickly become one of the Gedolei Hador. Anyway, he comes to see me, and Baruch Hashem, G-d arranges it that he gives me $200 as a Rosh Hashana present. I thank him, I thank Hashem, and then I give the money to my wife so she can go and buy the food she needs for Chag.*

*A few days before I'm meant to be flying off to Uman, there's a knock at the door and there's some holy Jew standing there with an envelope. He gives me the envelope, no questions asked, and inside there are 1500 shekels worth of gift vouchers for the local mall. There are vouchers for food, vouchers for clothing, vouchers for the kids' shoes, yishtabach shemo! We only buy the stuff on sale, so I even managed to squeeze in a new dress for my wife, but do you understand? Even in the hardest circumstances, G-d sends you the miracles you need to turn everything around.*

*Right. So now, my wife and family are all set. The bills are all paid, they have what they need for the holiday, and I need to borrow the $700 that I need to get to Uman. I also really need to keep my plan a secret from my wife, because she's developed an allergic reaction to the word 'debt' - and unfortunately, she hears that word at least three times a day in our home.*

*So really against my will, I pay a visit to the local loan gemach, which most of my friends used to help them pay for their trip to Uman. I come away with $700 - exactly the amount I need to buy my ticket, and I'm not planning to spend a shekel more. I'm going to take my sleeping bag, ten pitas, five cans of tuna, yishtabach shemo, I'm set.*

*I go to the travel agent, I book the ticket, I check that my passport is still valid, and my wife puts it away in a drawer to make sure it doesn't get lost. The day before my flight, I'm packing all the stuff I need to take, and I go over to the drawer - no passport! I go through the whole drawer, turn it upside-down - no passport!*

*My wife's gone out to a Torah class, so I can't ask her if she's seen it. I decided I was going to go to sleep at 9pm so I could get up at midnight and pray Tikun Chatzot, the Midnight Lament, because I wanted to do some hitbodedut before the trip and pray that everything would go smoothly and that I'd get to Rabbeinu with a few more mitzvahs under my belt. But now, my wife's only going to get*

# The Stolen Light

*back around 11pm, so I decide that really, I don't have any other choice and I'd just have to wait up for her and ask her about the passport.*

*She comes home, and I'm lying on the sofa half-asleep, because I've spent the last hour and a half giving each of the kids some attention, and when you've get eight kids, even just five minutes each of quality time can take a lot of effort. But I'm happy to spend the time with them, because they are so sweet. You know, our kids are really all that matters in life. Do you know how amazing it is to leave behind children that are going to say kaddish for you, who will learn some Mishnayot for the memory of your neshama, your soul, and who will continue walking your path after you're gone?*

*So like I was saying, in the end my wife only gets home at ten past midnight, because she ended up chatting with a friend after the class and stayed together talking for an hour. So she tiptoes into the apartment so as not to wake anyone up, but I've been worrying about my passport for three hours now, and as soon as she opens the door I awake and jump up like a wild animal: "I have no idea where my passport is! Have you seen it anywhere???"*

*She got a real shock, which really she's entitled to do, because she's walked into all my stress, plus she just accidentally smacked her head into the door and it really, really hurts, and I can tell she's a bit upset with me, because she has a funny look on her face. While she's still wincing from the pain, she starts being sarcastic: "Shalom, my beloved wife. How are you doing, my love? How was your class?"*

*I know she's right. "Sorry, my beloved wife. How are you doing? How was your class?" She's soooooo right to be upset with me. I've spent hours listening to classes on shalom bayit, and how you're meant to treat your wife, but then as soon as I get a bit stressed, it all goes out the window and I forget all the good advice I've learned.*

*Both of us start looking for the passport, and we go through every single drawer in the house, then every single cupboard, then we go through all the kitchen cabinets, then we look in the bathroom, the toilet - where don't we look? For the next four hours, we turn everything upside down; there isn't a single bag or container we don't look in, or a single drawer we don't open. Even on Pesach, I don't make this much effort to go through everything.*

*Around 4am, my wife collapses, exhausted, while I spend a few more minutes looking for the passport. By this point, I've come to the conclusion that one of the kids must have been playing with it, and they probably know where it is. So now, I have to wait until they wake up and have already missed the right time to say Tikun Chatzot, and also the best time to do my hitbodedut. At night, you have some real peace and quiet, and your brain works differently. Just as Rabbeinu tells us - the night-time is when the world stops running after all the daily earthly nonsense, and at that point expanded consciousness, or mochin dgadlut, becomes accessible. Isn't that right, brother?"*

I'm just standing there nodding away as he talks, even though I have no idea what's he's going off about. Geez, these people can talk the hind legs off a donkey.

*"While I'm waiting for the kids to wake up, I decide to go to the mikveh. I immerse 310 times, and each time I go under the water, I yell out to G-d to please help me find the passport, because that evening at 8pm, I'm supposed to be flying out. Brother, I got filled up with so much light. After that, I went and prayed with the sunrise minyan, and asked all the chevra there to pray that I would find my passport. They start crying out to Hashem with me, because they're already used to all the things that can go wrong at the last minute when you're trying to get to Uman for Rosh Hashana. Everyone knows that the bigger the obstacles, the greater your desire to overcome them.*

*So I come home all psyched up, and what do I find? My wife is still passed out, and my kids are going wild because this has never happened before. It's not every day that you see your mother passed out in the kitchen, and my kids are getting worried that something serious is going on. They ask me one question after another, until finally I get them to quieten down enough to ask them if they've seen my passport.*

*Shloime tells me that he saw Rivky playing with it. I run off to Rivky's bed, but she's still asleep, so I start singing a Shwekey song that I know that she likes, to try and wake her up: "Rachem, rachem al yisrael amecha, rachem..." After a while, she finally wakes up. I help her to do al netilat yadayim, then ask her as calmly as I could where she put the passport she was playing with yesterday.*

*'Abba, I DIDN'T play with the passport,' she tells me in a very defensive voice. I try to coax her into telling me what she did with it, but she clams up and starts clamouring for me to get her some chocolate milk. Just then, Nachman, her cute but naughty four-year-old brother, spills his chocolate milk all over himself and starts wailing and crying hysterically. He's so loud that he wakes up my wife and the rest of the kids. Now that everyone's awake, I start questioning the whole family like an ace detective, asking each kid if they've seen my passport. No one owns up to knowing anything about it but they all offer to help me look for it, so for the second time in less than a day, we turn the whole house upside down.*

*This time, I also go through the kids' room with a fine-tooth comb; for two hours, I'm checking the toy boxes, the bookcase, under the beds. Nothing. Nada. No passport. I start to feel quite down about the whole thing. Then, I pull myself together, and decide I need to make an urgent trip to Misrad Hapnim, the interior ministry/passport agency, to find out what I need to do now.*

*I get there just as everyone is on their morning coffee break. I don't want to bother anyone when they are in the middle of eating their sandwich, G-d forbid, but I just want someone to tell me if there is any chance that they could sort me out a new passport in the next hour, so that I'm not just standing around in there wasting my time. But as usual with these government offices, there's no one around to even ask, so in the meantime I sit down and wait and start talking to G-d instead:*

*'G-d, please sort out my passport!'*

*Sometimes, these conversations with G-d are very humbling, because you suddenly find yourself talking to G-d about sorting out your entrance visa to the Ukraine or getting a new passport in record time, and it strikes you how much of your life is taken up with mundane things that really don't seem to be all that important. But, like Rabbi Natan explains[1], if you really believe that everything - even these small things - are from G-d, then of course you need to talk to G-d about them.*

*Ten minutes go by, and still the desks are vacant. I try to judge them favorably - maybe they're chewing each sandwich mouthful thirty times to make sure it's easy to digest as per the halacha, and while they're eating, they're also concentrating on the kabbalistic intentions they need to raise the holy soul sparks contained in the food back to G-d... As I'm thinking this, one of the workers comes out with a sign, saying that the office is now going to be closed for staff training until 1pm.*

*'What!?' I ask him. 'Why do you need to have staff training right now?!' He glances at me with cold disinterest.*

*'I have a flight to Uman booked at 8pm tonight, and I've lost my passport,' I tell him, with big, mournful, puppy-dog eyes.*

*'So stay in Israel,' he says, turning his back on me. What a chutzpah! Who is he to tell me where to go or what to do? I get really angry, and this urge to show him what people with emuna can do wells up inside me. We can get to Uman for Rosh Hashana, even when government clerks like him are standing in our way.*

*'You stay in Israel. I'm going to Uman,' I tell him, but I regret saying it as soon as the words leave my mouth. I don't need to give this guy any more excuses for not helping me.*

---

[1] Rabbi Natan was Rebbe Nachman's most prominent student

*'You can bet I'm staying here,' he says. 'I'm not crazy enough to want to leave my family and Eretz Yisrael just to go and spend Rosh Hashana with a bunch of Russian Nazis.'*

*Right, so now I know what I'm dealing with. Not only does he not have the zchut to go to Uman for Rosh Hashana (because you know, Rabbeinu has to invite you to come here) - he's also anti anyone else going. I realize that by the normal way of things, this guy is definitely not going to help me. So I try a different tactic:*

*'My brother, I love you, and I'm sorry that I spoke to you like that. I'm desperate to get to Uman, because my whole life depends on making the flight tonight. If you were in my shoes, what would you do?'*

*His demeanour softens a bit, because 'words from the heart enter the heart', and he tells me: 'Your only chance of getting an emergency-issue passport is if you go to our branch in Kfar Saba. There's a clerk there who loves you guys, and she'll do whatever it takes to get you another passport. Good luck, and I hope you make it to Uman.'*

*I give him a hug goodbye, and I ask him for the names of him, his wife and his kids, so I can pray for them when I get to the Tzion (Rebbe Nachman's gravesite). He writes it all down for me, and then he gives me 50 shekels for the trip as well. Unbelievable!*

*I call my wife to tell her what's going on and I ask her to get my bag ready, because I'm going to swing by and pick it up and then race off to Kfar Saba - a three hour drive from Tzfat - where hopefully, this clerk is going to help me get a new passport. Then with G-d's help, I will tear down the highway to the airport and hopefully get on the flight at 8pm.*

*I drive a 30 year old station wagon which runs on miracles at the best of times, even when I'm just cruising around the corner to buy groceries. It drives ok as long as I don't go too fast, but I haven't got the time to take it easy today (not that I'm going to break the speed limit, G-d forbid, because keeping safe and healthy is also a big mitzvah), but I put my foot down, and I hit 65 mph. Almost.*

*I grab my bag, say goodbye to my wife and kids, and drive off in the direction of Kfar Saba. It's already 1pm; I get to Kfar Saba at 3:00 and go straight to the Misrad Hapnim - or at least I try to go straight there, but get lost and end up driving around for a half hour trying to find the right place. Finally, I get there and jump out, parking the car haphazardly on the side of the road. I run off to the office - and it's closed. It's only going to re-open tomorrow morning, long after my flight has already gone. My last chance of getting on the plane just evaporated.*

# The Stolen Light

*Dejected, I head back to my car, and a traffic cop is already standing there writing me a 250 shekel ticket for parking illegally. I don't even try to argue with him. I thank G-d for giving me the kapara - hey, it's just money, after all - and who knows what judgements are being sweetened as a result of me getting that ticket? I get back into the car and debate turning around and going back home to Tzfat, or staying here overnight and trying again tomorrow. In the meantime, I need to inform the travel agent that my ticket is available in case someone else wants to buy it. Maybe I'll be able to get another ticket for tomorrow, which is the last day I can fly out before the Chag starts.*

*I start driving, not paying attention to the fact that I'm talking to the travel agent while driving the car. The same traffic cop who gave me the parking ticket now pulls me over again, and this time gives me another fine for using the cell phone while driving: 750 shekels! Once again, I don't try and argue with him, I just thank him, and thank Hashem, and accept Hashem's judgement with love.*

*I believe wholeheartedly that I'm going to get back every penny I spend trying to go to Rabbeinu for Rosh Hashana, whatever I spend and even more. It's just like Rabbeinu said: 'whoever gives to me, I'm going to give back to him much, much more.' I've seen that happen with my own eyes. Each year, whatever I spend getting to Uman, Rabbeinu pays me back, and then some.*

*One year I was so poor, I can't even begin to tell you how bad it was. And it was the same year that my eldest boy was going to turn seven, and I just had to bring him with me to Uman. Even my wife was telling me that whatever it took, we had to find a way to get Shmuel to Uman before his seventh birthday."*

"What's the big deal with getting your son to Uman before he was seven?" I wanted to know.

"What? You don't know about Rabbeinu's promise? Rebbe Nachman promised that any child who was brought to his tomb to say the Tikun Haklali at his kever before he turned seven would stay 'clean' until he got married."

"What on earth are you talking about, that he'll stay 'clean'?" I asked him. "I wouldn't make all the effort to *shlep* my kid here just for that." After all, it would be much cheaper just to get the kid to take a bath every day... My new friend tells me that 'clean' means clean from any spiritual blemishes in the areas of personal holiness and modest behavior. OK, you might think that's obvious, but how am I supposed to understand all these mysterious chassidic code words?

*"As I was saying, that year I needed to buy two tickets - one for me, and one for my son Shmuel. I went to the bank - I was desperate, and at that point I really didn't have anything to lose - and end up in front of a clerk who already knew me*

*very well, inasmuch as he's the one calling me every two days to tell me that I'm way over my overdraft limit, and I need to deposit a few thousands shekels pronto.*

*I take my credit card out of my wallet and tell him that in another two weeks my son and I need to fly off to Uman. Is there any way he can increase my overdraft limit, even temporarily, so that I can buy the tickets and put them on my card?*

*He smiles an incredulous smile, like he can't quite believe that I've just asked him to increase my overdraft limit, and says to me: "How on earth do you expect me to agree to that? You don't even have anyone I can put down as a guarantor for the additional debt!" I ignore his obvious antagonism and tell him, "Rabbeinu Hakadosh is going to stand guarantor for me!"*

*The clerk starts laughing, and decides to have some mercy on me. He starts tapping away at his keyboard, fills in all the necessary forms, and it pings back a few seconds later: permission denied.*

*I grab a few seconds to talk to G-d, and tell Him that I'm only doing all this for the massive mitzvah of taking my son to Uman. I ask the clerk to put the request through the computer again, and can see he's starting to get a bit impatient with me. He sends it off again, and again it comes back: permission denied. Even though he's actually a really sweet-natured guy, the line is getting longer and longer, and I can see he's getting stressed. Pretty please, I ask him, just give it one more try. If it doesn't work, I'll leave. This time it pings back with a wonder of wonders: permission received. They increased my overdraft limit exactly by the amount I asked for!*

*The clerk is looking at me with a stunned expression on his face; he can't believe they gave it to me. Before he can say anything else I run straight off to the travel agent to book two tickets, before anyone can change their mind. I come back home exhausted but thrilled, and that year, Shmuel and I made it to Uman.*

*That year was tough; it was packed full of tikunim and soul-corrections. When Pesach came, I didn't even have enough money to buy matzot and wine, let alone fish and meat. I decided to take three of my kids along to go and see my parents and see if they could help a bit. They're usually quite generous anyway, but their giving enthusiasm definitely gets more pronounced when they see their grandchildren.*

*Also, I figured that if I took the kids, it would also help my wife, who needed a bit of peace and quiet to get on with cleaning the house for Pesach. She could use some time without the kids disturbing her every two seconds asking for candies or messing up the stuff she's just tidied.*

# The Stolen Light

*I make sure everyone is showered and nicely dressed, and then we set out for my parents. On the way, Natan, my three year old, disappears. I ask Shmuel, my eldest, to help me find him, but none of us can see him anywhere. I start praying intensely, because I know my son, and in the five seconds since I've last seen him, he could have gotten anywhere.*

*I hear some strange rustling noises coming from the big green garbage dumpster near to me. When I take a look inside, of course there he is. 'Natan, Ribono Shel Olam! What are you doing in there? How did you even get inside that thing?!'*

*My son pops his cute head out of the dumpster, smiles his sweet smile, and tells me, 'Abba, there's money in here!' I look at what he's waving around in his hand, and it looks like a 200-shekel bill! I come closer, and I see that the money is the genuine article, the real deal. 'Where did you get that?' I ask Natan, and my son, may Hashem bless him, rummages around in the dumpster and comes back out with a tattered envelope that he hands me. I open it up and can't believe my eyes: inside are forty 200-shekel notes, which is exactly the extra amount I added on to the overdraft so that I could get to Rabbeinu for Rosh Hashana, may the Tzaddik's merit protect us. It's just like I said: Rabbeinu, the light of lights, pays you back whatever you spend to get to him, and then some.*

*I kiss the envelope, and then I thank Hashem and also my little Natan'aleh, who sometimes likes to pretend that he's naughty - but who's really just a little tzaddik in disguise. Of course, I didn't use the money immediately. I called up my rav to find out the law in this case on hashavat aveda, or returning lost things. He told me to hang on to it for six months and if no one came forward with recognizable signs that would prove it was their money, then I could use it. When my father heard the story, he told me to go ahead and use the money already, and if anyone showed up at my door, then he'd happily reimburse them out of his own pocket. Man, we had such a happy Pesach that year.*

*But let's get back to this year's story. So I've just been fined 200 shekels for illegal parking and 750 shekels for talking on the phone while driving, and now I'm standing next to the car by the side of the road where I got pulled over by the traffic cop talking to my wife on the cell. Suddenly, the phone starts making the beeping noise that tells me the battery is about to die. Of course I forgot to bring the charger with me, so I tell my wife the whole story as fast as I can, and ask her what to do. She tells me to stay there in Kfar Saba and to see if I can get the passport tomorrow and fly out on a different ticket. If I can't, then either I'll come home then, or I'll go and join the gathering of Breslev chassidim in Jerusalem or by Rabbi Shimon Bar Yochai in Meron.*

*I tell you, my wife is such a tzaddeket; so full of self-sacrifice. Really, our wives are the genuinely holiest people, because they are the ones who stay home with the kids over Rosh Hashana while we're away. And not just on Rosh Hashana -*

*they're looking after the kids all year round! Believe me, they really deserve a medal. After all, the only reason they volunteered to come down to this earth in the first place was just to help us, their husbands, get through all the tikunim that we need to go through to fix our souls.*

*Anyway, while all this is going on, I tell myself that I believe with perfect faith that I'm still going to get to Uman for Rosh Hashana this year. Now that I'm unexpectedly stuck in Kfar Saba, I realize what good mazal I had that the clerk gave me 50 shekels for the trip. I take the money and find a local mobile accessories store where I buy a new charger for my phone. Realizing I don't actually have anywhere to go to where I can charge the phone, I ask the employee if I can plug my phone in there at the shop for a few minutes.*

*I figure that I'm just going to park the car somewhere near the Misrad Hapnim and sleep in it overnight, and that way I'll be first in the line when it opens in the morning. I decide to make a few calls on my mobile while its still plugged in, although they don't recommend that you talk on it while it's still charging because the radiation is at its most dangerous. But I didn't worry about all that, because I believe that 'it's the sin that kills, and not the snake.'*

*I call up my travel agent, Derech Tzaddikim, and tell them what's happening. They tell me that because I booked the ticket on a chartered flight, there's nothing they can do to help me. Or to put it another way, I can't get back any of the money that I borrowed to buy my ticket. I just spent $700 for nothing. They tell me that the last flight out is leaving tomorrow, and at the moment, it's fully booked. They aren't going to know until 11am the next morning if there will be any cancellations.*

*After I speak to them, I get another call from my wife telling me that she thinks I forgot to pack my tefillin. There's at least a chance that I can track down another plane ticket by the next morning, but there's no chance that I'm going to find another pair of tefillin by then. What am I going to do about morning prayers if I don't have any tefillin? I thank G-d for the problem, because for sure, it's all for the best. In the meantime, my phone's all charged up, and while I'm disconnecting it from the wall, one of the workers in the store comes over and asks me if I'm going to Uman for Rosh Hashana. I tell him that I really hope so, and he gives me 50 shekels and asks me to pray for him that he will find his wife this year. Ribono Shel Olam, what amazing divine Providence! You know why? Because when I left Tzfat, I didn't even know if the less than a quarter tank of gas I had was going to get me to Kfar Saba.*

*So I find the nearest gas station, and literally a meter away from the pump, my car runs out of gas. Yishtabach shemo, what miracles I'm getting! I push my car the last little bit up to the pump, and then I fill it up with 40 shekels worth of gas, because I want to keep the other 10 shekels in case I need it for something important, like getting into the mikveh tomorrow morning. I drive back towards Misrad Hapnim, and this time, I find somewhere legal to park. Now, I need to find somewhere to pray Mincha and Ma'ariv, so I look around and I go into the first synagogue I see.*

*It happens to be an old-style Sephardi synagogue, full of decent salt-of-the-earth Sephardi folks, and I really enjoy praying Mincha with them. I stay on to hear the halacha class between Mincha and Ma'ariv, and then after Ma'ariv, I ask one of the gabbais where the nearest mikveh is, and if it would be ok for me to sleep in the synagogue. I also inquire if by chance he knew of a pair of tefillin I could borrow to pray with tomorrow morning.*

*That holy gabbai, that tzaddik, looks me up and down, and then invites me to come home with him to eat some supper. Everything was so beautifully and simply arranged. We ate, we talked, we learned some Torah, and after two hours together, he invites me to stay over in his home, as his guest. His wife makes up the room for me with new linens and a washing cup right next to the bed. Just before 4am, my host wakes me up to come with him to the mikveh before praying; he pays for me to get in, he gives me shampoo and a towel... I tell you, you see how Rabbeinu takes care of every small detail for us, even though we don't deserve a thing?*

*I pray at the sunrise minyan using a set of tefillin given to me by the gabbai. Afterwards, we sit down together and learn a page or two from Chok L'Yisrael, and he tells me that the tefillin I used belonged to his son, who was killed in the Second Lebanon War. But that's not the really amazing thing: the really amazing thing is that his son and I have exactly the same name.*

*The gabbai tells me to take his son's tefillin to use in Uman and return them when I get back. I was so touched by this man's quiet nobility and generosity. Before yesterday he'd never seen me before in his life - and now, without any exaggeration, I felt like he was treating me with the same love and concern he'd give to his own flesh and blood.*

*At 8am, the gabbai escorts me to Misrad Hapnim, and that's when we find out that the clerk I'd come to see was on annual leave until after the holiday. At that point, I have to admit that I nearly gave up. I try to talk to one of the other clerks, but he just brushes me off in a really rude way. I try a different clerk instead, but she just yells at me that I should sit down and wait my turn. Brother, I'm the only customer there.*

*The gabbai sees what's going on, and he calls his friend, who calls his friend, who calls his friend who actually knows the clerk that I initially came to see. I'm not exaggerating: within half an hour, the clerk is standing there in front of us, and she's telling us that now she understands why her vacation to the Dead Sea got messed up. She tells us that right now, she should have been in the Caesar Hotel, except that they called her last night to tell her the hotel had a fire and they were cancelling all the bookings. I'm thinking to myself, 'Wow! Rabbeinu arranged that fire, just to help me!' It really is true that the whole world is made for us, just like it says.*

*Right away, chik-chak, the clerk sorts me out with a new passport. The gabbai insists on paying for the passport photos I need; and he insists on paying Misrad Hapnim their fee for sorting out the passport, all in cash, no questions asked. I tell him he should get to work already - he's helped me so much! - but he won't hear of leaving me until he sees that I'm all sorted out, and right now, he's doesn't care about anything else. I thank G-d. I thank him. I've got my new passport in my hand, and now - I somehow have to buy a new ticket.*

*The gabbai tells me to come with him to his office and call the travel agent from there so as not to waste the charge in my phone. I put another call in to Derech Tzaddikim, and they tell me that they have no cancellations, and can only advise me to go to the airport and see if I can get a connecting flight to anywhere that will end up in Kiev. I say goodbye to the gabbai, and thank him with all my heart for all the kindness he's shown me. He gives me 200 shekels as a parting gift - and I'll tell you something, if he'd known that I didn't actually have the money to pay for a new ticket, I'm certain that the tzaddik would have insisted on buying me one himself. It's now 10:15am, Erev Rosh Hashana.*

*In the meantime, I call up my wife and ask her to check in with the local travel agents on what connecting flights there were and if there were any seats available on them. I'm on shpilkes for an hour, waiting for her to call me back, when the phone finally rings, she tells me that there's a flight leaving to Germany in an hour and a half. There's a four-hour stopover before the connecting flight, which arrives in Kiev at 4pm. The Chag comes in at 7.30 pm, and there's at least a three hour taxi drive to get from the airport to Uman. What do I want to do?*

*I figure that if worst comes to worst, I'll end up in some Ukrainian forest for Rosh Hashana. It's definitely not ideal, but if that's what G-d wants, who am I to argue? I ask my wife to give me the travel agent's number so I can call and confirm the booking. 'How are you going to pay for it?' she wants to know. There's that question again.*

*I tell my wife I'll call her back, and call my childhood friend who's already in Uman, but not because he has any money. He doesn't, but what he does have is a massive overdraft limit on his credit card, and that appears to be the only way I can pull it off at this stage in the game. He answers the phone, but he can't really hear me properly. From all the background noise, I can tell he's standing right next to the Tzion. My heart fills with joy, and I ask myself, how on earth could a person pass up the chance to be part of that holy gathering, that Ukrainian Har*

## The Stolen Light

*Sinai? I give my friend a very quick history of the recent events, and he tells me that he'd love to help me but the credit card is at home with his wife. If she agrees that I can put the ticket on the card, he'd be thrilled. I ask him to call his wife up and soften her up a bit, but he tells me it's better if I call her directly - she'd be more likely to say no if he called her up to discuss it first.*

*So I take a deep breath, and I call her: she can't speak right now. It's 1:10pm on Erev Chag, and the travel agent is going to close in another hour. What else can I do? I start praying and calling out to Hashem. Half an hour later, she calls me back. I explain what's going on, and at the beginning, she just keeps telling me that she and her husband are already weighed down with debt and can't possibly take on any more. And what's more, she doesn't know if the card will go through even if she does let me use it.*

*I promise her I'll get her the $700 in cash before the beginning of the holiday, but I just need to have a credit card to actually buy the ticket now. Those turn out to be the magic words, and she agrees and gives me the card details. I call the travel agent that my wife found and book the ticket to Germany, with the connecting flight to Kiev. All told, it comes to $1050. For a minute, I wonder if I should just cancel the whole thing; after all, I told my friend's wife it was only going to be $700, and I'm obligated to be a man of truth and keep to my word. What's more, I said it in such a way that it probably has the halachic status of an oath – nothing to trifle with.*

*I tell the travel agent I'll call them back, and I call back my friend's wife and tell her that it's going to cost a bit more, and that I promise to send her the full sum, in cash, before the beginning of the holiday. By some miracle she agrees, and I book the ticket. Now, I have an hour to get to the airport and make the flight, and I still need to get through check-in.*

*This time, I drive like a lunatic - I go through red lights, I drive on hard shoulders, I'm ignoring all the speed limits, and I get to the airport half an hour before the plane takes off.*

*I realize that if I park the car where I'm supposed to, I will miss the flight. My hands are tied, so I drive up to the airport gates in the taxi lane and leave my car there, amongst all the white taxis. I leave the keys in the ignition and pray that some good-hearted, honest person would understand the situation, and park my car in the right place.*

*I grab my bag and run into the airport to find the booth where my ticket is supposed to be waiting for me. There's some tourist waiting there in line, and I tried to explain to him in English why I needed to go ahead of him, to get my ticket, but he's clearly not understanding a word I'm saying. Miraculously, he lets me go ahead of him anyway, and I realize that he was yet another one of many, many kindnesses G-d was sending me this trip. It took the clerk five whole minutes to print the ticket out, and I grab it and run off to check-in as fast as my legs would take me. I tell them to check me in at the speed of light - my plane is five minutes away from taking off at this point - and literally a minute before they closed the doors, I get on board.*

*On the way to Berlin, I'm looking around at the other passengers, and I realize there isn't a single other chareidi Jew on the whole plane. I start pondering to myself how on earth I'm going to come up with $1050 cash to give to my friend's wife like I promised, when I suddenly realize that I haven't got an entrance visa for the Ukraine!*

*I get back on the phone to Derech Tzadikim and ask them to please send to Berlin airport the visa I already paid for from the previous flight that I missed. They tell me it's impossible to do that, and so now, I'm faced with a really serious problem. If I get to Kiev without the visa, either they'll send me straight back to Israel, or I'll have to spend the whole of the Chag stranded there in Borispol airport. I start crying my eyes out, mamash like a little boy; all the stress and the anxiety I'd been through the last couple of days suddenly catching up with me.*

*An older man who I thought was German is sitting next to me. When I start crying, he asks me in Hebrew what the problem was, and if he could help in any way. I pour out my heart to him and tell him the whole situation, and what do you know? My new best friend happens to work at the Israeli embassy in Berlin. I thank G-d, I thank Rabbeinu, and I thank my new friend, who's already busy on the phone, half in Hebrew and half in German, trying to arrange me a visa. Half an hour later, he tells me with a big smile on his face that the visa is waiting for me at Kiev airport. I literally start jumping for joy. I give him a big hug; thank him and Hashem again, and for the rest of the flight we spend the whole time talking about emuna, Rabbeinu, the Holocaust, and why I made teshuva. It was a really interesting conversation, and he asked me a lot of difficult questions. Some things I had answers for and others I didn't, but even when I didn't know what to tell him, he was still very respectful.*

*Now, let me tell you how amazing Jews are: I booked the flight last minute on a non-Jewish airline, so it was obvious that they couldn't order any kosher food for me. My friend, once he realized that I wasn't eating anything, also decided not to eat the non-kosher food, so that he wouldn't upset me. The pintele yid is still alive in every single Jew, even though we've been in exile for 2,000 years.*

*We get to Berlin, and my friend accompanies me until the gate for my flight to Kiev. We part with another hug, and he asks me to call him from Kiev and let him know that the visa arrived. I promised him I would, and the next thing I know, I'm on the flight to Kiev. Once again, I look around, and it doesn't look like there's a single other Jew on the plane. It's 3pm and the flight is going to take an hour and a half, which means I'll get to Kiev around 4:30pm. The whole flight, I'm praying that there won't be any more 'miniot', difficulties, regarding the visa. Suddenly, it hits me that I don't have any money to pay for the taxi from Kiev to Uman. No Russian taxi driver even so much as looks at you if you can't show that you're carrying at least half the money for the trip. I stop praying about the visa, and start praying about the taxi.*

*To cut a long story short, I was in dvekut with Hashem for an hour and a half. Everyone around me was talking in German, Russian, who knows what, but I was off in my own world and I didn't notice anything else. I get to Ukrainian passport control, and by some massive miracle, the visa was already there in an envelope waiting. The Ukrainian officials rolled out the red carpet for me, as they thought I was connected to the embassy in Germany. I barely noticed all the special treatment, because finally, thank G-d, I made it to Ukraine for Rosh Hashana.*

*I exit the airport and start looking for a taxi; maybe there would be a Jewish taxi driver who would have some mercy on me. But then I decide maybe that's not such a good thing to pray for, because he might drive back to Kiev on the Chag, and it would all be because of me. I can't help but daydream about how I'm going to make my phantom Jewish driver stay with me in Uman and celebrate Rosh Hashana by Rabbeinu...*

*I stop what I'm doing, I look up at the sky, and ask G-d to help me, the way a child would ask his Abba to help him. Just then, I notice three very stressed chareidi men running out of the airport towards the taxi line, like some modern-day version of Avraham Avinu's three angelic visitors. I run after them. One of them shouts at me in English: 'Are you going to Uman?' I yell back: 'Yes! Are you?' They motion for me to come with them, and we run off to the nearest taxi without saying another word to each other, because we already feel like long-lost buddies.*

*The driver tells us the trip is going to cost $400, which is the most ridiculously inflated price I ever heard in my life. The Ukrainians know they can charge whatever they want on erev Rosh Hashana, and they just love fleecing the Jews at every opportunity. The other chassidim either don't realize or don't care that they are being charged an astronomical price, and they pile into the taxi. One of them sits up front next to the driver, and tells him that if he can get us to Uman in two hours or less, he'll get an extra $100 tip.*

*Now the driver is all tanked up with adrenalin to get his big tip, and it almost goes without saying that he's also tanked up with a quarter bottle of vodka. None of us are over the moon about that, but everyone knows that just like a car needs gas to drive, a Ukrainian needs vodka to function. It's like water for them. Nevertheless, I tell my fellow travellers that the only way we're guaranteed a safe, peaceful trip is if we immerse ourselves in learning Rabbeinu's Torah while en-route to Uman.*

*I also tell them upfront that I don't have any money to pay for my share of the ride, but that when we get to Uman, I'm sure I'd be able to find someone I know who would lend me the money. They tell me straight away not to worry about it, and to just enjoy the trip without feeling bad about anything. They really were bona fide angels.*

*We start learning Lesson 6 from Likutey Moharan. One of the chassidim explains that although he's a Satmar chassid, he's getting really into Breslev teachings, and he starts sharing some amazing ideas about making teshuva, and about making teshuva on the teshuva you already made. I thought that only formerly secular people like myself had to make teshuva, but he taught me what the idea of making teshuva on your teshuva really means. His words went straight into my heart.*

*As we're travelling, I tell them all the miniot I'd been through just to get to the current stage where we were all sharing the taxi together. Don't get me wrong, I wasn't complaining; I told them right from the start that I knew all these difficulties were all for my good, but it was possible that as I gave over a little bit of a feeling that G-d didn't really want me to be in Uman that year, and that I felt a bit rejected by Him. I guess partially, I felt a sense of unfairness - they were also getting to Uman at the last possible minute, but unlike me, at least they didn't have to worry about how they were going to pay for everything. For whatever reason, they were on a level where they didn't need to go through everything I'd been through in the last 48 hours.*

*That's when Kalman, the Satmar chassid with Breslev tendencies, started telling us about some of the miniot that he'd been going through with his wife and her father, and a whole bunch of other Satmar chassidim in his circle that were very against Breslev generally, and especially against people travelling to Uman for Rosh Hashana. He'd lost a lot of social standing and had been humiliated and criticized a great deal for his attachment to Breslev, and particularly for his wish to travel to Rabbeinu for Rosh Hashana. He had no idea if his wife was going to let him back in the house when he got back home, because he'd simply run off to the Ukraine at the last minute without telling her, in case she tried to stop him.*

*Kalman knew that when a person is trying to come close to the True Tzaddik, he's going to get a lot of abuse, and that the abuse and the arguments themselves are actually what give him the merit to get closer and achieve previously unattainable spiritual levels. We learn all this from Rebbe Natan, who epitomized self-sacrifice and self-nullification, and achieved the loftiest of spiritual levels.*

# The Stolen Light

*Kalman's words were sincere, the words of a man with a broken heart, and they made a deep impression on me. All traces of my previous bitterness and worry disappeared, replaced by a deep, profound feeling of joy. I felt even happier a few minutes later, when one of Kalman's friends put a call in to a good friend of his in Israel who lived very close to the friend who'd lent me his visa. Kalman asked him to be his shaliach, or messenger, to give my friend's wife the $1050 in cash that I owed her. I tried to talk him out of it, but he told me that he'd already decided that he really wanted to give some tzedaka to a genuinely deserving poor person before the holiday, and that I fit the bill exactly. Hashem was looking out for me right until the end.*

*We spent an hour and a half like that together, sharing experiences, friendship and powerful moments of prayer and Torah, really something out-of-this-world, until we pulled up to the Tzion - which is where I met you. Ashrecha! Thanks for all your help, my dear brother. What's your name, by the way?"*

"Now, we have to take the stairs all the way up to the ninth floor," I tell him. "My name's Avi. Nice to meet you." We start to climb. I'm not ashamed to tell you that I found the whole stairs thing a complete nightmare, because I'm just not cut out for walking up nine flights. All my life I've lived in a villa, and the nearest I got to walking up any stairs was in high school when I had to go up half a flight to get to math class, and even then I just used the elevator. It's only because I'm pretending to be religious that I'm killing myself like this. I thought I was going to have a heart attack. To calm down, I started muttering to myself that everything's for the best, and then I nearly had another heart attack because I realized I was starting to talk like them. OMG, I was becoming a *frummie*! But I relaxed again, and told myself that all this effort was going to be worthwhile when I actually got down to doing the job I'd come here to do.

Meanwhile, my mysterious *chassid* friend was taking the stairs two and three at a time. And if you thought he couldn't climb stairs and talk at the same time, you'd be dead wrong: the whole time, he's telling me about all the other miracles that happened to him in previous years. Even while he was breaking the world record for stair climbing, he still didn't keep quiet for a single second.

When we got up to the apartment, there were only ten people there. The table was already set with most of the dips and challah, so we just had to sit and wait for everyone else to arrive before we could do *Kiddush*. A few times, I tried to see if I could quickly sneak some food before anyone would notice, but every time I got near the table, someone else would come over and stand right next to me.

At 10pm we finally made *Kiddush*. I have to tell you that the atmosphere around the table was actually really nice, with everyone sending out loving vibes to everyone else, and trying to help in whatever way they could. No one mentioned a word about the extra guest I'd brought home with me for supper - they just set another place, found him a chair and presto! He was one of the *chevra*, just like everyone else there.

The leader of our little group was called Nachman. He put everything he had into making *Kiddush*, and everyone around the table closed their eyes, apparently lost in spiritual ecstasy. I thought it was a great moment to maybe try and steal a carrot or something, but my conscience got the better of me. I'd waited this long, I may as well wait the extra minute it was going to take for him to do *Kiddush*. Ten minutes later, he was finally done - but then everyone got up to go wash their hands. The apartment was really crowded, and even just getting to the sink was a whole saga. You had to move the chairs out of the way and then move them back, depending on who was standing up and who was coming back to the table. Our group also included a few kids, who needed help reaching the tap or reciting the blessing. To put it another way, we started saying *Kiddush* at 10pm, but it was only half an hour later that I actually managed to eat a bite of bread. You'd think that after all that, we'd just get on with the actual meal, but even then you'd be wrong - because now it was time for the *simanim*.

The whole *simanim* ceremony was like something out of the Passover Haggada. The whole *chevra* was clearly really into it, and they didn't care how long the whole thing was taking or when they'd actually get to eat something real. They were all in their element, making a big blessing on every little morsel, and then linking it to some symbolic thing or another. For example, they'd hold up a plate and say, 'May it be Your will that You dish out justice to our enemies.' Or they'd hold up a glass and say, 'May it be Your will that You make our souls as clear as glass.' And so on and so forth, until they'd gone through every item on the table.

I was watching all this with bemusement, but it wasn't all bad. I managed to eat at least a whole challah by myself - with humus - without blowing my cover. How? Before each slice, I simply made a big show of saying: 'May it be Your will that Hamas (humus…) should disappear off the face of the earth…' so that they could see I was really joining in with the whole vibe they had going on. My stomach felt a bit happier, but I was still waiting until we got to the meat.

Next, they brought out a massive tray of different salads and drinks, all the while discussing the amazing praying, the amazing *chazzan*, and dropping in little *divrei Torah* from *Rabbeinu* all over the place. Every second word was '*Rabbeinu* said this', or 'Rabbi Natan explains'. I have to tell you that honestly, a lot of what they were saying was really amazing, profound stuff that deserved to be thought through and properly digested. But I didn't come to Uman for mental stimulation, so I deliberately kept out of their deep conversations and tried to let it all bounce off me as much as possible. I spent most of the night trying *not* to see how great a lot of the people were, because I didn't want to get confused and pulled off track.

# The Stolen Light

I consoled myself that I had a job to do in Uman, and it didn't involve praying, getting religious, or thinking deep thoughts about the purpose of life. Let *them* pray; let *them* get more pious; let *them* worry about what they were really doing down here. I came here to hit the jackpot, because in Uman, there was a whole sea of money just waiting for me to dive in. Like I've already mentioned, these *frummies* were all loaded with cash, and they were giving it out like candy. Wherever I looked, I saw *frummies* giving other *frummies* bucket loads of dollars or shekels. There was barely a conversation here that didn't end with someone giving someone else a whole bunch of cash. There were literally hundreds, thousands, and maybe even millions of shekels being tossed around here, and seeing all that money changing hands made me feel so happy. Why? Because like I already told you, I came to Uman to hit the jackpot.

So anyway, I'm really hoping that all these people will be going to sleep soon, because tomorrow morning, while they're jumping around and praying and getting themselves all filled up with happiness, I'm going to be happily jumping around from suitcase to suitcase, trying to get my empty suitcase filled up with cash. I literally left Israel without a cent to my name, but I'm planning to return cashed up, with enough money to fund at least a couple of very good years. In fact, if it goes as well as I hope, I'm also planning to come back to Uman every Rosh Hashana from now on, *bli neder,* hahaha.

I have at least two whole days to go through as many suitcases as possible. Not that I'm planning to steal everything they have, G-d forbid. I'm planning to take ten bucks from each person, but 10 times 30,000 still comes out to a very nice $300,000. Not a bad salary for two days' work... plus no one is even going to notice that the ten or twenty bucks is missing. On second thought, maybe it's better to take the $20, because that way I don't have to come back every year. Maybe I can just do this bi-annually, or maybe just once every three years or so.

Maybe you want to know how I'm so confident that they won't know that their money is missing until after I'm long gone. The whole of Rosh Hashana, they're not even going to go near their money. It's only after the *Chag* is finished that they'll even check, and even then, they probably won't realize that ten bucks, (or 20, or maybe even 30 bucks) is missing. It's not such a big amount, and they'll just think they miscalculated how much money they actually brought with them.

Yeah, I know that most of the people I meet here are telling me that they're on the breadline, and that every cent counts for them, but I don't really believe them. If they were really that poor, how could they
buy a plane ticket for $800 or $900 in the first place? And some of them are travelling with two or three kids in tow, so I think all the stories I'm being told about being poverty stricken are just fairy tales to try and keep away the evil eye.

Or at least that's what I'm telling myself to try and get my conscience to stay quiet, so it doesn't try to stop me from leaving here a rich man.

Why aren't they going to check their money over the *Chag*? Because it's *muktzeh!* And if you don't know what *muktzeh* is, let me try and explain it in a way that normal people like you and I can understand. *Muktzeh*, to a *frummie*, is like a suspicious package to everyone else. It's dangerous to even touch it. Just because I know what *muktzeh* is doesn't make me a *frummie* too, G-d forbid, G-d should help me, with no evil eye. I am a dyed-in-the-wool *chiloni, Baruch Hashem*, but I've picked up some basic ideas from my twin brother Motty, who is about as big a flaming Breslever as you'd ever hope to meet. He taught me everything I need to know to pull off my 'special mission' in Uman this year.

# The Stolen Light

## Chapter 2

*Let me tell you a bit about my twin brother, Motty, who became a baal teshuva, may G-d have mercy on us, and who persuaded me to come to Uman with him, and why I agreed.*

I know, you're dying to find out: how'd I even get to Uman in the first place? My brother Motty, may G-d have mercy on us, *Hashem* should be compassionate, *bli neder* and, *tizku le mitzvot*, came down with the dreaded illness – that is to say, he decided to get religious. This happened four years, two months, two days and four hours ago, when Motty was in the army.

Even now, I don't really believe his story about how or why he decided to make *teshuva*, even though he gives everyone the same line. I'm convinced that they must have drugged him, or brainwashed him, or stuck some magic '*teshuva*' powder in his coffee or something. Anyway, according to Motty, one day he was waiting at a bus stop opposite the prison at Beit Lid Junction to get the bus that was going to take him back to his army base. That was the place and time of the terrible terrorist attack that killed many people whom we both knew personally, may *Hashem* avenge their blood, and my brother's story starts there.

Usually, we'd travel back to base together, but that day I was feeling pretty unwell, so I stayed home and my brother headed out without me. He was standing there at the bus stop waiting for a few minutes like everyone else, when the terrorist, *yemach shemo*, detonated himself.

(May our enemies all blow themselves up, without hurting so much as a hair on a single Jew's head.)

A Breslever *chassid* was one of the other people waiting at the bus stop, and he was trying to sell those little pamphlets that they like to distribute, with the nice colorful picture on the front. He was going from soldier to soldier trying to sell these pamphlets for a shekel each. My brother told me that most of the people weren't interested and were being kind of rude to the guy. But Motty, my sensitive, kind-hearted brother, became upset about all the bad treatment the Breslever was getting.

So he decided to do something nice for him and to buy 10 of his little pamphlets. Of course, he had no intention of actually *reading* them; as soon as he got on the bus, he was going to dump them onto an empty seat for someone else to take. The Breslever got really excited about Motty - it's not every day he gets a soldier to buy ten of his little pamphlets - and started telling him all these *dvar Torahs*.

Like I told you, my brother's a really nice, polite guy, so he didn't tell the Breslever to get lost. Quite the opposite, in fact. He had a bit of time to spare while waiting for the bus, and it wasn't costing him anything - so why not talk to this young black-hatter, who was telling him how he'd made *teshuva*? Motty asked him how someone could make *teshuva* even before they'd done the army, because that seemed to him a pretty unusual thing.

That's when the Breslever started telling over his life story. When he was 15, around two years earlier, he was diagnosed with cancer. He underwent chemotherapy, radiation, and a big operation which successfully removed part of the tumor - but it wasn't enough. Every couple of months, the tumor just got bigger again, and started spreading all over his body. The doctors were not very optimistic about his chances of making it, and his parents were on the edge of despair. They'd spent so much time, money, and emotional energy on their son getting better, and now the doctors' prognosis devastated them. The hospital told them that their son's only chance was to travel to a specialist in America for an operation that would cost $30,000, after the rebate that their Israeli insurance would pay.

The family sold their house, collected money from relatives, and even made a radio appeal to raise the money they needed, because as well as the cost of the operation, they'd also have to fund after-care, flights, and accommodation while in the U.S.

Two days before they were to fly out, some *chassid* comes knocking at their door, trying to collect money to help him pay for his ticket to Uman for Rosh Hashana. Any other time, as soon as the *abba* opened the door and saw who was standing there, he would have just slammed the door in his face. This time he didn't. For whatever reason, he started crying his eyes out, and telling the Breslever *chassid* about all the terrible things that were going on with his son. Five minutes later, the son's name was all over Uman, thanks to the Committee for Miraculous Salvations, and was also being publicized in every Breslev synagogue and community in Israel, too.

# The Stolen Light

One of the well-known Breslev rabbis who heard the story got in touch with the original *chassid*, who was still standing there on the doorstep and told him to tell the family that if the *abba* and the son got on a plane straight to Rebbe Nachman's *Tzion* to pray and ask G-d for mercy, he promised that they would see some very big miracles.

Of course, all this imaginary miracle nonsense didn't really convince the *abba*, and just as he was telling the *chassid* 'thanks, but no thanks', his son suddenly came to the door and told his father that he was prepared to go to Uman. Not only that, he demanded that his father book the tickets right then, and take him straight to Rebbe Nachman's grave, so he could prostrate himself on the tomb and beg for mercy.

The *abba* was completely taken aback. Why was his son so keen on making this insane trip to Uman? The son explained that the night before, he'd had a dream where some wonderful looking man with a beard had appeared and told him, "Come and visit me, and you'll have a miraculous recovery. But first, you have to come and visit me." Of course, the son had no idea who was telling him that, or where he was meant to go, but then once the Breslever *chassid* showed up at his door and told them about Rebbe Nachman, the son was convinced that the two things were connected. So it was that a few hours later, the *abba*, the boy, and the Breslever *chassid* found themselves on their way to Uman.

When they finally arrived, father and son spent 10 straight hours beside the grave, crying, praying, confessing all the things they weren't doing right, and making lots of promises to G-d for the future. They guaranteed that if the son was cured of his terrible disease, they'd turn their lives around and make complete *teshuva*. They'd start keeping *Shabbat* and everything else, too.

They stayed stuck to the grave for hours on end, and the Breslever *chassid* told the son afterwards that his prayers had sounded like they were completely out of this world. It was impossible to stand too close to him, because his cries were piercing bystanders to the core. At the end of that gruelling ten hours, father and son both collapsed beside the *kever*. When they recovered, they travelled back to Kiev and caught the plane back to *Eretz Yisrael*.

The next day, ten hours before they were meant to fly to the U.S. for the invasive, extremely expensive operation whose positive results were in no way guaranteed, the boy asked his father to take him for one last check-up to his own doctors. As you're probably expecting, because the same thing seems to happen in a lot of these miraculous stories, something amazing happened: the doctors took the boy in for an X-ray to check the size of his growth - and they couldn't find it! It had simply disappeared (and may the same thing happen to all of our enemies, *Amen*).

From that day on, the young man decided to devote his life to bringing other people closer to the Doctor of the Soul, Rebbe Nachman of Breslev.

The young man finished telling Motty his miraculous story, and Motty turned to go. The Breslever kept him back a couple of minutes longer, because he wanted to give him his number in case he wanted to come to a class on *Likutey Moharan*, or buy another few dozen more pamphlets to give out to his friends (it wasn't every day that he came across such a soft-hearted sucker like my brother).

Motty told us that after he heard the *chassid*'s story, he figured he'd open one of the pamphlets, which happened to be called '*Hashem* is behind everything - there are no coincidences', and read a little bit. A minute later, the terrorist detonated his nail-packed explosive vest. Anyone who was standing close to him either died immediately, or was very seriously injured from the blast. The only person in the vicinity that escaped without even a scratch on him was Motty. He was sure the pamphlet he was reading had somehow protected him.

Of course, I tried to explain to him that it was just a matter of happenstance, and that statistically speaking he would have been OK even without the pamphlet. Let's just say he wasn't convinced. He said, "So you're telling me that I should be praying to statistics now, and saying thank you to statistics?!" From that moment on, Motty started to take on all sorts of new religious commitments in the merit of all the people who'd been injured in the blast, that they should have a complete recovery. First it was *tefillin*, then it was *Shabbat*, then it was keeping kosher.

Basically, within four months, we had a serious *frummie* at home. And then he started driving everyone else crazy with his *Shabbat* hot plate, and his *Shabbat* clock, and his taking all the cutlery to the *mikveh*, etc. He's still driving me crazy, but thank G-d, he got married pretty soon after he made *teshuva* and had twin boys, whom he named - what else - Nachman and Natan. Nowadays, he's not sharing a house with me and my parents anymore, just driving me crazy from his own home - so it's much less annoying and intense than it used to be.

To tell you the truth, I found my brother's radical lifestyle change pretty hard to get used to. The truth is I'm still finding it hard, but at the beginning I had this strong feeling that he'd somehow betrayed me, and I wanted him to just disappear from my life. You see, Motty and I are identical twins, and we're very, very connected. I love him an awful lot, and he feels the same way about me.

Before he grew a beard and *peyot*, it was completely impossible to tell us apart. When we were little, we used to pull the classic twins trick a lot, blaming each other for mischief that we'd done to get out of being punished or embarrassed. Our parents and teachers never knew which of us was the genuinely guilty party, so most of the time they'd let us both off with a warning. Right from the start of our lives, we were together - from the maternity ward right up until the army. Until, that is, he got infected by the '*teshuva*' virus.

Initially, I thought it was a fad, a passing phase, and that within a month or maximum two, he'd get over the massive trauma he'd experienced from being caught up in the terrorist attack and get back to normal. He'd start coming out partying with me again, and playing music with me again, and doing all the things we'd loved to do together. But the opposite happened: instead of getting over his bout of *teshuva*, it intensified to the point where we didn't really have anything in common anymore, and we kind of drifted apart.

Of course, he still wanted to hang out with me a lot, but he was always just trying to convince me to join him in his *teshuva* adventure, or telling me some new crazy idea he'd gotten, or giving me another book full of strange theoretical ideas about how to live my life. I honestly had no idea where he was getting all this stuff. One day, he came to see me with another fantastical theory, this time about something he called the '*yetzer hara*', or evil inclination. According to his latest amazing discovery, the *yetzer hara* was busy stealing all our light from us, which meant that we were living in terrible, impenetrable darkness, and we couldn't so much as see plain objects directly in front of us.

I got a bit snappy with him, and told him that if that was his issue, he should go and learn how to be an electrician - that way, he'd have as much light as he needed, whenever he needed it. But he didn't take the hint, and kept going on and on about how 'the Torah is light' and how the exile we're in is darkness, and how Rebbe Nachman revealed to us the Torah of redemption, which shows us how we can steal back this 'stolen light' that the *yetzer hara* stole from us in the first place, blah blah.

The whole conversation left me with a nasty taste in my mouth. By the end of it, I made it very clear to him that I wasn't interested in his new lifestyle, or new beliefs, or his stolen light theory, and that from now on it would be better for us both if we just accepted that we were heading in different directions, and stay out of each other's way.

At the beginning, my parents got really worried about what was happening to Motty, but they were still pretty happy with me. Then some time passed, and they started worrying about me, and decided that Motty was actually doing OK. After all, now he was married with children and was learning and doing OK for himself, financially. They made it out like Motty had really done something with himself, while me? I was like some social services case.

Of course, it definitely helped that my brother had married the daughter of a millionaire who'd also made *teshuva* the Breslev way, so he was really set on every possible level. As for me, I felt like somehow I'd fallen between the cracks and gotten a bit lost. My parents really wanted me to go university to learn a 'useful profession' and become a doctor / lawyer / accountant, but I knew I just wasn't cut out for that life. I'd had enough of school. But I also wasn't cut out for a life where I'd knock myself out working as a motorcycle courier, porter, or factory worker either, earning a measly 4,000 shekel a month even if it *was* cash in hand. So instead, I just stayed in my room day after day, playing my guitar and composing new songs, hoping that some time soon I'd get a break and understand what I was meant to be doing with my life.

In high school, my brother and I were in a band together and played at the year-end parties. We really loved the music we were creating, and anyone who heard me sing or play the piano would tell me I that I had a great musical future ahead of me. So even though my current reality was pretty lame, my future was already in the bag. One of the most upsetting things about Motty making *teshuva* was that he completely abandoned his music - our music - to go and learn in yeshiva. I simply couldn't understand how he could so easily walk away from our songs, and from me. What especially bothered me was that we'd agreed that after we finished the army, we were going to start recording some of our stuff. What would happen with that idea?

Anyway, a couple of months ago, Motty was at my parents' house eating something to break his Tisha B'Av fast when he suddenly got this crazy idea in his head that I should come with him to Uman for Rosh Hashana. He told me he could pick me up a ticket for a couple of hundred dollars, because there was some millionaire American who was crazy about *Rabbeinu and* was making 4,000 tickets available at a really cheap price - and personally supplementing the difference.

Of course, he wasn't so much talking to me as trying to convince my parents, who were still worrying about what I was going to make of myself. Motty, may he be healthy, has a real way with words, and he convinced them that my salvation was in Uman. He told them that each generation had its own problems and difficulties, and required its own special 'doctor of the soul' to help people get back on their feet. At one point it was Moshe Rabbeinu; then, Rabbi Shimon Bar Yochai - and this time, this generation, it was Rebbe Nachman of Breslev. My parents are simple, innocent people, and when Motty mentioned Rabbi Shimon, they got really excited, because they love Rabbi Shimon.

I still don't understand why, but every year, my parents would pack a tent and take the whole family up to Meron for Lag B'Omer. My brother and I hated the two days we'd spend there. It was a complete nightmare to be stuck in the middle of millions of other people, and we didn't even know why we were there. But come what may, we couldn't get out of going.

# The Stolen Light

So anyway, they bought all of Motty's explanations about why I needed to go, and proceeded to put a massive guilt trip on me that they were 'getting older, and only wanted the best for me, and even if I didn't want to go, I should still go to Uman *for them*'. I was sooooo not interested. What possible reason could there be to go to Ukraine, with all the *frummies* that were going to be there? But Motty, may he be healthy, wasn't put off so easily. Once he gets an idea in his head, he just keeps going until he pulls it off.

It was the same with the music. For his *bar mitzvah*, he decided that he wanted a guitar, and he persuaded me that what I really wanted was a piano. Our parents weren't so into the whole idea, but he just kept on at them for months and months until they caved in and bought us a guitar and a piano. He showed the same determination when it came to actually learning how to play them; he just kept going until he'd learned a new note, then a new chord - and he encouraged me to do the same with piano. It's really thanks to him that I learned how to play music, because if I'd been left to my own devices, I probably would have given up years ago.

Anyway, he pulled the same stunt now with Uman. Day in and day out, he was in my face with one argument after another. One day he showed up and persuaded me to go with him to Misrad Hapnim to get a passport 'just in case'. "You don't have to go anywhere," he told me, "but what's the big deal about getting a passport? That couldn't possibly be harmful."

A few days after we got the passport, he convinced me to come with him to Jerusalem to buy the plane ticket. "What's the big deal about getting a ticket?" he asked me. "The worst thing that happens is that you'll just give it to someone else if you don't want it."

OK, so now I had a passport and a ticket. Not that I had any intention of actually going, you understand. I was sitting in my room playing to myself, trying to compose a new song, when this amazing melody suddenly popped into my head. At just that moment, one of my friends came to visit me, so I played him my new tune. He loved it! He told me, "Avi, you have to record this! It's amazing!"

"Where am I supposed to find the money to buy the studio time?" I wanted to know. And then I told him about all the Uman nonsense that my brother was trying to force me into. Suddenly, his face lit up and he told me, "What's wrong with going to Uman? You can make a lot of money in Uman!" He told me that he had a brother-in-law who also had the Uman disease, and that each year he needed big financial miracles to get him there - but he always came back with a big stash of money.

What, was I going to beg strangers to give me some money? Not on your life! I wasn't some impoverished *shnorrer*….which is when I had the brainstorm of the century. I don't really know how I came up with it; it just kind of popped into my head. There were going to be 30,000 people in Uman, and everyone knows that the people there, the *chareidim* there, had tons of cash. And why did they have so much spare cash? Because they are eating for free and contributing NOTHING to the State of Israel. All the newspapers I read, all the media I absorbed, they all told me the same thing: the *chareidim* are bleeding the country dry; they don't work, they don't contribute anything, and in the meantime, we are paying them millions of shekels a month in handouts. They were *mamash* stealing my money! That's what all the talk show hosts were always saying. So I decided - I'm going to steal it back! After all, doesn't it say in the Torah that if you rob a robber, you're not held accountable? (It's amazing how I suddenly became such a big *Talmid Chacham.*)

My first reaction was to recoil from the idea: I wasn't a thief! But the idea kind of got stuck in my head, and I started to imagine all the things I could do with a few thousand shekels. Why not? Why not do it, just once, and then I'd be set for life? I could come back from there with a big stash of cash that would enable me to record a whole album, not just one song. And then I persuaded myself that if my album sold as well as I was hoping, I'd pay back every single person that I took the money from.

So now here I was in Uman, and pretty much the only thing I'd managed to do so far was eat. Bardogo, the cook, had really outdone himself in the kitchen - the food he was turning out was five star gourmet. My brother saw that I was enjoying myself and gave me a big hug. He was sure that I was 100% 'with the program', and that I was enjoying the food just as much as I'd enjoyed the praying. He had no idea what was really going on in my head - and neither did anyone else. To them, I was just a new recruit in the army of Rebbe Nachman's returnees to G-d, sitting there in my brand new white *kippa* (with the pompom on top) that I'd bought just before the *Chag*, waiting for *Rabbeinu* to start giving me my very own personal soul rectification - my *tikun*.

If you looked up the word 'tikun' in a Breslever dictionary, the meaning would be something like: The making of order out of chaos, with *Rabbeinu* himself putting everything exactly into place. That's how they all talked, and it was obvious that each person here felt more 'soul sick' and more in need of some radical spiritual surgery than the next. This one had come to Uman for the open heart operation, that one had come for the brain transplant... Honestly, I don't know where they got all their crazy theories from, but that's how they talked.

Everyone had just one word on their lips: '*tikun*'. What soul correction were they going to get this year, and how was it going to completely change their lives? But I wasn't thinking about my *tikun*; I was just hoping they'd go to bed already, because I was dead tired and already starting to worry that I wouldn't be able to wake up early enough the next morning to put my plan into action, G-d forbid.

# The Stolen Light

All of a sudden, I found myself muttering a little prayer to myself: "*Ribono Shel Olam*, Master of the Universe, do me a big favor and please get them all to sleep already. Please help me G-d, even though I don't really know You... and we've never really spoken before... and really, I have no idea why I'm even talking to You now... but that doesn't matter. Please help me G-d, even though I know you probably aren't so keen on what I'm trying to do here, but please help me do it anyway."

I caught myself saying it, and I was shocked: what was going on? I'd come here to steal a bunch of money, and now found myself in silent prayer asking G-d to help me pull off my heist. I felt totally confused - maybe I'd hung out with my brother and his friends for too long and also gone crazy? I tried to calm myself down by drowning myself in food, and ate much more than I usually do.

As I was busy stuffing my face, they all started singing again, and I just couldn't get it: what did they have to sing about all the time? What were they getting out of it?

"*Becha Rabbeinu nagila, becha Rabbeinu nismecha*[2]" - we'd sung that song once already; maybe even twice. When they finished that one, they started on another perennial favorite: "*Mi yiten li aver ka-yonah, iyoofa el Tzion hakodesh umana*[3]." They liked to sing that one every chance they got.

And finally, the Uman anthem: "*Ashreinu, ashreinu, shezachinu le'hitkarev le Rabbeinu, Uman Uman Rosh Hashana*[4]," which was definitely at the top of the hit parade for Breslev *chassidim* on Rosh Hashana.

I joined in with the singing - why not? I have a pleasant strong voice, and the crew loved it. They loved it so much, they asked me to sing another song. Even though I didn't actually know any of the words, I joined in anyway. Or at least I joined in with what was going on externally; in my thoughts, I was still planning how best to pull off my big heist tomorrow morning.

My plan was this: on the first day of the *Chag*, I was going to go around taking money out of everyone's suitcases, as I've already explained - although I still hadn't decided exactly how much I was going to take. I thought maybe I'd just play it by ear and take more money from the people who brought more with them, and less from the people who had less. There could be some suitcases that were empty, and others that were holding a fortune, and from those, maybe I'd even take $100.

---

[2] "In you Rabbeinu, we will rejoice; in you Rabbeinu we will be happy."
[3] "Who will give me the wings of a dove? I will fly to the holy *Tzion* in Uman."
[4] "How fortunate are we, that we merited to come close to Rabbeinu."

On the second day of the holiday, after I'd collected as many dollars as I could, I'd hire a taxi to take me back to Kiev and then just sit in some Ukrainian casino somewhere, sipping a tall drink until it was time to fly back home. Now that's what I'd call a really successful trip to Uman for Rosh Hashana, if only everything went according to plan.

Just then, they started singing: "*Ve kol asher, asher ya'aseh, asher ya'aseh, yatzliach,*" which roughly translated, means 'everything that you do, you'll succeed in'. I took it as a colossal hint from Upstairs that my plan had gotten the stamp of approval, and the divine forces were going to help me pull it off. My brother had taught me that everything that happens to us or around us, whether heard, seen, or experienced, is all just part of a grand message from *Hashem Yitbarach*. I figured I'd just gotten a clear hint that my plan was going to succeed - and what could I say, except *'Amen Sela!'*

## Chapter 3

*Let me tell you about Shraga the computer guy, and his bizarre dream.*

I'll tell you this - since the first minute that I agreed to join my brother on his trip to Uman, the whole experience has been like one enormous fairy tale.

When I told my brother that I would come with him, he hugged me and then danced with me for ten minutes. My parents were also on cloud nine, because now they were sure I was going to get the 'salvation' they felt I so desperately needed.

So we left for Uman, a group of four: me, my brother, and two of his buddies from yeshiva. One of them was Shraga, who used to be the director of a very successful high-tech company until he also caught the *teshuva* disease. My brother's other friend was named Gidon, and he *davka* came from a *chareidi* home. Great! What a fun *chevra* to be flying out with!

Most of the time, they were away with the fairies being all spiritual, or reading obsessively from a book called *Likutey Tefilot*, written by Rabbi Natan. And they were convinced that every single prayer in that book was written just for them - which goes to show you how divorced from reality they were, because the book was written more than 200 years ago. Nevertheless, every few minutes one of them would say to the other:

"Look at the amazing things that Rabbi Natan wrote here. It just can't be that he's talking about his own experiences, because what flaws did he have? What sins could he have been caught up in, the pure, holy soul that he was? G-d must have given him a spirit of prophecy, so that he'd be able to write this prayer just for me! It's like he's here right now, and understands exactly what I'm going through, and what I'm thinking and feeling."

And then they would stroke that book, and kiss it, and dance with it, which was just additional proof that they were all certifiably crazy.

We had decided before the trip to divide between us all the stuff needed for our stay. Initially, I thought I was flying out to get pampered in some five star hotel (although even I knew that a five star hotel in Ukraine probably wasn't a five star hotel anywhere else in the world). But very quickly, they let me know that we weren't going anywhere near a hotel, five star or otherwise. I'd be lucky to be sleeping in a room with fewer than five other people.

They told me in no uncertain terms that if the bed had a mattress on it, that was five star luxury in the Ukraine, and the same principle applied for the food. If I wanted to eat something good without paying a fortune for it, I had to bring it with me from Israel and cook it there.

So Gidon was given the job of bringing the fruit, vegetables, bread and spices. Shraga was assigned the fish, drinks, grape juice, wine, dessert, and snacks. My brother had to bring the chicken and meat - his father-in-law owned a big chain of supermarkets, so it was clear to everyone that he'd get his shopping at a bargain-basement price - and I was asked to bring all the plastic cutlery and paperware. I hate disposable plates, so I also brought along a real plate and fork for myself. Unfortunately, I never got to use them because I didn't *tovel* them beforehand, so their use was banned by the *chevra*. They wouldn't even let me sneak off somewhere to eat quietly by myself, so I decided to just immerse myself in the food instead and forget about my plate.

When you got down to it, the *chevra* was actually pretty nice, even though I was trying my hardest not to get too close to anyone on the trip - partially because I'm quiet and I keep myself to myself anyway, and partially because I didn't want to run the risk of getting any pangs of conscience when I wanted to steal their money later on.

So there I was, on the plane in the center of a row of seats, with Shraga on the right of me and Gidon on the left. They've become obsessed with talking at me, trying to convince me that there is actually a Creator of the world (I'm sure my brother put them up to this). They start bringing me all these scientific proofs, and to be honest, I didn't have the strength to fully get into it with them. I already learned from being around Motty and his friends that the best way to get them to leave you alone was by asking them how they got close to *Rabbeinu*, to Rebbe Nachman.

Shraga took the bait, and the pressure was off. And when Shraga was done telling me his story, I made a mental note to ask Gidon to tell his, because that should just about take us the whole flight. Listening to their crazy stories was clearly preferable to getting into complicated, pointless arguments about whether or not G-d existed.

I fixed my most interested look on my face, then turned to Shraga and asked him, "How did you get close to *Rabbeinu*?" And, just as I thought, I didn't have to say another word for the next hour.

This is Shraga's story:

*"It all started when I was 38 years old. At the time, I was a very successful businessman. I had a factory that was manufacturing innovative hi-tech products that we were supplying to big companies all over the world. We were just about to sign an exit deal with Tykon, a big company in Berlin, which had agreed to buy us out for 100 million euros.*

*All told, we were ten partners and 40 or so employees, each of whom had minimal stakeholding shares in the company. I was set to bring home seven million euros from that deal, which would set me up for life.*

*One night, I had a dream that I was sitting in front of a doctor, at his clinic that looked something like a spaceship. I was sitting there in silence while he looked at a bunch of x-rays and leafed through a bunch of official looking papers on his desk. Suddenly, he looks up and he tells me in an anguished voice: 'Shraga, you have only one hour left to live.'*

*He didn't say 'I'm so sorry, you only have an hour left...' or 'I regret having to tell you this, but...' He just gave it to me straight. I started shouting at him in a loud voice that ended in a sort of strangled cough. I asked him to clarify: 'Do I have exactly an hour left to live, or a bit longer?' I thought maybe I'd try to ease up the conversation a little by making my tone somewhat light, but he did not respond in kind. He said, 'An hour. Actually, now you have an hour minus a minute...' In other words, a minute had already passed since he'd first told me about my death sentence, and the clock was ticking.*

*'What are you talking about?!' I protested. 'I feel fine! I think you're looking at the wrong chart. You must have made a mistake, and you're talking to the wrong guy.'*

*'You're wasting your time!' he told me. 'Now, you have 58 minutes.' I got up and left.*

*In the dream, I left his clinic feeling shocked and depressed, and got into my car and started to drive. I had this vague notion that I was going to drive home and break the news to my wife, but then it hit me: I only have 55 precious minutes left to live! Why am I going to waste ten of them driving home? I realized there wasn't even any point in calling her up, because the conversation would be very difficult and painful, and would also take up a lot of time. In less than an hour, she'd find out that I'd just died anyway, so why waste the time that I still had? I had an hour minus ten minutes to live, what was I going to do with it?*

*The thought crossed my mind to go to my favorite restaurant and order my favorite meal. But I realized that with all the traffic on the way and looking for parking, I'd probably get there with just 10 minutes left on the clock and barely enough time to take the first bite. I would walk in, order, and probably die with food actually in my mouth. Not a pleasant vision.*

*So what was I going to do with the 45 minutes I had left to live? I know! I could drive to the beach and watch the last beautiful sunset of my life... I started berating myself for being an idiot - what was watching the sunset going to do for me, really? And that's assuming I wouldn't get stuck in a massive traffic jam on the way to the beach, either. As I was debating all this in my head, I realized I now had just 30 minutes left to live - and no idea what to do with them!*

*Suddenly, my alarm clock rang and I woke up with a start. It was just a dream! But what a nightmare - I was drenched in sweat. You could have wrung out my pajamas and filled a bucket with all the liquid. I got up and took a very long shower to try and wash off the sweat as well as the memory of the dream, which had really shaken me up.*

*I made myself a coffee and had a nice breakfast, but somehow couldn't shake off the dream. It was in the back of my mind the whole day. I couldn't concentrate on what was happening at work, and I was walking around like a zombie. My partners noticed that I was really out of it, but they chalked it up to stress about our big imminent deal. Of course, I didn't tell them what was really upsetting me. They were uber-rational business people, and would have laughed me out of town if I'd tried to explain it to them.*

*Even though we were literally a day or two away from signing our big deal with Tykon, I asked for a couple of days annual leave. My partners thought I was cracking up from the stress, or maybe that I'd gotten emotional about selling the business I'd helped build from scratch. They gave me the OK to take a two day break, and I took my wife and daughter and went up north. But even there, I couldn't seem to shake off the dream.*

*My wife felt that something was seriously going on with me, and she nudged me until I opened up and told her about my horrible dream. Of course, she was very practical back then, and played down the whole thing by telling me it was just a dream and I shouldn't take these things so seriously. There was no point even in thinking about it any more. End of story.*

# The Stolen Light

*But I asked her what she would do, if told that she had only an hour to live.*

*'I'd fold all the laundry, make sure the house was tidy, and prepare enough food in the freezer to last you a week. Then I would die, and that would be that.'*

*'What? Just like that? So simple?'*

*'Yes. Why, what would you do?'*

*'Well, that's exactly the problem. I got all disturbed because I really didn't know what I'd do if I only had an hour left to live, and it's really bothering me.'*

*'Why is that bothering you so much?'*

*'Well, let's take a minute and really think about this seriously. What are we doing with ourselves? We're just living like animals, running after money and careers, having kids, then dying. That's it? That's called 'life'? If that's all there is to it, what's the point? What's the point of being alive?'*

*'You sound like an angsty teenager! My love, what's really going on with you? Usually, people stop asking about the meaning of life by the time they're 16. By the time they get to our age, they already know what the answer is: there is no meaning! Live and let live, try and make your life as good as you can, leave a bit of money for your descendants, and then go to the grave peacefully. The only thing that we leave behind is a few memories in our children's heads and maybe a few impressions that we made on our grandchildren. Once they die, there's nothing to remind the world that we ever existed, except our gravestones, where people can come and see the day we were born and the day we died.'*

*'That's so depressing!' I told her.*

*'No it's not. It's just life. That's how it is.'*

*Wow, if even my own wife thought I was making my dream into a big deal over nothing, maybe I really had just cracked up from all the stress at work.*

*I came back to the factory and found out that the deal with the Germans had fallen through. Not just that, but everyone was blaming me for it, because I'd been the main contact person and had disappeared at the crucial stage. I didn't care so much, because at that point, I was completely wrapped up in myself and had become obsessed with getting an answer to the question of what one should do with only an hour to live. I asked all of my friends that question, and each one gave me an even more ridiculous answer than the last.*

*That's when it hit me, very depressingly: we're all just living like robots! How could it be that the driving force of this amazing creature called a human being, with all its wisdom, knowledge, and super-sophisticated internal systems and abilities, was just to eat good food, drive a fancy car, live in a nice house and have fun? How could it be?*

*For half a year after that, I was sleep-walking through my life; I couldn't focus on anything. One day, I happened to pass the security guard's hut at work and saw a poster advertising a lecture that was going to take place in one of the local synagogues, entitled: "Life after death: reality or make-believe?" 'OK!' I said to myself, 'that is one lecture that I really need to go to.'*

*But it wasn't so simple, because even the thought of stepping inside a synagogue was pretty stressful, and I suddenly worried that I was just setting myself up for some hardcore religious brainwashing. On the other hand, I could feel that I actually needed that sort of brainwashing right now, so I swallowed my misgivings and went inside.*

*The man delivering the lecture was a youngish-looking Rabbi, and he asked the audience: 'What's the point of us being alive when the world seems to be so full of suffering? Where are we all trying to get to in such a hurry? Where is the world heading? Is it even possible to have a happy, fulfilled life? Why are there such big differences between us, why is this one poor, and that one rich, and this one healthy, and that one sick? What's the point of everything? What are we doing down here?'*

*He didn't give us any answers. Instead, he quoted Rebbe Nachman: 'Rebbe Nachman taught us that when a grain of wheat is planted in good soil, it grows tall and strong, and no wind or thunder or lighting can damage it. Our emuna is an indication of our ability to grow - and when a person has emuna, they live a beautiful, good life.'*

*Ah, I got it: this lecture was going to be about 'emuna', and other Jewish missionary stuff. That was really not for me, so I got up to leave and started making my way to the exit. The Rabbi saw me get up, and addressed me directly from the stage:*

*'Don't go until you answer this: if you were at your doctor's office, and he told you that you only had one hour left to live, what would you do with that last hour of your life?'*

*'What?!' I think I must have screamed that out, because the whole audience turned around sharply to look at me.*

# The Stolen Light

*'Why are you specifically asking me that question?!' I couldn't believe the coincidence.*

*'I'm not just asking you, I'm asking every single one of us, myself included,' said the Rabbi. 'I think its something that anyone with even minimal awareness should be asking themselves, because who knows how long any of us really have left to live? Statistically speaking, any one of us could drop dead at any minute, even if he or she is the fittest person on the planet - or the richest, or the cleverest. We hear about these things happening all the time.'*

*It goes without saying that I sat back down and stayed to hear the rest of the lecture. If I'd have heard what he was saying even a couple of hours earlier, I would have completely ignored it and discarded all his ideas; I wouldn't even have wasted a millisecond of my precious time thinking about such ridiculous, superstitious nonsense. But now? After the amazing coincidence when he'd asked me my very own question, something opened up in my heart, and I was at least willing for the first time to give his ideas some space and fair consideration, which I never would have done before.*

*At the end of his lecture, I went over to him, and I told him about my dream. He smiled at me, and told me that he was so pleased that G-d had put the right words in his mouth to get me to stay. After that, I found myself driving the Rav around in my car, again because of a massive coincidence that resulted in his regular driver not showing up to take him to his next lecture. I volunteered to do it instead. I drove him around the whole night, and after that, I became his regular driver, taking him from lecture to lecture most nights. Yishtabach shemo la'ad, thank G-d, the King of the World, who turns all the thoughts in a man's heart to good.*

*It goes without saying that we talked the whole time. I asked the Rav what he would do if he knew he had just an hour left to live. Very simply and unassumingly, he told me that he would do a cheshbon hanefesh (moral inventory check) and make a personal accounting of his whole life up to that point. After that, he'd ask G-d to forgive him for all the sins he'd done. He also told me that the word for 'sin' in Hebrew, chet, came from a verb root that meant 'to miss the target', and that was really the deeper meaning of what happens when we sin, that we go off in the wrong direction and miss the point of why we're really alive.*

*I'd never heard anyone describe sins in that way before; whenever I heard the word 'sin', I'd always associated it with the most primitive, backwards modes of thinking.*

*Anyway, the Rav continued, his last act would be to finally thank Hashem for all the amazing bounty and kindnesses that He'd given him throughout his life.*

*When I heard that, I was blown away. What amazing clarity! What a way to spend your last hour on earth...*

*During our conversation, I started to realize that I was actually a sad, angry person, a boor and an ignoramus who was incredibly arrogant and disliked other people - and this was only the tip of the iceberg. I was stuffed full of bad middot which were really running the show without me even realizing just how bad it all was, or what was really going on. My attitude had always been, 'This is me - if you like me, that's great; and if you don't, you can get lost.'*

*For the first time, I started to see that I was an anger-prone, stingy racist. If I tell you a story, you'll see just how cruel and stingy I used to be. This story isn't about how I used to treat street-beggars or anything like that, because I used to just act like they didn't exist and completely ignore them. On the odd occasion that someone would actually come knock on my door, if I was in a good mood, I'd give them a shekel maximum. But even that I'd give begrudgingly, because I couldn't believe that these crooks actually had the gall to expect me to give them my money.*

*At the time, I was earning an absolute fortune - I'd regularly net between 50,000 and 60,000 shekels a month, and that's not including any bonuses or extras that I'd periodically be given. Some months, I'd come home with 100,000 shekels burning a hole in my pocket. I drove around in a fancy car worth half a million; I lived in a big house with a swimming pool and a beautifully manicured garden that cost 4,000 shekels a month just to maintain; I had one daughter and two dogs. Five or six times a year, I'd take the family on holiday abroad to a luxury hotel. We'd go skiing in Swiss Alps in the winter and hiking in the Austrian Alps in summer, and I enjoyed many other fringe benefits that I took for granted without even thinking twice. And yet, with all that luxury, I still didn't feel happy and content.*

*From the outside, it all looked amazing. I always had a carefully arranged smile on my face, I dressed in the latest Italian fashions, and I always seemed to have a bunch of clever things to talk about. But on the inside? I was in the pit of despair. I hadn't gotten in touch with what I was really feeling until I had my dream, because up until then I was completely obsessed with my work, being a success, and winning the race, so I never took the time to look inward.*

*So, now that you have some idea of how much money I had, let me give you an example of just how cruel and stingy I was to other people. I have a sister. At the same time that I was at the peak of my financial success, she was going through a very hard time. Nothing was going right for her - she hadn't managed to find Mr. Right, she hadn't managed to find her path in life, or a job that suited her. She was really in a hard place, and was barely able to scrape enough money together to even pay her rent.*

# The Stolen Light

*She was already 28, and had passed the stage where she could happily stay living at home with my parents. Desperately trying to hold on to her rundown 800 shekel a month basement apartment, she could barely even afford to pay that. She was living from hand to mouth and still eating most of her meals at my parents, who were consumed with worry and sadness about what was going to be with her.*

*I, by contrast, was earning a fortune, more than enough to have helped my sister out and to give her a much better standard of living. I wouldn't even have really noticed, because it would have made barely a dent in my own lifestyle. But why should I care what was going on with her? Why should I help her? She should get a grip on herself, pull herself up by her bootstraps, and make something of herself just like I'd done. No one had helped me to get to where I'd got to. I was a self-made man, and if I could do it, why couldn't she?*

*My credo was, 'anyone who helps themselves will succeed in life; anyone who relies on other people, won't.' Even when my parents came to try and wake me up a bit about my sister and encourage me to have a bit of brotherly compassion for her, it didn't change my attitude one iota. As far as I was concerned, I'd hit the big time, I was living the high life, and the people who were bouncing along the bottom were beneath me in every sense of the word.*

*Of course, the massive irony is that these days, I don't have the same assets that I used to and I live in a small apartment in Ramat Gan. Often, I find it very hard to keep afloat till the end of the month. But do you know who's helping me out? My sister! When she made teshuva, she found her husband - and Baruch Hashem, he's a pretty wealthy businessman, and Baruch Hashem, they're being very generous. My sister isn't just giving me a few shekels every month to keep her conscience quiet, she's giving me $1,000 dollars! And not only that, she's also taking care of my mortgage, and paying for all the nursery fees and school fees for my kids - and she's doing it all with a sincerely good heart, without holding a grudge for the way I treated her when the shoe was on the other foot. And I can promise you that if she hadn't made teshuva, it would be completely different; she'd be exacting payback now and not giving me so much as a shekel, just as I did to her.*

*It should go without saying that completely turning my life around wasn't an easy thing. For months, I was keeping everything hidden; No one, not even my wife, knew that I'd made teshuva. I used to leave the house very early (which of course, I blamed on work), then go to synagogue and put on my tefillin and pray there. On Shabbats, I suffered terribly, because I'd gotten to the stage where I really wanted to keep Shabbat according to halacha. I already understood how meaningful and beautiful and important Shabbat was and how big a problem it was to desecrate, but what could I do? My wife was so disgusted by anything even called 'religion' that there was no chance that I'd be able to try to sneak a Shabbat hotplate into the house, or to set things on a Shabbat clock. And if I'd even so much as mentioned the idea of not travelling on Shabbat - not going to the beach, or visiting her friends, or popping in on her parents, she'd have gone ballistic.*

*As I was getting more observant, albeit secretly, her anti-religious streak seemed to get even bigger and more strident. It was like her intuition had picked up on what I was up to, and subconsciously she was trying to uproot my newly-sprouted faith and practice before it could grow, by coming out with the most outrageous anti-religious comments she could think up. Or at least, that's how it seemed to me at the time.*

*This continued for a few months until the day that I decided to leave my job and sell my shares in the company. I was scared that my wife might be really angry and accuse me of making a stupid, rash decision, even though the company wasn't actually doing so well anymore. Without boasting, I was really the brains behind the company, and when I stopped putting all my time and energy into work, the company started to nosedive. It's not that I didn't want to work or didn't care about having a good income anymore, because of course I did! But I'd gotten to the stage that I had no other choice except to leave, because the company policy was to work on Shabbat and I just couldn't be a part of that anymore.*

*That evening, I told my wife that I wanted to take her to her favorite restaurant. I planned to finish off our romantic evening together by taking her to the seashore, where I'd finally stop living my double-life and come clean about everything that was going on. So it was that a few hours later, we were both sitting there by the beach, completely engrossed by the ebb and flow of the waves, as though it was the first time either of us had ever seen the ocean. And in some ways maybe it was, because it was certainly the first time I'd ever really noticed the waves, or thought about them in any meaningful way.*

*So we're sitting there, and I'm trying to find the right way to start the conversation off while avoiding her reflexive anger… As I'm still musing on what to say, she turns to me, and starts talking:*

*'Shraga, I have to tell you something to your face.'*

*I gulped. It felt like she was about to tell me that she wanted a divorce or something. Over the last few months, I'd obviously stopped being the successful, 'cool' person she'd married, and I was spending more and more time alone with my own thoughts, trying to sort a lot of things out. While I'd been obsessed with my quest for truth, she'd started looking for more attention outside of the house. So I braced myself for what I was sure was coming next.*

# The Stolen Light

*'I'm going through a spiritual process at the moment,' she said. 'I wouldn't call it a process of making teshuva exactly, but I'm definitely trying to get back to my roots, and to get back to the root of my soul, which is definitely bound up with Judaism.'*

*'You're what?!' I could barely speak, and my soul felt like it was about to burst out of my body.*

*'Shraga, please don't be angry with me, I know you hate religion and religious people, but I'm really talking about something else entirely. I don't want you to worry that I want us to sell everything and move to Meah Shearim, or that I'm going to start wearing a scarf on my head, but...'*

*'Why not?' I interrupted her. 'That would be great! Are you teasing me, or is this really true?' The thoughts were whizzing around my brain faster than the speed of light, and I felt a headache coming on, but my wife's smile just seemed to get bigger and bigger.*

*'No, I'm completely serious. I've been doing 'Shittat Yemima' self-discovery Torah classes for more than half a year now, and it's really connected me to all the 365 positive mitzvot, and 248 negative mitzvot.'*

*I wanted to scream, I wanted to dance, I wanted to explode, but I calmed myself down and I said: 'I've been involved in the 'Rebbe Nachman self-discovery through Torah' process for more than eight months now, and it's really connected me to all the 365 positive mitzvot and 248 negative mitzvot.'*

*'What? You're into Rebbe Nachman? I think I must be dreaming...'*

*'And if you're into Shittat Yemima, then I must be dreaming times two,' I replied. I didn't actually know what 'Shittat Yemima' was exactly, but I knew it was something to do with a G-d-fearing, religious psychologist named Yemima Avital who had developed a psychological approach based on Torah sources, and had helped a lot of people come back to G-d as a result.*

*For the next hour, we sat in silence just hugging each other and crying. It was like we were two little kids who'd gotten lost in the big city and just found each other again.*

*Of course, my wife was initially a bit wary about the whole Breslev thing; she thought I'd be dancing on rooftops and disappearing for hours while she'd be left to look after the home. But she's a methodical person, and decided to check out Breslev chassidut for herself. She spoke to some friends of hers about Breslev, and even booked herself a ticket to visit Rebbe Nachman's grave in Uman. There, her neshama simply got lit up in the most amazing way and from then on, she became the prime force behind our teshuva process.*

*One day I was sitting on the patio learning some Torah, when I heard her arguing on the phone to one of her friends who I'd always thought was quite anti-Breslev. That's the one who'd told my wife stories about 'the friend of her friend who had friends' whose marriage had fallen apart because their life had plunged into anarchy after they'd made teshuva, because instead of spending time with their wives and kids, the husbands were off all the time visiting the tombs of saintly dead people, or praying for hours in a field somewhere.*

*Sometimes it's very easy for people to make judgement calls based on a superficial understanding of what they think is going on, instead of making the effort to really understand the profound meaning behind certain practices.*

*In any case, I was really happy when I heard my wife challenge this friend's comments, and especially when she told her friend that dafka, she'd had the very opposite thing happen: when I'd gotten into Breslev, I'd taken a giant step closer to becoming much more of a family man. 'These days, he takes the trash out, he washes the dishes, he changes the kids' diapers, he goes shopping, and he makes a point of asking me how I'm doing every day. In the past, he used to wake up, leave for work at 7am, and only come home at midnight. Most of the time, we communicated by phone.*

*'Sure, he was bringing a lot of money home, but he himself was hardly ever around. These days, he's bringing in less money, but at least he's around the house now, and who cares if he wants to talk to G-d for an hour a day? Isn't that the whole point? Doesn't the Prophet Isaiah tell us to 'take your words with you, and return to G-d'? Take your words and go and talk to G-d for an hour! If you tried it yourself, you'd see some amazing changes in your own life.'*

*By the end of that conversation, she'd even managed to convince her friend to come with her to Uman, and see for herself. Today, that friend is as devoted a Breslever as you can be.*

*A lot of water has gone under the bridge since then, seven years ago. We had another four kids and my wife is pregnant with our sixth, with G-d's help. You see brother, how G-d arranges everything in our lives with precise detail?"*

"Wow, what a cool story. It sounds like something straight out of a movie", I told him, and I honestly meant it. But I didn't want to give them a second of quiet, because if I did, I knew they'd start trying to fill it by giving me a whole class on *emuna*, or telling me a whole bunch of stuff about 'Divine Providence'. So I turned to Gidon, and I asked *him* the question of questions: "And you? How did you get connected to *Rabbeinu*?"

# The Stolen Light

## Chapter 4

*Let me tell you about Gidon, who told me all about his genius brother Betzalel, who got lost in chutz L'aretz; and about Jeremy the famous artist and his son; and of course, a bit about himself, too.*

"I was born chareidi, which means that I was born into a chareidi home, with everything that goes along with that. Like every chareidi boy in Israel, I went to cheder, then I went to yeshiva katana, and afterwards to yeshiva gedola. I prayed three times a day, I kept Shabbat, and on the face of it, my life looked like it was going to go the standard route that life takes when you're a normal chareidi boy who's doing OK in yeshiva (or maybe, without boasting, who's even doing quite amazingly well in yeshiva).

I came from a good home with a good pedigree and everything was going along just swimmingly, until the day when everything exploded - because of my brother.

No one was really paying attention to what was going on with my older brother, the next one up from me. I was sixteen at the time, and he was 18. A really gifted learner, he was completing his third year of studies in yeshiva gedola. The Rabbis at his yeshiva were already talking about what a bright future he had ahead of him in the world of Torah; he was going to end up a big Talmid Chacham.

But while all this amazing holy stuff seemed to be happening on the outside, no one knew, or would even have believed, what was really going on inside my brother. He didn't have anyone he could talk to or confide in about what he was really feeling and thinking, and even if someone did try to talk to him, he was always careful to sweep all his real issues and problems under the carpet.

*Not that I'm talking about massive problems here, G-d forbid, because it really wasn't like that. Yet. If he'd just had someone to talk to at the beginning before everything spiralled out of control, things would probably never have come to a head the way they did. Our parents (may they be healthy and live for many long years) were devoting all their time and energy to learning Torah, living Torah, and helping Am Yisrael.*

*My father is a very well known Talmid Chacham who spent the vast majority of his time out of the house. Either he was in the synagogue or beit midrash learning Torah with his various chevrutas, or he was flying all over the world trying to raise money for worthy causes. One time it was to help a yeshiva, another time he was fundraising for a young man who needed to pay for a life-saving operation, another time to help a family in financial meltdown... You get the picture.*

*My mother was the headmistress of a Beis Yaakov high school for girls, but when she wasn't working, she was involved in a host of voluntary activities to help the community. We were a relatively small family for our neighborhood - just eight kids. The brother I'm telling you about was number five, and I'm number six. Four of my older siblings were already married with their own children, and we were used to a life where our parents were very rarely at home. All of the remaining kids adapted to that reality and made the best of it however we could. But my brother is a sensitive introvert, and he never really made his peace with our parents being out so much. Of course, he never said anything to anyone about it, but as time went on he became increasingly bitter about the situation, and eventually his sadness turned to anger.*

*He became increasingly disappointed and then resentful that our father never came to his yeshiva to visit him and see how he was doing, like he saw the other boys' fathers doing. No one took the time to send him little care packages from home, and no one even really called to check up on him, I guess because he was so successful and doing so well at school. But despite all his achievements in learning, my brother felt completely alone in the world. One time, he came home for Shabbat - the first time he'd been home in three weeks - and my parents weren't there because they were spending that Shabbat at some important seminary for girls.*

*Despite it all, I think that most of my siblings, including my brother, still appreciated my parents, because they really were trying to do things for altruistic reasons, le'shem shamayim. No one was paying them for all the volunteer work they were doing, no one was giving them any medals or putting up any plaques for them. They were working with joy all the time, just to try to spread more of G-d's light in the world.*

# The Stolen Light

*The day after that Shabbat when my parents were away, my brother didn't turn up at his yeshiva. Two days passed, then three, until finally the yeshiva got in touch with my mother to ask what was going on. Where was my brother? My mother had no idea, he certainly wasn't at home. My father was off fundraising in chutz l'aretz and wasn't scheduled to fly back to Israel for another week - and in the meantime, no one knew where my brother was. There was a sense of mounting hysteria as we started to call around to all the hospitals and police stations. This continued for two weeks, until my parents got a phone call from my brother. He told them that he was in New York.*

*He said that he was doing fine, and that they shouldn't worry about him. He didn't want to give them his contact details in America, but said he'd call them again when he could - and that was that. In some ways, a big stone dropped off everyone's hearts, because at least he wasn't dead, G-d forbid, or lying comatose in a hospital after being injured in some terrible accident. But in other ways, it was like a big boulder had just been dropped on us from a great height. What was he doing in New York? What was going on with him?*

*My father waited for him to come home for one month, then two, and then he ran out of patience. Like I said, he used to fly a lot to chutz l'aretz to fundraise, so he decided to go to New York and look for my brother. He went to every Jewish community he could think of - yeshivas, synagogues, you name it. Nothing. He spent a whole month in New York trying to find my brother, with no luck. The day before he was due to come back to Israel, he was sitting at a travel agency office in sunken despair, watching someone flick through a magazine - when one of the pictures caught his eye. One of the male models looked extraordinarily similar to my brother, but my father immediately pushed the preposterous thought out of his head, because that's the last thing his son would be doing. And so that was that, my father returned to Israel. He circulated a picture of my brother around all the Jewish communities in New York in case someone had news about him, but it was a dead end – he heard nothing.*

*Four heart-rending months passed, months where the whole family was in limbo. One day my father got a call from a friend of his telling him that my brother - his son, the Talmudic genius - was working as a hugely successful model for a very famous fashion house. His pictures were in magazines all over the world, and he was clearly making bundles of money - and bundles of shame for us, his family. The man advised my father to sit shiva for my brother, as it looked like he was sunk so far down into the klipot, it would be impossible to get him out again.*

*My father hung up the phone, and actually had a minor heart attack on the spot. He was taken straight to the hospital, where he was treated and released. For the next week, my parents were a bag of nerves as they tried to come to terms with what had happened. They went to visit every Gadol HaDor for a blessing; they gave thousands of shekels to charity, had yeshiva students go pray at the Kotel, at Kever Rachel, at the tomb of Rabbi Shimon Bar Yochai, and a bunch of other places too. They had people praying everywhere."*

"But not by *Rabbeinu!*" Shraga laughed.

*"Of course not! Not even the shadow of a thought of praying by Rabbeinu ever crossed their minds. My parents didn't really know anything about Rebbe Nachman himself, but they did know that Breslev was some weird fringe group far away from proper Judaism.*

*While all this was going on, no one had actually spoken to my brother for around six months. He hadn't gotten in touch with us, and we hadn't managed to track down the company that he was working for. Then a letter arrived which spelled out exactly what my brother had gone through, and where he was now. That letter was heartbreaking in the past tense, and absolutely horrifying in the present tense.*

*My brother had completely cut himself off from our world, and switched his life in the polar opposite direction, may Hashem have mercy. It looked like really, there was no choice but to sit shiva for him. I myself didn't read the letter that he'd written on ten sheets of paper, but saw the devastated faces of my parents after they'd read it, sitting in our living room with rivers of tears running down their cheeks. My parents weren't really to blame for what had happened, but neither was my brother, as you'll see.*

*In the yeshiva where he was learning, there was an American student who from the outside looked as though he was a good yeshiva bochur full of yirat Shamayim, but who really was about as far from Yiddishkeit and G-d as you could get. This boy started pressuring my brother and really twisting his arm to come back with him to America. He told my brother that he had a cousin who was a millionaire and would help them set up some sort of export business. The plan was that when they'd made enough money, they would go back to yeshiva and continue learning.*

*Even now, I have no idea how all these ridiculous ideas influenced my brother so much. He was always so far away from the making money obsession, because his real love was learning. He just wasn't into following the latest fashions or anything like that. Later on, when we actually got to talking about it, I realized that the lack of love and attention that my brother felt drastically weakened his ability to see through the lies he was being told.*

*So anyway, this 'friend' bought my brother a ticket to America just like he said he would; his cousin really was a millionaire, just like he said he was - and for the first few weeks, this cousin took my brother all over the place, to the beaches and the pubs. Initially, my brother was in total shock. He came from a very sheltered yeshiva environment where his entire reality was defined by Gemara and halacha, and now suddenly found himself shoved into this outside world of chaos and destruction.*

*But by the third week I guess he felt it was too late to turn back, and may as well just get on with his new life. The cousin arranged for my brother to get a new American-style haircut and bought him a new wardrobe of modern American clothes, and the path from there to becoming a full-fledged supermodel was a very short one. The cousin owned a men's fashion magazine, and that's how just two months after my brother left the yeshiva world in Israel, he found himself living in an expensive penthouse in New York, driving a new luxury car, and earning tens of thousands a dollars a month as an in-demand male model.*

*Of course, he still laid tefillin whenever he could, and sometimes even with a minyan; and he tried to keep Shabbat as best he could, in his own way. But when he was on location on a Caribbean Island, it wasn't so easy. The really interesting thing is that my brother would still take a massechet of Gemara with him even on his photo shoots and learn a few minutes of Gemara every day. But from the outside, it looked like he'd become completely secular, and slowly what was on the outside seeped inside, until how he looked and how he acted were the same. By a massive stroke of luck, at least he didn't marry anyone unsuitable.*

*Two years passed, and I got to the age where a man is supposed to get married. My father had stopped all his fundraising trips abroad, because everything that had happened with my brother had sapped all his energy and left him a weak, broken man. So I decided that there was no choice but for me to go to America myself, to try and raise the money I needed to pay for the wedding.*

*Of course, at the beginning my parents were less than keen for me to go to chutz l'aretz by myself. As it happened, I found a Rosh Yeshiva who wanted to travel at the same time as me, and I thought I'd just stick with him and go to the same places he was going to ask for donations. What can I tell you? New York completely overwhelmed me. I found all the people, cars, and buildings really stressful, but when it comes to making a Jewish wedding, what won't you do?*

*One day, the Rosh Yeshiva I was travelling with didn't feel so well, and I decided that maybe I'd also spend a relaxing day at home. I was staying at the house of a chareidi man in New York, who had an open-door policy for anyone who came collecting for charity from Israel. There was a magazine lying around - how it got there in the first place, I have no idea - and on the front page was a picture of... my brother! I didn't know whether to laugh or cry. The last time I saw him, he was wearing a suit and a black fedora; now, he had gelled hair, a pair of jeans, and his shirt was opened almost to the waist. It looked like him, but it really wasn't him.*

*I started to argue with myself: 'Gidon, you have to go and find him. You were his closest sibling; for sure he's going to be very happy to hear from you.' I didn't even know where to start, so I asked the son of my host to help me, because I could see he was a computer whiz and knew how to use the internet. I asked him to help me track down the number of this famous model, who I used to know from yeshiva, and who was like a brother to me before he got trapped in the klipot (I didn't tell him straight that he was my brother, but that way, I also didn't lie too much). The son was really touched by my story, and he made a super-human effort to track down the phone number.*

*I dialled that number feeling so much pent-up emotion and quite afraid, because who knew what sort of reception I was going to get when my brother heard who was calling?*

*'Hello?'*

*'Hello? Who is this?'*

*'Gidon.'*

*There was silence, and he hung up. He was in shock, I thought to myself. I debated whether I should try to call him back. Just then, the phone rang. I didn't know whether to answer it or not because it wasn't my house, and the odds were high that it wasn't for me. But then I decided to pick up anyway, because I could always just take a message.*

*'Gidon?'*

*'Betzalel, my dear brother, how are you doing?'*

*I wasn't sure about calling him 'my dear brother', but in the end, the words just came out by themselves, in one big rush.*

*'Where are you?' I could hear he was crying.*

*'I'm on 47th Street.' I realized that the son of my host was listening in on my call from another phone somewhere else in the house.*

*'I live on the next street over.'*

*'You're kidding me! I've been here for two weeks already, and I can't believe that I haven't bumped in to you on the street or something.'*

*'Maybe you did see me, but you didn't recognize me.' A hint of shame was in his voice.*

# The Stolen Light

*'I'm looking at a picture of you right now, on the front page of a magazine. Is that really you?'*

*'Listen, do you want to come to me, or shall I come to you?'*

*'I'll come to you. Wait for me at the corner of 47th Street and I'll be there in another five minutes. It'll be much easier for you to spot me than it will be for me to spot you.'*

*'Yeah, you are definitely right about that, my dear brother.'*

*Not in a million years did I think I'd ever hear him call me his 'dear brother', quite the opposite: I was certain he wouldn't want to have anything to do with me. If I'd been in his shoes, I for sure wouldn't want to see anybody who'd remind me of who I used to be, and who I really was.*

*I didn't want the son of my host to follow me, so I ran out the front door so fast that I nearly forgot my hat. I ran to the corner and waited for my brother to come. I waited 10 minutes. Nobody. Then suddenly, I heard a car beeping at me from the street. I looked over and saw a really fancy car with tinted windows, the sort that big government ministers or important mafia types get driven around in back home. A couple of seconds later, the back window opened and inside I saw my brother, the Torah genius, sitting there in all his glory, with a gelled quiff that made him look like some sort of human rooster. He told me: 'Jump in.'*

*I was a bit embarrassed but I got a grip on myself and got in. I noticed that he looked very uncomfortable and was blushing, and his face turned all the colors of the rainbow. I just fell on him, and hugged him, and told him: 'I have missed you so much, my brother. What's going on with you?'*

*His entire cool seemed to melt after that, and suddenly he looked so pathetic, so miserable. All his money and all his luxury - even his chauffeur-driven car and fancy clothes and status symbols - it all suddenly looked so cheap. To tell you the truth though, somewhere deep down inside me I was still a bit envious of all his success. There was my millionaire brother, and then there was me, going from house to house to collect ten bucks here, or $18 dollars there. Maybe by the end of a whole month of knocking on doors, I'd come away with a maximum of $800, and that's only if G-d helped me and things went well.*

*I needed to raise $30,000 to pay for the wedding. I thought I'd have to ask my parents and future in-laws to take out some more loans and make some more promises, even though they were already up to their necks in debt. But my brother was loaded. He could cover the whole cost of paying for the wedding* with a snap of his fingers, and maybe he could even help me pay for the first year's rent on the apartment, too.

It would be like the biblical partnership between Issachar and Zebulun, except that I already knew that there was no way my parents would let me accept any money from someone they considered to be a first-class heretic...

We drove for five minutes until the car turned into the underground parking lot of a very luxurious building. The parking attendant flashed my brother his most flattering, horrendous big grin, and my brother tipped him a dollar. The elevator attendant gave my brother an even bigger fake grin, and also got a dollar. It took us five minutes to go all the way up to the 120th floor, and then I found myself in the most luxurious apartment I'd ever seen, loaded with every pointless, time-wasting gadget ever invented.

'By the way, just so you don't think that I've turned into a complete goy, there's a synagogue in this building, on floor 88. Do you want something to drink? I've got disposable cups, and you don't need the water to have a hechsher, do you?'

'I'd be very happy to have some water.'

'So now, tell me: what's a serious yeshiva bochur like you doing in a terrible place like this?'

'In another couple of months, I'm getting married, be'ezrat Hashem.'

He flashed me a big smile, and I could see that he was genuinely happy for me.

'Mazal tov! Mazal tov, my brother!' He gave me a hug, and I started to feel a bit nauseous from the overpowering smell of his aftershave.

'So, have you been missing me?'

'Missing you? It's like you're not even alive any more. Our parents sat shiva for you.'

There was a pregnant pause.

'Really? I feel like I'm not alive any more. Maybe I'm alive in body only, but certainly not more than that.'

Was he having regrets?

'Will you come to my wedding?' I asked him straight out, because I wanted to give him the chance to open up and to really start talking to me.

## The Stolen Light

*'I'm not even 'alive'. How do you expect me to come to your wedding?'* He smiled at me, and his wise eyes were full of sadness.

*'You're still alive to me! You'll always be my successful Torah genius brother. I love you.'* I went over to him and made an enthusiastically loud blessing on my water, and he responded with an equally enthusiastic 'Amen'.

*'I don't know if I'm going to come to your wedding. But in the meantime...'*

He went over to a massive plasma screen on the wall in the middle of the salon that had to be at least 55", which was hiding a picture, which in turn was hiding a safe - and opened the safe.

Inside, there were stacks of notes. He took out one of the bundles of money and gave it to me.

*'This is to help with the wedding,'* he told me. *'There's $20,000 there. But don't tell our parents that it's from me, because if you do they won't let you use my tainted money. Bli neder, I'll send you a bit more money soon. I'd like to pay for your first year's rent, bli neder.'*

I didn't want to touch the money, not because I didn't want to take it, but because I didn't want my brother to see just how desperate I was. With that one present, he'd solved the problem of how I was going to pay for the wedding, and also taken all the stress off me about how I was going to pay our first year's rent. After a little while, I took the bundle of money.

*'With what you just gave me, I could go home right now,'* I told him.

*'So go! There's really no reason why you should stay in this morally corrupt place a second longer than you have to.'*

*'The same thing applies to you...'*

I put the money on the table. Behind me, the afternoon sun was streaming in through the window, and I looked at the clock on the wall and realized that in another ten minutes it would be shkia - sunset.

*'Can we go down to floor 88 and pray Mincha?'*

He made a face, but said:

'I'll come and pray, just for you. It happens to be my day off today, so I don't need to get anywhere urgently. But you should know that in the two years that I've lived in this building, I've only been down to that minyan once.'

I was over the moon that he wanted to come and pray with me. We went down in the elevator, and this time I gave the attendant the dollar tip. He gave me such a big grin that all I could see were two rows of shiny white teeth.

My brother pinched my cheek and whispered to me, 'Are you a millionaire, now that you're giving away all your money to the elevator attendants?'

We got to the synagogue at just the right time, I was the ninth man and my brother the tenth. The guy leading the prayers gave us a royal greeting, like he was welcoming the Moshiach. He gave us both a siddur and then immediately started to pray Mincha.

I'm not exaggerating when I tell you it was the sweetest, nicest praying I'd heard in years. I glanced over at my brother and could see that he looked somewhat wistful. How could he not? The praying was so beautiful that it was bound to melt anyone's heart, even a heart made of stone.

When we finished Mincha, I asked my brother to stay with me to do the Ma'ariv prayer too. The praying was so sweet that he agreed without making a fuss. In the meantime, the prayer leader had sat himself down at the head of a table in the synagogue, and the other members of the minyan came and sat next to him - and let me tell you, no one there looked like they were 'frum from birth'.

The prayer leader himself also didn't look so chareidi; he looked like an artist or singer or something, but you could see his yirat Shamayim shining off his face. My brother and I grabbed an empty corner of the small shul which was furnished very nicely and simply, and very different from the usual kitsch style of most American synagogues.

'Do you want to learn something together?' I asked my brother, hesitantly.

'Sure, why not? If I'm already here praying, I may as well learn something as well. Let's do it properly. I'm happy to dedicate one day a year to my Yiddishkeit.'

I couldn't believe my ears! I ran over to the synagogue library feeling full of enthusiasm and hope and prayer. What could we learn together that would fan the spark into a flame, and get him to come home with me? Maybe some Gemara? Maybe some 'Strive for Truth'? What? What should I pick?! I turned to the Ribono Shel Olam and asked him to help me make the most of this *opportunity - and at exactly that moment, the prayer leader started speaking. Just as his praying sounded so sweet and beautiful to the ears, so did his words.*

*'With G-d's help, today I'd like to start learning some of Rabbi Nachman's stories with you. Rabbeinu told these stories towards the end of his life, when he could already see that even his Torah couldn't help us forever, because eventually we would all be so lost in the dark. So instead, he started to hide his light in stories that would have the power to illuminate even the darkest places, and to pull us all out of the spiritual mud that we've gotten stuck in and has hardened our hearts. OK, let's start to read through, and then we'll explain as we go along. Really, you'll see that I don't need to explain anything, because each one of us can, and really should, explain to ourselves what we're getting out of each story. Where am I in this story? What is this story highlighting to me? What's it trying to teach me?'*

*After some lengthy deliberations, I'd finally decided on Mesillat Yesharim, ('The Path of the Just'), so I took the book off the shelf and went back to my brother to start learning it - but I could tell he wasn't really listening to me. Instead, he was straining his ears trying to listen to what the prayer leader was saying. I stopped talking. I knew that the prayer leader was talking about Rebbe Nachman, and that was enough to quiet me down.*

*What I knew about Rebbe Nachman was that his followers danced on top of vans as they were being driven around the streets of Bnei Brak, playing music that was loud enough to shatter your ear drums. Those vans parked all over the place, making it hard for people to move around and causing no end of traffic jams. They annoyed half the residents, and amused the other half, but even the people who quite liked them didn't think of them as Torah scholars or people of learning. They related to them as though they were a particular type of street entertainer, just dressed up in 'frum' fancy dress. Or at least, that's what I thought about them then, although even at that time I knew I was wrapped up in my own preconceived notions. But if my brother was finding Breslev interesting, who was I to get in the way? The prayer leader continued talking in his beautiful, sweet way:*

*'The Rebbe spoke up and said, "While on my journey I told a story. Whoever heard it had a thought of repentance.'*

*Hmm, thoughts of repentance are always good, I thought to myself. If only my brother would have a 'thought of repentance'! But then I realized it was probably also a good thing for me to have a 'thought of repentance', because after all, Elul was just around the corner. If I was being honest, even though the yeshivas were full of trepidation over the upcoming Day of Judgement, I hadn't been feeling so religiously inspired and enthusiastic about it myself lately.*

*The man continued: 'If I could take a few moments before we continue the story, I'd just like to briefly explain some of the tremendously deep ideas that Rabbeinu is hinting to us by way of his introduction, because amazing profundity is contained in that one simple sentence. You could write a book just on that one sentence, because each of us needs to understand that every single day that we're alive is another part of our journey. Each of our neshamas has come down to this lowly material world that's called the world of 'Asiya', or action/implementation, in Kabbalistic thought - from the very highest spiritual worlds.*

*Now our souls are travelling through this world, and every step of the journey is being dictated by Divine Providence. From the smallest actions to the biggest dramas, nothing is a coincidence; absolutely everything is being arranged from Above. The soul is being directed at all times and in all circumstances according to its spiritual root and according to the specific tikun, or spiritual rectification, which it needs to achieve. That's the sole purpose for all its journeys in this world, throughout its lifetime. Everything is just to help our soul fix whatever spiritual flaws it has that need repairing. And we need a lot of encouragement on this journey of ours to avoid all the obstacles and traps that are being set for us by Amalek, which has the same gematria as the word 'saffek' in Hebrew, meaning 'doubt'.*

*We learn this from Rebbe Nachman's teachings in Likutei Moharan, the second part, Lesson 19, which states: 'The tzaddik falls, and gets up'. In the Hebrew, if you take the end letter of each word, it spells out 'Amalek', because Amalek gets us to fall down by filling us full of doubts, and doubt is the biggest form of galut, exile, that there is. When we're travelling on our path and then get filled up with doubts about G-d and faith, rachmana litzlan, we need an awful lot of spiritual strengthening to know how to deal with our problems. We need to know in advance how to overcome all the spiritual obstacles, sins, and failures that Amalek tries to put in our way.*

*'And in this story, that's exactly what Rebbe Nachman is trying to teach us. He's showing each of us how to successfully traverse this world so that we can get to the world of truth. And we can't let our sense of embarrassment stop us from doing what's required in this world, because the world to come is really the place where we'll feel ashamed and embarrassed of our sins. The bigger the sin, the bigger sense of shame we'll have, and it's much better to own up to our flaws and feel embarrassed in this world, then to be embarrassed in the next.*

*Let's start the story: "There was once a king who had six sons and one daughter. This daughter was very precious to him and he loved her the most and spent a lot of time with her. One time, he was alone with her on a particular day and got into an argument with her. He inadvertently said, "May the Not Good One take you!" At night she went to her room. In the morning, nobody knew where she was. Her father was very upset, and he went looking for her everywhere. The viceroy stood up as he saw that the king was very upset, and asked to be given a servant, a horse, and some money for expenses, to go and search for her.*

*"He travelled back and forth for a long time, through deserts, fields and forests. He looked for her for a very long time. While he was travelling through the desert, he saw a path to the side. He composed his thoughts: 'Since I have travelled for so long in the wilderness and haven't found her, I will go along this path, and maybe I will come to an inhabited area.' He continued travelling for a long time, until at last, he found her..."*

*Just then, one of the other members of the minyan pointed to his watch and signalled to the prayer leader that it was time to pray Ma'ariv, and that he should move it along.*

*'Ok, it's time to pray Ma'ariv. Maybe you'd like to lead the prayers?' He pointed to me, the obvious Israeli, but I did what every other yeshiva bochur would do, and politely refused.*

*'Maybe you'd like to lead the prayers instead?' he asked my brother.*

*'I'm not worthy of leading the prayers,' my brother answered, 'and especially not after such a beautiful Mincha. But I'm happy to listen.'*

*The prayer leader smiled at us, and went forward to start praying Ma'ariv. He davened with the deep joy and animation that I'd very rarely witnessed in the congregations I'd prayed with over the last few years. At the end of the prayers, the prayer leader started dancing in a circle with most of the other congregants. Only my brother and I weren't joining in. The prayer leader danced over to us, and somehow managed to include us in the circle in a very natural way. For five minutes, we all danced together, and I really, truly enjoyed it. I enjoyed it even more because my brother was also there dancing.*

*When the dancing finished, the prayer leader announced that there was going to be a netz, or sunrise minyan the following morning, and then everyone started to leave. My brother went over to talk to the prayer leader, and I followed behind him quietly to hear what would be said.*

*'Who is the king, what are the six sons, who is the princess, and what does it mean that the Evil One took her away?'*

*'You just asked all the right questions!' the prayer leader told him. 'But in order to give you the right answers, we'll have to stay here and talk all night. If you're not in a rush to go anywhere, I'm happy to sit down now and to start talking it all through with you.'*

*My brother looked at me, then looked back at the prayer leader. I said a silent prayer that he'd agree. The way the prayer leader spoke, with such sincerity and warmth, I was sure something good was going to come of it.*

*'I'm free now, if you are. I don't know if I can stay here all night, but let's get started and see where our conversation takes us.' I started smiling to myself.*

*'Before we get started, let's first have a little something to eat,' replied the prayer leader. "You can't fight Amalek on an empty stomach. I'm Jeremy, by the way, nice to meet you.'*

*Jeremy took out his mobile and made a quick call while he walked over to the bookcase, removed three books, and sat himself down at the table. He motioned for us to sit next to him.*

*'In a minute we'll have some food, all kosher l'mehadrin, Badatz New York,' he told us. We smiled at him, and then he began his explanation. 'Before we start, I want to tell you some general ideas about Rabbi Nachman's stories, the "Sippurei Maasiot", as they're called in Hebrew. Firstly, everybody has to try to find themselves in each story, and to come up with their own interpretation of what the story is really telling them, using the hints the Tzaddik is giving them. But in order to really get the right messages, all of Rabbi Nachman's stories require simplicity. We have to throw our brains and our intellectual airs out the window. We have to listen to the story as simply and innocently as we can, then try to figure out what advice we're actually being given to help us on our journeys to get closer to the Creator of the world.*

*'OK, with that in mind, let's get back to your questions. You asked me 'who is the king'? The King is the King of the world, G-d. The six sons represent the six sefirot of chesed (kindness), gevurah (limitation), tiferet (harmony), netzach (eternity), hod (glory), and yesod (foundation). These connect to the six orders of the Mishna that discuss the aspects of the six working days of the week, namely kosher (fit), pasul (unfit), tamei (ritually contaminated), tahor (ritually pure), assur (forbidden), and muttar (permitted). The princess is prayer, because Hakodesh Baruch Hu values our prayers more highly than anything else. G-d gets enormous enjoyment from every single word that His Jewish son or daughter says to Him.'*

*'Are you talking about the Shmoneh Esrei?' I asked him.*

*'I'm also talking about that, but not only that,' Jeremy replied. 'Rabbeinu was really referring to the prayers that come straight from our hearts, the prayers that are a reflection of our real selves, and not just the ones that Chazal wrote*

*down for us more than 2,000 years ago. I'm talking about the prayers where you really tell G-d what's going on with you.'*

*Jeremy opened one of the books he'd brought to the table, and started reading: 'The yetzer hara and the sitra achra are aspects of oppression that enslave and burden all of creation with endless problems and errors, until people exchange the world of truth for the world of lies. The suffering that people endure causes them to go astray from the path that leads to good, eternal life. Instead, people follow the yetzer hara down a path that leads to hell, and to a life of tremendous suffering that is more bitter than death even in this world, and all the more so in the world to come. There is no greater oppression in the world than the oppression of the yetzer hara, and the main way a person can be saved from it is through prayer and supplications. A person should always strengthen himself to pray to Hashem that He should draw him close to His true service, come what may. Then certainly, the yetzer hara will not be able to fool him.'*

*As he spoke, the room seemed to fill up with happiness and awe. We sat there rapt, until someone knocking at the door broke the silence. A young man with long hair and a big woollen kippa on his head walked in and started handing us all sorts of snacks, telling us, 'Everything's got a good hechsher.' Before he left, he looked at my brother and asked him: 'Hey, are you the guy who models for 'Baron James' in all the magazines?'*

*'As it happens, I am.' I could see that my brother was blushing.*

*'You know, I just knew you were Jewish. I had a bet with my friend that you were. I told him that you had the eyes of a Talmid Chacham. Thanks man, you just won me my bet!' And then he left just as quickly as he had come.*

*'That's my son, as you probably figured out for yourselves. Up until a couple of years ago, he was in a wheelchair, and the doctors were telling us that he was permanently paralyzed and would never walk again. But Rabbeinu thought differently, and got him out of his wheelchair and back on his feet. If I tell you what happened to him, you probably won't believe me.'*

*My brother had taken one of the cookies, and was looking at it with a really stressed expression on his face: should he say a blessing on it, or not? Jeremy seemed to understand the struggle my brother was having, and with immense wisdom he told him: 'The blessing you make on that is shehakol, not mezonot.' Now, my brother had no choice; he had to make the blessing. I turned to Jeremy and I asked him: 'I'm sorry if this is a rude question, but you don't really look like you grew up frum. Did you?' I had a feeling this guy had an interesting story, and I wanted to hear it.*

*'Everyone has their own story of how they went looking for their own Lost Princess, which represents their emuna, their happiness, the simplicity of their soul, which the Evil One stole away from them," he replied. 'In his story about the Lost Princess, Rabbeinu is showing us that the place where we can find the Lost Princess is none other than in the Evil One's own palace. And the strangest thing is that in that evil palace, there is no end of 'happiness', and wealth, and servants, and glory, and honor. This world is full of superficial things that appear to be very good, and very tempting, but are really just evil. And that's why the Lost Princess can't wait to escape from there.*

*I'm a world-famous artist, and each one of my pictures sells for tens of thousands of dollars. My work is exhibited in the best museums, and the critics all write rave reviews about me and my art. Sometimes, they even go as far as to say that I'm a genius who's blazing new trails in my field, and that my paintings are the most exciting thing to hit modern art in the last century. I have all the money a person could want, as you can see for yourselves. I bought this apartment just so I'd have my own private synagogue close to home. I have another apartment that houses my studio, and a third apartment where I actually live. To put it another way, I have plenty of money, I have critical acclaim and amazing success in my chosen field, and I have everything that any artist could ever really want.*

*My life was really pleasant and good until my son, who you saw a little while ago, was involved in a serious road accident that left him paralyzed from the neck down, and unable to speak. As I already mentioned to you, the doctors said that in their opinion, my son was going to stay permanently paralyzed forever. We took him to the best doctors and to medical experts all over the world, and none of them held out even the tiniest bit of hope that my son would ever recover the use of his limbs. We understood from everything those doctors said that the only thing left to do was to cry.*

*As a massively successful and egotistical artist, I actually took the news surprisingly well. I was so wrapped up in myself that it was relatively easy for me to express any pain that I felt through my art. What's more, those pictures started selling for a premium, because the media got hold of the story and made a big deal out of it, like they do. They find some tragedy, and then commercialize the whole thing and it stops being about people, and starts being about dollar signs. But my wife took the news very, very hard. She just couldn't accept the very bleak future the doctors were describing for our son. He was our only child, and we only managed to have him after years of waiting and many failed attempts to have children.*

*Anyway, at this point my wife was working as the head manager of a chain of malls. One of her staff members had taken two weeks off, then come back to work wearing a head-covering. My wife got worried that maybe this worker had cancer and that the treatments were making her hair fall out, so she went over to*

# The Stolen Light

*speak to her, and ask her if there was anything that she could do to help her. She told the worker that she shouldn't feel that she had to go through everything alone, and that she was there to support her with whatever she needed.*

*The young lady started laughing hysterically, and told my wife that there was nothing bad going on; if anything, it was quite the opposite: for the first time in her life, she'd found light, reality and meaning in her life. She explained that in the two weeks that she'd been off work, she'd converted to Judaism and married the love of her life in Jerusalem. My wife was stunned. She'd known this woman for over ten years, and she was the most goyish goy you could ever hope to meet. She was obsessed with making money, achieving status, and obtaining all the superficially good things in life. What possible connection could there be between this woman and Jerusalem, or Judaism, for that matter?*

*Like me, my wife was Jewish, and she simply couldn't understand what had drawn this woman to convert. But she wanted to know, so she cancelled all her meetings, cleared her desk, and sat with her staff member for four hours while the woman explained why she'd taken such a big step and converted to Judaism.*

*This is what she told my wife: 'As you already know, I was engaged to Boaz, a secular American Jew who had absolutely no connection to religion.. His parents left Israel thirty years ago to move to the States, and he was born here and grew up feeling that he was 100% American. He followed the same path towards 'success' that all the other pampered American kids do, and decided he wanted to study medicine. He became a very successful doctor, and today he's very much in demand as one of the top orthopedic surgeons in the country.*

*His parents were not thrilled that he was marrying me, a shiksa, but they didn't make such a big fuss about it. Everything was arranged, and we were meant to be getting married at one of the fanciest wedding venues here in New York. Then something happened to Boaz that completely changed everything.*

*Boaz was on the ward one day when a religious Jew and his 16-year-old son were admitted. They'd both been seriously injured in a very bad road accident. The father's whole body was paralyzed and he'd been in a coma for two months. The son's situation wasn't much better: a massive sliver of glass had entered his brain, and all the doctors, including the biggest experts in the field, had decided that attempting surgery to try to remove the shard was far too risky. It was lodged in such a critical place that even the smallest movement could cut all the nerves and leave him permanently paralyzed, or worse.*

*Boaz was the attending physician for the injured father, and one day he was talking to the man's wife, explaining to her that there was zero chance that her husband would ever walk again. They'd done hundreds of X-rays which all told the same story: the man's nervous system was shot to pieces, and no operation could help him. Boaz suggested that it was time to take her husband off all the machines, and let nature take its course.*

*Later on, the paralyzed father explained what had been happening to him while he was hearing this conversation go on over his head. Even though he was in a coma, he could hear every word, and was shocked to his core. He saw his wife standing in front of him, completely shattered by what she'd just heard - but he couldn't do a thing. He couldn't move, or speak, or even gesture. So this man, who was a devotee of Rabbi Nachman, started to pray wordlessly from the bottom of his heart, in the merit of Rebbe Nachman of Breslev. He asked Rebbe Nachman to intercede for him in Heaven, and to ask the Ribono Shel Olam to heal him. He was silently pleading like that for an hour, and took all sorts of resolutions upon himself if he would only be healed.*

*In the course of his prayers, he fell back into a very deep sleep. He dreamt that a good-looking Torah scholar appeared in front of him, and started to dance in the most extraordinarily beautiful, graceful way. As he was dancing, the scholar was also talking to him, and telling him the most amazing words of Torah, which penetrated straight into his heart and caused him to feel the most enjoyable sensation he'd ever felt in his life. An unusual beautiful-coloured light and a powerful warmth were radiating off the Torah scholar's body, and they affected the injured man in such a profound way that he simply didn't have the words to properly describe what it felt like.*

*After a while, the Torah scholar turned to him and asked him, 'Why aren't you dancing with me?' The father replied, 'I'm completely paralyzed. The doctors are saying that I will never walk again.' The Torah scholar told him, 'Stand up. You can move now.' But the father argued with him: 'I can't! I was in a terrible accident, and now I'm completely crippled!' But the righteous man didn't back down; he came closer to the father and held out his hand, which was radiating the most amazing sparks of light, and told him, 'Give me your hand, and come and dance with me.'*

*In the dream, the father held on to the Torah scholar's hand and slowly sat up in bed, and then stood up. Then he started to dance with the scholar. They danced for an hour, and the man was so filled with joy and contentment that he felt he was out of this world. Of course, he was overjoyed about the massive miracle that meant he was now standing on his own two feet again, but the dance itself also filled him with tremendous joy. The scholar turned to him and told him, 'My name is Rabbi Nachman, and you are now one of mine. I want to ask you to change your name from Menachem to Nachman, and to promise that you and your son will come visit my grave in Uman, and that you'll spend a whole month there absorbed in prayer.*

# The Stolen Light

*'If you can make me this promise, then you will walk again, and your son will undergo a very simple operation to remove the glass splinter from his brain that won't harm even so much as one hair on his head.'*

*It goes without saying that Menachem the father gave his word to do all these things - and then he woke up. At exactly the same time, the nurse who was responsible for arranging his blood transfusions and medical injections came into his room. It just so happened that the regular nurse was off duty. The replacement nurse apparently hadn't read all the patient notes, and didn't know that she was dealing with a patient who couldn't move or speak.*

*Instead of giving him an injection, the nurse instead plunked down some pills in front of Menachem, and then went off to deal with the next patient. Menachem wanted to shout out to her that he was paralyzed, but he couldn't make a sound. Instead, he put out his hand towards the pills - and his hand obeyed his brain, and grabbed them. He had no idea if he was still dreaming, but decided to try to sit up in the bed. Ten seconds later, he was sitting up. Following this, he decided to try and stand up on his feet.*

*At exactly that moment his wife came into the room and started screaming, 'What are you doing?! How are you standing up?! You're paralyzed, you're crippled, you can't stand up like this!' But she was so shocked that she wasn't just saying these things quietly to her husband, she was screaming her head off. A second later, the whole ward was gathered around his bed, trying to see what was going on, and Menachem broke into a dance, just like he'd been doing in his dream. Then he started singing. It goes without saying that everyone who saw what had happened was shocked to the core.*

*Boaz became completely tongue-tied with shock. He just knew that the hand of G-d was at work here. They took Menachem off for more X-rays, which showed that his nervous system, which until half an hour ago had been completely crushed and mutilated, was now working perfectly fine again, as though he'd never been in the accident in the first place.*

*Menachem, who was now called Nachman, asked the doctors to re-examine his son, and take him in for the simple operation that Rabbi Nachman had described to him. And just as he said they would, the doctors managed to remove the glass shard with no complications or problems, in a simple half-hour procedure.*

*After witnessing all this, Boaz couldn't just continue on as though nothing unusual had happened. He started to ask questions, as befitting a serious deep thinker. He's not the sort to accept anything without first testing it out, experiencing it, and understanding it for himself. He decided to fly out to Uman with Nachman and his son, and was there for four days. When he came back, he was a completely new person, 'lit up', like they say in Breslev circles. He sat down with me and told me straight that he'd no longer be able to marry me unless I agreed to convert. I wanted to know what that entailed, so he arranged for a Rabbi to come and sit with us for two whole days, to go through all the aspects of the Jewish faith.*

*Nachman's miraculous story combined with Boaz's new 'light' and the powerful explanations of the Rabbi worked their magic on me, and for the last year I've been secretly studying the Jewish laws and beliefs. Last month I went before the conversion board, and that's it! I'm officially a believing Jewess! Of course, now my parents are very upset with me, and Boaz's parents are also very disturbed at the new direction our life has taken. If they weren't so keen on him marrying a goy, I can tell you that they're even more upset that he married an orthodox Jewish convert. But we don't care, because our life is so content and fulfilled now that we've embraced this new way of being. We know that we're on the right track now. My husband is still working as a doctor, but these days, he takes a lot of advice from his Rebbe, Rabbi Nachman of Breslev, and he knows that if he gets stuck, the Big Doctor above him is always ready to help out.'*

*'My wife heard the story of the goy-who-is-now-a-believing-Jew and immediately left work,' Jeremy continued. 'She went to the nearest travel agent and booked three tickets to Kiev; then she came home and barged in on me in my studio, yelling so loudly that I immediately thought something terrible had happened. 'You, Shneur, and me are flying out to the Ukraine tomorrow, to Uman, to pray at the tomb of Rebbe Nachman of Breslev. I've already bought the tickets,' and she put the tickets down on my worktable.*

*I saw that my wife was 100% serious. I didn't really understand what she wanted from me or why I had to come with her to the Ukraine, to whatever tomb of whichever dead Rabbi, but my heart understood that my wife needed to do this because the whole situation with Shneur, our only child, had completely devastated her. At the same time, I had a pressing deadline to finish a painting for a collector that had been ordered a while back. I didn't know what to do. I started to think it over: maybe it would be good to visit somewhere different, somewhere new, and to see new sites and observe different people. Maybe that would help my artistic process... But then, I started to argue with myself: I have no idea what's waiting for me there, and it's really hard to travel anywhere with a wheelchair, even when it's not to Rabbi Nachman's tomb in the middle of nowhere.*

*I'm not ashamed to admit that I'd never prayed before. I'd never put a kippa on my head, never so much as exchanged a word with a chareidi Jew. I come from a secular home, and I'd been secular all my life. In my house, no one ever spoke about religion or about the fact that we were Jewish. The fact that I'd married a Jewish woman was a complete coincidence - I'd only found out that she was Jewish after we got engaged, because we hadn't even bothered to discuss each other's religious persuasion beforehand. What mattered was our 'chemistry'; our connection with each other. Who cared what our backgrounds were?*

*Anyway, to make a long story short, the next day I found myself at Rebbe Nachman's tomb. I was completely at a loss - I didn't know what to do with myself. The enclosure around the grave was completely empty. No one else was there apart from me, my wife and Shneur. I asked my wife what we were supposed to do now, and she told me that the lady who converted had told her that we needed to kiss the grave, and then start asking for whatever we wanted.*

*I went up to the grave, glancing around to make sure no one else was there to see me do such a moronic thing as kissing a bit of marble, and gave it a very casual, half-hearted kiss. My wife also walked over to the grave and kissed it, and then just started talking and talking. I'd already told her that she needed to talk for both of us, because while I was very good at expressing myself via my art, I wasn't so good at expressing my thoughts and emotions any other way.*

*We both sat down next to the tomb, and while my wife was talking, I took out a sheet of paper and started sketching the scene of my wife and wheelchair-bound son by Rabbi Nachman's grave. I heard my wife sobbing, and for once, I really felt some of her pain. I stopped sketching for a minute - and when I tell you what happened next, you'll probably think that I was hallucinating. But all I can tell you is that what happened next completely changed my life.*

*As I told you, I'd just finished sketching my wife, and now I started to concentrate on drawing my disabled son, Shneur. First I sketched his head, and then afterwards, I started sketching his body. As I was drawing, I noticed that he'd moved his head, which he hadn't done even once in the two years since he'd come out of the rehabilitation ward. Then he opened his eyes and started talking loudly in Hebrew - but I had no idea what he was saying, because we only spoke English at home, and Shneur himself had never learned Hebrew. But I'm watching my son having a conversation with someone - even though no one else was there - and I remember him saying in Hebrew: 'But I can't walk!'*

*There was something otherworldly in his gaze, and I stared at him in terror. Of course, the artist in me wanted to capture that look of heavenly awe that he had in his eyes, but the shock of hearing him speak in a language that none of us knew completely unnerved me. The next thing I knew, he had his arms out in front of him, as though someone was standing right there in front of him asking Shneur to give him his hands, and then he just stood up and started taking steps, one after another.*

*I started screaming: "Lise!!" My wife had her head down on the grave, but she lifted her head and I could see her eyes were red from crying. She saw our son, then put her head back down. Then a second later, she lifted her head up again -*

*and fainted dead away. At exactly the same time that my wife fell to the floor, Shneur also fell to the floor, and I also fainted. I felt like I had no choice. I have no idea how long all three of us were out cold like that on the floor, but after a few minutes I woke up, then awoke my wife, and together, we roused our son.*

*I was terrified that I'd hallucinated the whole scene that had occurred before I fainted, but it hadn't been a dream. We pulled Shneur to his feet and walked him around the grave enclosure for a few minutes, to check that we hadn't just imagined the whole thing. When we could see with our own eyes that our son really had been healed, we stood there hugging and shaking and crying, and we were so indescribably happy just like we were the day he was born, after 20 years of infertility.*

*As we digested the miracle that had just taken place for Shneur, we asked him to tell us exactly what had happened to him. Initially, it was really hard for him to speak, but he told us that he'd suddenly seen a very handsome, impressive-looking man standing in front of him with a long white beard and deep blue eyes that were filled with light. The man told him to stand up in a language that he didn't know, but that he apparently could understand. My son felt so much trust for this man that he simply started walking with him, step after step, as the man was saying something - which today we know were words of Tehillim - Psalms.*

*My wife explained that she had been begging the holy man who was buried there to perform a miracle for her. She'd promised him that if he did a miracle for her son, she would make teshuva - and from that day on, she'd be a completely kosher Jew. The miracle had indeed taken place for our son, and now it was my wife's turn to fulfill her part of the bargain.*

*We came back home, and it goes without saying that our doctors were in a total state of shock when they saw the miracle that happened for Shneur. Baruch Hashem, he started learning Torah, and despite the fact that he dresses like a hippy, today he is a fully observant Jew, and gets up every single night to say Tikun Chatzot and do hitbodedut. He's a serious Gemara learner, and has also written a commentary on Likutey Moharan, though he's not ready to publicize his work because he's worried it may not be quite ripe yet. But with G-d's help, I hope that he'll be ready to publicize the book in the near future.*

*Of course, my wife was the driving force behind our teshuva. She connected with her employee who had converted and learned all the religious laws and principles she needed to live as an orthodox Jew. All this happened when I was already 64 and my wife was 62 years old, but we continued getting stronger and stronger in our religious beliefs, and we made a lot of changes in our home.*

*At the beginning, it was really hard for me. But after I started to get a taste of how good it was to keep Shabbat, and how sweet the prayers were, how energizing and amazing and enlightening doing hitbodedut was, and how stimulating it was to learn Likutey Halachot, I really started to get into the whole religion thing, and now it's probably fair to say that I'm more stringent than she is.*

*But the biggest miracle was yet to come. A little while after we made all those massive changes, my wife discovered that she was pregnant. She gave birth to our daughter, Odelia, when she was 65. We didn't get into the Guinness Book of Records, but we got one of the sweetest presents we ever received...' The artist finished telling his story, and his eyes were filled with a tremendous light."*

Gidon finished the fascinating tale of Jeremy and his son Shneur. We were still on the plane, flying at a high altitude above the clouds, and I started to feel a bit 'elevated'. Maybe, the plane was starting to fly a bit too high? Gidon continued telling his story:

*"Both me and my brother Betzalel were completely blown away by the story of Jeremy, the holy artist and hidden tzaddik, who lived on the 88th floor of the luxurious building on 47th Street and had his own private minyan.*

*His story really gave me a lot of chizzuk, and I decided that the first chance I got, I was going to go and visit Rebbe Nachman (without my parents knowing, naturally). It was enough that one of their kids had gone off the derech; if they knew that another one was going a bit crazy, it would have completely broken them.*

*Jeremy's story also changed the direction of my brother Betzalel's life, but the changes were initially very small. From that day on, my brother started to attend Jeremy's classes and joined his minyan. Slowly, he got stronger, and eventually started to keep Shabbat. He asked me not to tell my parents anything about what was going on - not about the money he'd given me, or the changes he was experiencing in his own life - so that they wouldn't have any massive expectations about him that he wouldn't be able to live up to.*

*After two months, Betzalel quit his modelling career, and gave me another surprise when he called me two weeks before my wedding to tell me he wanted us to meet up again, this time in Uman. I got really emotional when I heard that, and wondered if this time I should tell my parents about what was going on. I was scared to even broach the subject with them, but my Rav agreed to act as the go-between and told my parents about everything that had happened with my brother and me from the minute I first laid eyes on him again in New York.*

*Surprisingly, they were really happy about it all, and wanted to hear more about the forthcoming trip to Uman. The main hope for them was that I come back to*

*Eretz Yisrael with my brother. They'd gotten to the point that they just wanted him back, even if he came back a Breslever. They'd accept him however he was.*

*So this is what happened: I flew out to Uman on 'Love Day', Tu B'Av. There were hundreds of people there. We spent a very inspiring Shabbat by one of the main Breslev Rabbis, and then we travelled to Medzibuzh to visit the grave of the Baal Shem Tov before going on to visit the grave of Rabbi Natan in Breslev. It was there, in Breslev, that Rabbeinu's light finally penetrated into my brother's heart. He stood there, in front of Rabbi Natan's grave, and was arguing and talking to him as though he could actually see someone right there in front of his face.*

*'Give me some peace and quiet! Let me live my life the way I see fit!' For more than an hour, that's how my brother argued with Rabbi Natan. He'd put forward an argument, and then fall silent as though he was getting a response. Then he'd put forward another argument, and so on and so forth until finally he collapsed sobbing on the grave for the next two hours.*

*It goes without saying that he came back to Israel with me for my wedding. His reunion with my parents was one of the most emotional things I've ever witnessed in my whole life. At the beginning, the meeting was rather formal and cold, as though they hadn't really missed each other at all. It had the feel of a business meeting, until my brother suddenly exploded into a heart-rending confession that was in turn full of apologies and accusations.*

*My parents also let rip, and told him everything that they'd been carrying around in their hearts for the last couple of years. By the end, it all turned out well and everyone learned whatever lesson they needed to learn. It was such a happy wedding.*

*Sadly for both my parents and me, at the end of the celebrations my brother decided that he was going to go back to New York to live, where he could be close to his rebbe, the artist-tzaddik Jeremy. Together, they're teaching a lot of people about Rebbe Nachman's path and bringing a lot of people back to G-d. My brother goes to shiurim and rounds people up to come hear Jeremy speak, and then he turns their hearts around and encourages them to make teshuva. They have a community of around 18 baalei teshuva, most of whom are Israeli, and the rest Americans.*

*My brother got married to an Israeli girl who came to study music in the States but instead caught Rebbe Nachman disease, and they already have three little Breslevers: Nachman, age 4, Natan, age 3, and a little baby girl. My parents are happy, my brother is happy, I'm trying to always be happy, because being happy is a big mitzvah - just like Rabbeinu teaches us."*

## The Stolen Light

Gidon finished his story just as the plane's landing gear slid down into place, as the plane was approaching the runway at Kiev airport. I have to say that both their stories were very fascinating, and I thought to myself that it was a shame that no one had turned them into a movie script or something. One of my friends was studying at film school, and I thought maybe I could tell him the stories and he'd turn them into a film - which could be another way I might make a bit of cash from the trip.

If I came away from Uman with as much money as I hoped, maybe I would produce films about this *chevra* myself... In the meantime, back in the apartment on Pushkina - where was the meat already? I was scared that someone else was going to start telling another *dvar Torah* or story, and then I'd have to wait at least another hour before I could actually get to the chicken.

## Chapter 5

*Let me tell you about Aharon the Litvak, and about the long route he had to take to get to Uman, via Romania.*

Sitting opposite me at the table was someone who looked like he was *frum* from birth - not a *baal teshuva*. His name was Aharon, and we'd spoken a bit that morning. In the course of our chat, it became evident that he wasn't a Breslever *chassid*, and was even something approaching the opposite: a *Litvak*. The only reason he was in Uman was to close a business deal, and he really wasn't into the whole Rebbe Nachman/Rosh Hashana thing. If anything, he was even quite 'anti', and was making light of Breslev in general, with its emphasis on making *tikunim*. He said that being outside of Israel for Rosh Hashana would wreck a lot more than it would fix.

When we spoke for a little while before the *Chag*, he'd told me he was pretty upset to be caught up in all the craziness going on around him. To top it all off, he was scared of flying and detested travelling by coach bus. He'd left *Eretz Yisrael* with a group Sunday morning on a flight headed to Romania. From there, they were supposed to catch a bus to the Ukrainian border, and by the next morning at the latest, they should have already been in Uman. On the way, they were also scheduled to visit the grave of Rabbi Yisrael, the Baal Shem Tov, in Medzhibuzh.

That was what was plan. In reality, they'd only gotten to Uman on Thursday morning, having spent four whole days of stress and headache on the road. And what was the point? In just a moment, you'll hear him tell his fascinating story in his own words.

In the meantime, Aharon told me that if he'd known beforehand what he was really signing himself up for, he'd never have agreed to the trip. He was acting as the agent of a very wealthy friend of his, who wanted to buy a few apartments in Uman as an investment. This friend was also not a Breslever, and had no intention of becoming one. He was a businessman who was only interested in the financial bottom line, and according to him, buying apartments in Uman was a very profitable line of real estate to be in these days. He'd buy a run-down apartment for $30,000, fix it up nicely, then make a lot of money renting it out. He claimed that if he bought a couple of apartments, he could make enough money off them every year to be on easy street. Every year, there were tens of thousands of *chassidim* and other tourists coming through Uman, and the demand for rental units was very high.

Aharon had no plans to be in Uman for Rosh Hashana, but his wealthy friend had called him up a day before the flight and told him that he'd closed a couple of real estate deals and needed Aharon to be his agent to pay the money, sign the necessary documents using his friend's power of attorney, and to get the keys. Aharon was just the middleman in the deal.

But why was the roundabout flight to Romania, and not directly to Kiev? Because the rich friend had a business acquaintance he knew in Romania, and he figured that Aharon would go and visit him for an hour or two to discuss a couple of future deals that they might want to join forces on before the bus came to take him into Ukraine.

It goes without saying that Aharon was unhappy about leaving Israel and his family for the holiday. The man should live long and be healthy, but he looked like he wasn't a day over 30 and already had six kids, with number seven likely already on the way. It was the first time he'd ever left his wife and children by themselves on Rosh Hashana, and he just didn't get how the Breslevers could do it year after year. He told me that he'd said to his friends that they were all 'trampling on *mitzvot de'oraita* just to keep some *minhag*.'[5]

I had no idea what he was talking about, but I went along with him just as I was going along with everyone else there, pretending to be whatever they wanted me to be. But truthfully, I also didn't really understand how you could celebrate Rosh Hashana without your wife and kids, even though I didn't yet have a wife and kids. So on that point at least, I genuinely agreed with him. Aharon's wife and kids had gone to be with her parents, just like it is with all the other Breslevers. In those circles, everyone knew the joke that the Hebrew letters for '*Elul',* the month leading up to Rosh Hashana, stood for 'I'm off to Uman, and my wife's going to the in-laws'. If the feminists ever got a whiff of what was going on, they'd have a field day with it.

The *chevra* started singing yet another song, and while they were doing that, Aharon the *Litvak* told me his story:

---

[5] 'Breaking Torah laws just to keep some mere custom'.

*"From the moment I left my house, I had a feeling that the whole trip was going to be a disaster. I hailed a taxi to take me from Bnei Brak to the airport, and I wasn't paying attention to who was driving it, but just my luck: it was a 'Na-Nach' guy, complete with the big crazy white kippa. I was really tired, but the guy didn't give me even a second of peace to try and nap.*

*The minute I got into his cab he popped a CD into the car radio, a Torah class from one of the big Breslev rabbis, and then he tells me: 'Listen up: you are about to hear a CD that is going to completely change your life!'*

*You know, I was born to very religious parents, who in turn were born to very religious parents who came through the Holocaust with their faith intact, despite the horrendous circumstances they experienced. My family is also related to the famous rav, the Nodah B'Yehuda, if that means anything to you. And now, this born-again Breslever, who probably only made teshuva two days ago, had the gall to tell me that his CD was going to transform my whole life.*

*I asked him to turn the sound down a bit, because as I explained to him, I was really tired, and had a headache. 'If you're really worried about your head, you need to immerse it in some Torah learning,' he told me. 'Pay attention to what you're hearing, because from this minute on your whole life is going to change!'*

*Apparently I had no choice, and whether I liked it or not, I had to go along with him. My bad luck continued when we hit a big traffic jam, which slowed us down a lot and unfortunately meant that there was ample time to listen to the CD. I listened to that blasted CD until it was coming out of my ears. I'm not pretending to be Rabbi Akiva Eiger, or the Vilna Gaon, or the Chazon Ish, or anything like that, but to put all the false humility aside, I studied at a bunch of top-notch yeshivas, and I made sure not to waste a minute of my time. I was a serious learner.*

*And now, what was I being forced to listen to on the CD? The rabbi telling me that the evil inclination wanted to ruin my life. Wow! What a big chiddush! But that's not all: the rabbi was also telling me at every possible opportunity that I was really a nothing, a nobody; that my learning wasn't worth anything, and how much of a shame it was that I wasted so much time on it. Ok, he made his point already. So what was the earth-shattering bottom line bit of advice he wanted to give me? This: I shouldn't let anything get me into despair! I couldn't believe what I was hearing. But then, he went on to emphasize that 'you shouldn't fall into despair and get sad and depressed, even if you just committed the worst sin in the world. Just continue on, as if nothing happened.'*

*The rav made the same point over and over again, as though he was delivering the most ingenious Torah insight since the Torah was given to Moses at Sinai. All the time this was going on, the self-satisfied cab driver kept looking at me through his rear-view mirror, to check if I really understood the 'amazingly deep' piece of advice I just heard and to see whether my life had already changed.*

*To be honest, I was a bit scared of the cab driver, and just smiled at him so that he'd hopefully think that I'd seen the light, and was now busy trying to internalize it. He clearly believed this, because when we eventually got to the airport, he gave me the CD as a present and then added insult to injury by telling me, 'I'm relying on you to spread the word in your community, immediately!' He then winked at me like I was on his payroll, and sped off.*

*I took the CD and put it into my valise, with the firm commitment that the first chance I got, I was going to break it into pieces to make sure that no other Torah scholar would waste their time listening to its moronic advice, chas v'shalom.*

*I got to Romania and found out that I was one of a group of 36 people who were continuing on to Uman. The leader of our group was a guy called Alex, and he did the roll call. I didn't know anyone else there, and that was fine with me because I just wanted to learn Torah during the journey without any of these religiously lightweight goofballs bothering me. We arrived in Bucharest, and that's where we got our first surprise of the trip: Instead of sending us a big coach bus with enough seats for 36 people, they sent us a 14-seat minibus - and there was no one around to complain to about it.*

*The leader of our group spoke Russian, and the Romanians spoke English about as well as I speak French, so we realized that we didn't have any other choice but to figure out how we were going to get to the Ukrainian border on our own, by train. To their credit, the majority of the group reacted to the situation relatively calmly and peacefully. Most of the group were newly observant Jews from North Tel Aviv who were just about as cool as you could get. When they heard the news, they reacted by exclaiming 'bring it on! Let Rabbeinu's tikunim begin!'*

*But I was pretty angry. I hadn't paid good money to have this hitch, or this 'tikun' or whatever. I told everyone that when we got back, I was going to sue the company for this oversight. Most of them just smiled at me, and told me I should drop the facade of 'normal' already, and get used to the new reality we were entering where we were sure to encounter many obstacles and snags.*

*Some of the group had brought along their food for Rosh Hashana in Styrofoam boxes packed with ice. They had maybe another 10 hours until the ice started to melt. I'd travelled light, with just my small valise, a few cans of tuna, and some snacks like Bamba and Bissli. Nonetheless, I found myself helping load up the van with boxes belonging to people who'd brought along half their house. Having to do that was less than pleasant and contributed to my growing frustration with the whole situation.*

*By nature, I'm a fairly moody person, prone to quick bouts of anger and depression - and I could sense that my mood was starting to plummet. Most of the group, however, seemed to be in a great state of mind, and you might even say they were happy.*

*We made our way to the train station, the whole way the chevra reminding each other about guarding their eyes, and talking a whole load of divrei Torah. We got on a train and presently arrived at the Ukrainian border, where the second big surprise of the trip was waiting for us: no one knew what had happened to our entry visas.*

*The group leader, Alex, called up the company who'd organized the trip and asked them to send the visas straight to the border. The head of the company explained that he himself was currently en route to Uman, and was actually talking to Alex from the plane. He told him that when he got to Kiev, he'd do his best to arrange the visas from there. It was already 4pm, and the group decided to pray Mincha, hoping that in the merit of our prayers, G-d would change the whole situation around for the best.*

*I really struggled to pray, because the worry about how this all would be resolved was weighing heavily on my heart. By contrast, the rest of the group was singing and shouting their prayers, and praying with tremendous joy and achdut - unity. After a whole hour of praying, they even started dancing, while the Russian and Romanian passport control clerks stood off to the side watching. They might have enjoyed the spectacle or they might have been laughing at us, but one thing's for sure: they were certainly getting some free entertainment.*

*Once again, Alex called the head of the travel agency, who by this time had arrived in Kiev. The man told him that everyone had already gone home, and that he was hoping to be able to sort it out first thing the following morning. That meant that we either had to spend the night there at the border, or we'd have to go back to Bucharest. The decision was put to the vote and most of the group opted to stay at the border, partially because they wanted to be able to get across as soon as the visas were sorted out. Also, a lot of the people in the group couldn't afford to pay for a night in a hotel, even if it was only a 1-star establishment.*

*We were very fortunate that most of the group was planning to camp out when they got to Uman, so in the blink of an eye, they put up seven tents. We ate a meager supper, and then all 36 of us managed to somehow squash into the tents, which gave us some protection from the cold night air.*

*I was very close to falling into a serious depression. I stayed in a corner trying to fight off my disturbing thoughts, and couldn't even think about learning or praying. In the middle of the darkness, one of the chassidim switched on a flashlight and started reading some Torah aloud. And what Torah was he sharing with us, at full volume? Exactly the same Torah I'd heard in the cab, that a person shouldn't stress himself about anything - especially not about the things that his yetzer hara was telling him, because the yetzer only wants to get us depressed and make us crazy.*

*This time, I realized I was less upset about the advice - not least because it helped me to get to sleep much faster than I'd otherwise hoped, and I think I even fell asleep with a smile on my face.*

*We awoke at the crack of dawn the next morning, feeling rather frozen. I was shocked by the attention to religious detail being displayed by the chevra, who at first glance looked like they were ignoramuses, or at best, a bunch of ordinary guys who wouldn't know the finer points of halacha in the slightest. But they were very concerned that every member of the group should do 'netilat yedayim' according to halacha.*

*I really needed a cup of coffee to help me wake up like I was used to at home, but noticed that I was the only one into that. Everyone else seemed to be following Rabbeinu's advice based on the Zohar, where he cautions his followers not to drink so much as a cup of water before they've prayed. The chevra were following his advice to the letter in complete simplicity, but that didn't stop one of them from kindly making a cup of coffee for me.*

*In the time it took me to get myself organized and dressed, I realized that some of the group had already gone for a dip in one of the streams that was close by the border, and that most of the other people were already wrapped in their tallitot and wearing their tefillin. What can I say? I never in my life prayed the morning shacharit prayers like we prayed that morning. We did birkat hashachar at 7am, and only by 10am did we get to aleinu leshabe'ach. It was the first time I'd ever experienced praying where every word counted, and where every single word of the prayers was sung so beautifully. I started to feel quite bad that I hadn't really appreciated the chevra, and that up until a couple of hours ago, I'd even been belittling them.*

*After the prayers were over, Alex went off to the border control building to see if the visas had come through yet. While he was doing that, the guys organized a communal Tikun HaKlali recitation, and for an hour, they were shouting out the Psalms. It took me a quarter of an hour to decide that I was going to join in with their screaming. Before I started, I looked around from side to side to see if anyone was looking at me - and that's when it hit me. I was living a lie. Instead of worrying about the 'inner dimensions', I was obsessed with appearances and worrying about things that really didn't matter. Here I was, stuck in a completely foreign country along with 35 other people who were all busy saying the Tikun*

*Haklali, and all I was worrying about was what the goyim would think about me. I was never going to see these Romanians again!*

*Suddenly, I started shouting out the words along with everyone else, and felt like each second I was shedding more and more of my hypocrisy, and dropping the mask of pretending to be some sort of 'normal' person who was part of a 'normal' gathering of people. I suddenly realized just how much I wasn't really being me. After I had that breakthrough, I just didn't care what anyone thought about me anymore. I stopped listening to my evil inclination, which was just trying to bring me down into unhappiness and anger.*

*What an amazing, ingenious, stupendous piece of advice I'd heard the night before! On the face of it, it had seemed like following it would only lead to anarchy and disorder, but now I really understood its profound depth. That advice about not paying any attention to the yetzer hara contained the most potent weapon that a person could possibly have against their worst enemies, namely self-deception, complacency and hypocrisy. The chevra gave me a big hug once we'd all finished saying the Tikun, and told me that I'd given them a big spiritual boost that morning - though really, it was the other way around.*

*Alex came back from border control and asked us if we could pray more quietly, because the passport control people on both sides of the border were starting to get upset about all the noise. Then, he told us something much more serious and worrying: the visas had simply disappeared into thin air, and no one could find them. Now, we had to choose between three courses of action.*

*The first option: To go back to Bucharest, and try to celebrate Rosh Hashana there.*

*The second option: There weren't any more direct flights between Romania and Israel in the next two days, but the chevra could try to return to Israel via several different routes, although it would be very complicated to try and arrange all the different flights home via Italy and Germany. In addition to the financial complications that that option entailed, there were also a number of procedural difficulties that wouldn't be so easy to solve.*

*The third option: To go to the Ukrainian embassy in Romania, and see if they would issue new visas for the group.*

*None of the options sounded particularly attractive to us, but that's what was on the table, so the group decided that everyone should go and do an hour of hitbodedut, and after that, they'd reconvene and decide what course of action to take. Alex also called someone in Uman and asked him to go and pray for us in the Tzion.*

# The Stolen Light

*So each one of us went off to find his own private spot to pray. For me, it was the first time I'd ever spoken directly to G-d; there was no siddur, Gemara, or book of Psalms acting as the go-between. I suddenly realized just how far away from G-d I really was. I felt so estranged from Him. I made myself a promise that I would come back to this topic again and explore it further, once we'd gotten through this current crisis - this tikun.*

*As I was doing hitbodedut, there was this sweet Breslev baal teshuva guy standing close to me. The whole hour, he was crying non-stop; he was clapping his hands, dancing, shouting, and talking to G-d so naturally and freely that you'd think he was talking to his best friend. I was so envious of him, to the very depth of my soul. This guy certainly grew up in a completely secular, spiritually devoid environment, with parents who didn't even have a minimal connection with the Creator of the world. But look at him now - what vitality he had! The man was completely uninhibited, and truth was radiating out of every pore of his body. His prayers were completely energized by the pure emuna that was bursting out from his vocal chords. What was his secret? What was Rebbe Nachman giving him that I hadn't been given? What was I missing?*

*The hour of hitbodedut passed, and then the Breslev guy turned to me and told me, 'I have absolutely no doubt that we're going to be in Uman for Rosh Hashana.' He started dancing with me, and together we danced back to the central meeting point. We took the vote, and the majority decided that we should find the nearest Ukrainian embassy and ask them to issue us new visas.*

*Alex and two other members of the chevra collected everyone's passports, then took a taxi to get to a village that was a two hour drive away. We stayed at the border and opened a kollel and a couple of shtieblach that were unparalleled in the history of the world. We learned Torah for many long, uninterrupted hours, and then davened with incredible joy and happiness. We went off for long hitbodedut sessions in the evening, we danced... In short, from 1pm Monday afternoon until 8pm Tuesday night when Alex got back with his good news, we were in some sort of gigantic holy trance. All we cared about was learning Torah and praying in a minyan.*

*Alex told us about the miraculous help they'd had in arranging the new visas. They'd gotten to the village where the Ukrainian embassy in Romania was located, and now I'll let Alex tell you more or less in his own words what happened there:*

*'We got there, and sitting in front of us was a jaded, indifferent female clerk, who greeted us in an incredibly rude way because we'd dared to interrupt the incredible monotony that was her usual day at work. She was even more annoyed with us when she realized we weren't going to look at her, and ordered us to maintain eye contact while speaking to her.*

*I tried to explain to her that it was nothing personal, but I probably would have gotten further if I was talking to a wall instead. Anyway, she informed us that the visas would only be ready in a week from today, minimum, and that it could even take longer. I tried to explain to her that we just had to be in Uman by Wednesday, but she got all sarcastic and told me 'And I just have to be in New York on Friday.' I guess that was supposed to be a joke.*

*I tried to laugh to lighten things up a bit, but that just got her even more upset at me. As we spoke, I suddenly realized that I didn't know where my cell phone was. Simon was with me, so I asked him to please go and look for it in the taxi, but the taxi had already taken off - apparently with my cell phone.*

*I asked the clerk if I could make an urgent call from her phone instead. She made a face, but then let me do it, because even she could see that really, she didn't have a choice. I called my father, who was already in Uman, and I told him everything that we were going through. My dad shouted through the phone that I shouldn't get depressed or fall into despair! He really encouraged me, and told me that for sure, we were still going to get to Uman for Rosh Hashana.*

*Just then, an older man in his fifties came out of one of the inner offices. He was very well dressed and put together, and I figured that this must be the senior manager of this remote branch of the Ukrainian embassy. He wanted to know what all of the noise was about, and the clerk started telling him about these crazy, unreasonable people who were really bothering her.*

*The boss motioned us over and told us to follow him into his office so he could understand what all the fuss was about. I told him what the problem was, and as soon as he heard the words 'Uman' and 'Rebbe Nachman' he asked me, 'Are you talking about the saint who's buried in Uman?' 'Yes!' I told him, and for a minute, I wondered if we'd stumbled across a hidden Jew in deep cover.*

*He went on to explain why he'd gotten so excited, but not before he'd stepped outside to give the antagonistic clerk an order to get on with arranging the visas we needed ASAP, so that they'd be waiting for us at the border no later than lunchtime tomorrow afternoon. The clerk was obviously very disappointed with the turn of events, and she gave us a hearty evil glare, but what could she do? Orders were orders.*

*In the meantime, I asked the boss about his connection to Rebbe Nachman, and he explained that he'd been flying into the embassy from Kiev every week for the last ten years. A few months ago, for the first time in his life, he decided to make the trip by car instead. As he drove, he got to a turn-off and a signpost that said 'To the Tzaddik', in Russian.*

# The Stolen Light

*He's a curious person, and was dying to know what a 'Tzaddik' was, so he turned off the road and followed the sign. Within a couple of minutes, he found himself at Rebbe Nachman's burial place, together with a few hundred other people. He parked and asked one of the passersby what was going on, why were there so many people gathered here? They told him that a very big tzaddik was hidden here, who'd already helped a massive amount of people.*

*The embassy boss asked if it would be OK for him to try and speak to the tzaddik himself, and then they told him that he'd been dead and buried here for more than 200 years. Now, he was really curious! How could a dead 'tzaddik' who left the world more than two centuries ago still be helping the living? The passerby explained to him the whole deal with Rabbeinu, and a few of the people standing close to them joined in their conversation.*

*One person told him about the miracle he'd got by Rabbeinu to have children, someone else chipped in about how he'd been miraculously cured from a horrible disease, someone else explained how he'd finally gotten married after a visit to the Tzaddik. There was also a gentile standing there who overheard what they were talking about, and he went on to tell them about the miracle that had happened to him too, through Rabbeinu.*

*The boss really took it to heart, hearing all these amazing stories of how a dead tzaddik was still helping hundreds of thousands of people. He decided on the spot that if a dead person could help so many living people, than a living person could certainly help that dead person. He made a vow that he would do whatever was in his power to help the Tzaddik continue to help even more people. Then he got back in his car and drove off to Romania.*

*Four short months later, we showed up in his office, and he immediately grasped that he was being given a personal invitation to help the Tzaddik - and that's exactly what he was going to do.*

*We were completely shocked when we heard his story, because it was a real glimpse of just how exact and individually tailored all of Hashem's actions in the world really are. We thanked the boss profusely, and then the grumpy clerk came in to the room and told us that the passports had all been faxed over to Kiev, and the visas would be ready to be collected between 2pm and 4pm the next day. Then she told us that we needed to pay around $400 to order the new visas.*

*I explained to her that we were talking about a group of really poor people, who simply didn't have that sort of money available. If we were lucky, we could probably scrape together $40, but that was it...*

*The boss sat up straight, and told us, 'I promised to help the tzaddik, and I'm going to see it through until the end. Don't worry about the $400 - I'll cover it* *myself.' Suddenly, I realized that we couldn't be dealing with a real Ukrainian embassy official - the man must be Elijah the prophet, in disguise! I simply have no other explanation for the amazing miracles that happened to us in that embassy bureau...' And with that, Alex finished his tale.*

*As you might expect, the place exploded in singing and dancing, and the joy carried on until the early hours of the morning. The experience energized me in a way that I'd never, ever experienced before. I like to dance at weddings, but with quite a few little breaks here and there, to eat some food, or smoke a cigarette outside, or to chat with a friend for a while. But here, I found myself enthusiastically dancing and singing for hours on end.*

*Until that point in the trip, I'd really thought to myself that I was doing my friend a massive favor by coming to Uman for him. Now, I started to think that he'd done me the massive favor. I called my wife to share some of the happiness I was feeling, and I think she was a bit shocked by all the light beaming over the phone line. But she was really pleased for me that I felt so joyful, and it was the first time I can remember that my wife told me that I sounded happy.*

*'What, don't I usually sound happy?' I wanted to know. 'No,' she replied. 'Usually you sound stressed, and now you're sounding happy, relaxed and confident.' And truly, that's exactly how I felt. I was surrounded by real friends, and the glue that had bound us so closely together was nothing other than prayer and learning Torah. There were no vested interests, there was no social pressure, victory-seeking, or 'keeping up with the Joneses'. There was only a true desire to do G-d's will.*

*It was so incredibly refreshing.*

*Well, we thought the story was pretty much over at this point, but we were wrong. There was still another twist to come. The visas were dispatched urgently to the border by the following afternoon, as we'd been promised. Alex had arranged for a coach bus to come pick us up on the Ukrainian side - and wonder of wonders, it actually showed up on time. We were all ensconced on the bus, making good time though the Ukrainian countryside and looking forward to our first shower in three days and our first night's sleep on something approaching a normal bed... when the last bombshell got dropped on us: three of the members of our group were missing.*

*Alex was making loads of frantic phone calls trying to track them down, until finally he found them at a hotel in Bucharest where they'd been staying. We were supposed to have picked them up before we headed to the border. After another round of discussions, they finally decided to take a cab to the border, and were on their way there presently. It was a real inconvenience, but the right thing to do was to turn the bus around and journey the two hours back to the Romanian*

# The Stolen Light

*border to pick them up. And after that, bli neder, there wouldn't be any more delays.*

*In spite of everything that we'd been through, the chevra unanimously agreed to turn back. Once there, we had to wait another four hours until they actually showed up. We picked them up, and then with the last of our strength, got back on the bus and made the six-hour journey to Uman, where we finally arrived early Thursday morning.*

*Physically, we were all completely and utterly exhausted by the time we reached our destination. But as soon as we stepped off the coach bus, most of the chevra got a new wind, grabbed their suitcases, and ran off in the direction of Rebbe Nachman and the Tzion.*

*I was so tired that I could barely stand on my feet. Thank G-d, a bunch of Russians pulling Stalin-era hand wagons ran up to me shouting: 'Wan dollar; too dollar, meester', so I gave them my luggage. All I wanted to do was to grab a shower and go to sleep, but decided that before I went to bed, I would first just step into the Tzion for a few minutes to say the Tikun Haklali.*

*When I got there, it was an incredible scene - there were hundreds of people at the Tzion, maybe even thousands, all buzzing around like they were in a beehive or something. This one was praying, that one was saying tehillim, another was saying the Tikun Haklali. People were crying out, dancing, there was a group who was trying to learn. I stood there looking around, not believing what was going on. It was 4am! What were all these people doing here? Why weren't they in bed, asleep? The whole place was full of such joy, such enthusiasm, such vitality.*

*I was standing there gazing at the scene when one of the chassidim came up to me, and without even saying a word, pulled me into a circle of dancing men. So I ended up spending another half an hour of my life dancing, and yearning, and passionately longing to get closer to Hashem. I was crying my eyes out, sobbing in a way that was beyond even when my father died, may his memory be for a blessing.*

*The dancing stopped, and I started saying my Tikun Haklali. There was an old man standing right next to me - 80 years old if he was a day - who was also busy saying the Tikun HaKlali, but with such care and precision. He was pronouncing every single word so carefully and with such happiness and enthusiasm, the way a child would recite it. I was transfixed and couldn't stop staring at him, but he didn't notice because he wasn't paying attention to anything except his prayers. Rivers of sweat were pouring down his face from all his intense concentration. I drew a lot of strength and inspiration from that old man, and for the next hour, I also took the time to say the Tikun Haklali properly.*

*The minute I finished, the original sweet dancing chassid from the bus came up to me again to tell me that they were just about to start doing the slichot prayers at the Kloiz Synagogue, and that he'd saved me a seat there. Of course, before we went there he insisted that I go and dunk in the mikveh - together with about 1,500 other people. Usually, I only go to the mikveh before Yom Kippur. Not for one minute did I ever think that I'd be using a mikveh with so many other people, but even that experience was surprisingly tolerable. So much so, in fact, that afterwards I decided that I was going to start dunking in the mikveh every day.*

*Baruch Hashem, we went over to the Kloiz to say slichot, and even though I was so incredibly exhausted, I still managed to stand up for the prayers the whole way through. And even then, I still didn't go straight to sleep. First, I went back for another visit to the Tzion, where I said another round of the Tikun Haklali, and only after that did I collapse into bed."*

Aharon finished his story, and only after he stopped speaking did I see just how tired he looked, even though his eyes were sparkling. He seemed like such a nice guy that I had to make a real effort to get a grip on myself and my emotions, so that I wouldn't be tempted to deviate from my big plan.

Already from the morning when I'd first heard a bit of his story, I'd decided that Aharon's suitcase was going to be the first suitcase on my hit list, because I figured from what he'd been saying that he was carrying with him something in the region of $250,000 in cash. I didn't yet know how much of it I was going to take, but one thing was for sure: it was going to be a lot more than ten bucks. On second thought, maybe I'd just take the whole thing, especially if I wasn't managing to get the money I needed from other people. In one go, Aharon's suitcase would bump me up very close to the $300k I was hoping to make from this trip. And if I managed to steal a lot from other people too, even better.

They started singing '*Ashreinu, ashreinu*' again, and I started to get really excited about the huge amount of money that I was going to have in another couple of days - it would be enough to buy me my own apartment in Tel Aviv. I really fancied the idea of buying a penthouse right on the beach... Most likely, I'd also give my parents a few thousands shekels to get them off my back and reduce some of the pressure they were putting on me.

**Chapter 6**

*Nachman, the head of our little group, shares some words and insights from Rebbe Nachman.*

Apart from my brother, every other person around the table seemed to have on average at least seven or eight kids. But Motty was still newly married, so even though he was only 22 and had just two children, by the time he hit 40 I was pretty sure he'd also have ten or twelve. What a frightening thought! How can anyone raise so many kids? If I even think about having one kid, I start to feel weak and my legs start to shake.

The unofficial leader of our little *chevra* is called... Nachman. I was pretty sure he was *frum* from birth. He has 15 kids of his own, plus another one that he adopted. It's impossible for me to understand what was going on with that. What, 15 of his own kids weren't enough for him, and he had to go and adopt another one? Madness. And the cherry on top was that the kid who he adopted had Down's syndrome. If I had a heart, all this would have broken it.

At least tell me that the man lives in a mansion somewhere, and has a football field and a swimming pool in his back garden... No. He doesn't. He lives in a one-and-half room apartment. What? How can you fit 15 kids in one-and-a-half rooms?! I figure some of his kids must sleep on top of the fridge, and on the table, and in the bath, and in the sink. Otherwise, I have no idea where he puts them all.

My brother had told me some amazing stories about this guy, Nachman. He manages a *gemach*, which spells out the first letters of the words '*gemilut chassidim'*, or 'good deeds' in Hebrew. Nachman's *gemach* gives out medicines. That means that when someone's having a coughing fit in the middle of the night and they run out of Acamol, he's the address they go to. It doesn't matter what time of night, if they lost their baby's pacifier, they can go to Nachman for a new one. And it's not like he's even getting paid to do it, ~~because he's crazy~~ because he's doing it out of the goodness of his heart. Normally, if you wake someone up in the middle of the night for anything, they charge you at least double.

On top of running the medicine *gemach*, Nachman also has a clothing *gemach*, which he runs out of his storage room. He has mountains of clothes tucked away in there. Anyone who doesn't want their old clothes anymore simply sends them off to Nachman. His wife fixes whatever needs fixing, washes it, organizes it, and then sells it for around a shekel per item. The buyer, usually a person on the poor side, gets to wear something that's nearly as good as new.

Isn't that amazing?

Every single day, Nachman's wife makes three square meals for her own 15 kids and also devotes a great deal of time to looking after the adopted kid with Down's. When she isn't doing that, she's sewing and washing and fixing clothes, all for a shekel. And what's more, Nachman is supposed to have a real head for business, which means that he isn't working for a shekel because he can't hack it in the real world - he's working for a shekel because he's probably the world's biggest sucker.

But that's not all: Nachman also runs another *gemach,* which gives out interest-free loans. My brother told me that hundreds of thousands of shekels go through his hands every month, even though sometimes he himself doesn't know where his next meal is coming from - and all of this is happening in an apartment that has one-and-a-half rooms!

My brother has been to Nachman's for a few *Shabbatot* already, and he told me that usually, in addition to his own large family, there are at least another 10 guests around the table and the children are serving the food. They used bookshelves to divide the apartment up into rooms, and two of Nachman's married children and their spouses with their own small children also live with him, and everyone gets along just fine. According to my brother, the atmosphere is so peaceful and calm in the apartment that it feels like a little bit of *Gan Eden*.

So this famous Nachman is the one who's leading our group tonight, and he's here in Uman with four of his children, two of which are already married, and the other two who are in their teens. And the biggest kicker of all is that Nachman himself is only 44 years old.

By the way, I forgot to tell you my name: I'm Avi Neuman. A lot of people think that my brother and I maybe 'Ashkenazied' up our surname, because we both look like we come from the Indian sub-continent or something, but there is actually a very simple explanation. My mother is Iraqi, and we both take after her side of the family. That's also the reason why every year, we had to celebrate

# The Stolen Light

*Lag B'Omer* in Meron (against our will), and how she managed to finagle my very Polish father into coming along, too.

My dad is a little bit anti-religious, probably because all of his family got killed in the Holocaust, and he's really angry at G-d. He believes in Him, but he's furious with Him, which is why he *dafka* goes out of his way to do things that he knows G-d doesn't want him to do. I could try and explain it more, but you can see that it's all pretty complicated.

OK, Nachman the *chassid* is starting to talk now. He looks like he's full of interesting, wise things to say - which is great, as long as he keeps it all short and to the point.

*"Gut yom tov, gut yom tov! Ay, ay, Ashreinu, that we are all here tonight in Uman, by Rabbeinu, the holy Rebbe Nachman, the holy pious one and light of all lights. Ashreinu, that we all had the merit again this year to put Rabbeinu's advice into practice, and that we merited to come to this place, at this time, to celebrate Rosh Hashana with Rabbeinu, who himself is of the aspect of Eretz Yisrael, and of the holiness of Eretz Yisrael."*

I can see that everyone else is nodding their heads at Nachman, but his words seem to have really rubbed me up the wrong way. I try to keep my cool by diverting my attention into the snacks on the table. These crazy people and their crazy ideas. I'm going to keep myself busy by eating the pistachios, and let these nut jobs get on with their nutty ideas and conversations. Nachman starts up again so enthusiastically that he looks like he's going to burst from excitement.

*"Rabbeinu himself told us on a few occasions that he could do tikunim, spiritual rectifications, on Rosh Hashana that he simply couldn't achieve at any other time of the year. And Baruch Hashem, everyone here can feel that special sense of spiritual elevation that you just don't get anywhere else in the world. It's that heady mix of togetherness and joy. We're sitting here all squashed together by this shaky table, drinking out of glasses that date from the Dark Ages, but our souls are soaring up to the spiritual heights! What do we care about all the material lacks and deficiencies? When we're by Rabbeinu, we're elevated up to a spiritual plane where all physicality ceases to matter. Ashreinu, ashreinu."*

He pauses, and everyone starts singing - what else? - "Ashreinu, ashreinu, ashreinu, that we have the merit to get close to *Rabbeinu.* Uman, Uman, Rosh Hashana, Uman Uman Rosh Hashana."

You know, at least on that score, Nachman was exactly right - the situation in the apartment was pretty difficult, and not just because of the overcrowding or the fact that we were sitting on rickety old chairs. The whole place was done out in extremely bad taste. The owner seemed to have stuck up any old roll of wallpaper he could find in the market place, and there didn't seem to be any aesthetic harmony between the different parts. Here, there was a bit of green wallpaper decorated with triangles, and right next to it was some purple wallpaper with a leaf pattern. He'd stuck some wallpaper with menacing-looking lions and panthers on the ceiling, and I really have no idea how he wasn't scared to sleep in the flat when we weren't there. If he had kids, they'd be traumatized and scared stiff of animals for life - or at the very least, they'd want to be zookeepers when they grew up - assuming this Ukrainian even had kids.

From what I could tell, he was drunk from the moment he opened his eyes in the morning until he closed them at night; or to be more precise, until they shut themselves down under the influence of vodka. Every single time I saw him, he'd be swigging at least a cup or two of vodka. But you know what? Even with all his drunkenness, that guy still knew how to make some serious money.

Let's do a simple calculation: there were 30 of us lodging under his roof. Each one of us was paying $250 for the privilege of staying there, which equals: $7,500 cash. He was getting half up front, and the rest once the *chag* was over, and you can be sure that he wasn't paying any taxes on it. That said, the local mafia was probably going to take their 50% cut, but he was still getting more than $3,000 for less than a week's work.

All he did was make the shabby beds every day (their antique mattresses stuffed with prickly straw) and occasionally sweep the floor. The rest of the time, he'd moved into the garbage room at the bottom of the building, and that's where he stayed. These Ukrainians really had no shame; the only thing that mattered to them was making money. But the truth was that in one week, he could earn his entire salary for a year. If I'd known where he stashed his money, I would have also robbed him…

By nature I'm really not a thief, so it's a bit strange even to me how I'm so obsessed with stealing money at the moment. But you know what? I've realized that these days, everyone's a thief. Everyone's trying to pull the wool over everyone else's eyes. Every day, the news is full of yet another prestigious person who was caught with their hand in the cookie jar. Sometimes it's a judge, sometimes it's a politician who was caught taking hefty bribes for thousands and thousands of shekels - and that's just the ones we know about. The ones we don't know about, *Hashem* should have mercy on us.

Man, where did that '*Hashem* should have mercy' stuff just come from? All the influence from these *frummies* is starting to seep into my psyche! I have to be really, really careful that I don't also catch '*teshuva* disease'. From what I can see around here, it's already a full-blown epidemic.

# The Stolen Light

When Nachman starts talking, it's really difficult to get him to stop. I got stuck having a really long conversation with him the first day I got here, and I'm sure Motty put him up to it. He was telling me a whole bunch of amazing things, and he also gave me twenty bucks. He was trying to explain to me what I actually needed to do in Uman - things like 'how to talk in front of *Rabbeinu*' and stuff like that. I actually didn't understand most of it, but I was still enjoying myself, and every now and then I'd let out a 'wow!' or a 'pssshhhhhh!'

Everyone else seems to hang on to his every word, as though he's always revealing some profound insights and deep understandings. And me? I act like a monkey, and just ape whatever everyone else is doing (although the thought has crossed my mind that maybe *they* are the real monkeys in this picture, and that I am the only real human being. But I digress). Anyway, Nachman was reading something aloud to them, and they were all raptly listening to him, like he was telling them the most gripping story they'd ever heard, full of cliff-hangers and twisting plot lines - and me? I didn't understand a word of what the man was saying.

*"The main principle underpinning all the work we do on Rosh Hashana, Yom Kippur and the whole month of festivals is that we need to be constantly clarifying the point of truth, wherever it might be, in the merit of the True Tzaddik, who enables us to uncover the whole truth to the fullest extent possible. On Rosh Hashana, Yom Kippur, and the ten days of repentance, we are clarifying the truth by way of the holy work done by Am Yisrael. We do this by crying out to Hashem, and supplicating Him, by acting charitably with one another, with the sound of blowing the shofar, and with all of our efforts to make teshuva, each one according to his own aspect...*

*Afterwards, on Sukkot, we are tasked with the job of clarifying the truth through our external physical work, such as eating, drinking, and sleeping in the Sukkah. Together, these form the basis of the whole mitzvah of Sukkot, inasmuch as these things teach us to know and believe that by way of real truth, we can rely on G-d and feel close to Him, no matter where we encounter Him in our lives. But we can also learn from the aspect of the arba minim, which includes all the different categories of Am Yisrael and include the willows, which represent the aspect of those who are very far away, and who have neither taste nor smell. And by way of truth, we can discover that even these distant ones give Hashem nachat ruach, and glory and splendour, by way of the point of truth that is to be found in each one of them.*

*And this is why on Simchat Torah, everyone is given an aliya to go up and read from the Torah - to show that every member of Am Yisrael has a share in the true Torah. Because the whole point of truth is to bring closer, and not to distance. We have to clarify the point of truth that's in every single one of the Children of*

*Israel, even those who are the furthest away - because that is what G-d truly desires.*

*Furthermore, we find that Rabbeinu, zichrono levracha, taught that the anthropomorphic attribute of truth came to G-d, and asked Him not to create the world, because it would be full of lies. But G-d not only didn't listen to 'truth', He cast it down to earth. As it's written, 'You will send truth down to the earth'. And after that, Hakadosh Baruch Hu said that truth will rise up from the ground, ostensibly referring to the attribute of truth which didn't agree that the world should be created. We know this, because the fundamental point of truth is G-d Himself.*

*It stands to reason that after G-d created the world, He needed to create it in accordance with His fundamental truth, but Hashem's truth is very profound and lofty, because 'very deep are His thoughts'. This is so much so, that even the attribute of truth itself, which was a holy angel whose very essence was 'truth', couldn't plumb the depth of Hashem's thoughts, when it came to His truth.*

*This 'misunderstanding' of G-d's original thought brings about those situations where sometimes, one friend argues against another, because it seems to him, according to his truth, that his friend is straying from the correct path. But when he argues with his friend, he can just end up distancing him even further from Hashem.*

*This 'misunderstanding' is the cause of all the arguments and disputes in the world. Sometimes, a person even accuses _himself_ of wrongdoing, and distances himself from Hashem Yitbarach, also through his own 'truth', because he knows the truth about himself, that he is blemished and very far from G-d. But when a person does this, he causes himself to despair and to be even more distanced from Hashem. But a person who is connected to Rabbeinu never, ever despairs, because he already knows this lesson - and thus he is truly alive at all times. Ashreinu, ashreinu, how good is our portion!"*

Everyone was paying rapt attention to Nachman's speech, and seemed to really enjoy it. If I'm honest, even I warmed up to what he was saying by the end, but I didn't let myself get too carried away by it all. I didn't want to risk getting pulled off track from doing what I came here to do. 'Aspects, *sefirot,* worlds' - it really seemed like these guys were living on a completely different planet, but it also looked like their planet was doing them a lot of good. It would be interesting to see if they were still enjoying it so much in another two days, of course, when all their money had been stolen... Nachman continued:

*"Today, we came here on eagles' wings. Yes, we had to pay a few dollars. Yes, we've all had our share of difficulties and obstacles. Maybe we didn't have the money, maybe our wives weren't happy about our making the trip, or maybe our*

*parents weren't keen on us coming here. But all these things pale in comparison to the difficulties we experienced twenty years ago, when Russia was still firmly locked behind its Iron Curtain. Then, the trip demanded tremendous self-sacrifice. We had to travel on forged passports, disguise ourselves as other people, and pay thousands of dollars for the privilege of visiting the grave for just a few short minutes, before returning to Eretz Yisrael. We were literally risking our lives and our liberty with every step we took, it was such a frightening endeavour. But what was more frightening for us was the prospect of not coming to the holy city of Uman, and not visiting Rabbeinu's holy Tzion, in order to fulfill the Rebbe's holy request."*

What 'holy city' was he talking about?! Surely not this ugly, undeveloped town that was filled with primitive *goyim?* There were still people here who didn't have modern plumbing in their homes, and got their water every day from a local well. You have to wonder how the Ukraine could have more lakes and iron quarries than it could possibly use, and still have so very many poor people in every corner. It's nothing short of miraculous. The *chassidim* all say that *Rabbeinu* cursed the Ukraine that it would never be a prosperous country because of all the terrible decrees they enacted against the Jews, and all the murderous pogroms they conducted here. Nachman continued on:

*"I remember the first time that I visited Uman, after the fall of the Iron Curtain. There were about 200 chassidim here, all of us full of joy and emotion. We were still a bit scared of the authorities, but we'll all remember that Rosh Hashana for many years to come. We met some old English-speaking Ukrainian man here, who saw us walking around Uman. He ran over to me and said, 'Now, I really believe that your God is the true G-d and that He's going to win.' I asked him why, and he told me a shocking story.*

*He'd been the neighbor of two Ukrainian women, whose hobby was killing Jewish children. That was their greatest pleasure in life. At that time, there were many Jewish parents who were trying to save their children from the Nazi beasts by paying local gentiles to hide the children in their homes or in remote villages. Also, there were Jewish kids who would run off to the forest a minute before their parents were rounded up onto the trains that would take them to their deaths. These women would go and hunt those children down, and then murder them just for fun. Many children were murdered in this terrible way, and the neighbour was sure that he was witnessing the end of the Jewish people. And the truth was that for a number of decades, he didn't see a single Jew anywhere, and he was sure that we'd become extinct, chas v'shalom.*

*Now that he was seeing us all here in Uman once again, freely walking around looking the same way that the Jews had looked before World War II with our long beards and our kippot, the old man understood that they really had lost, and that we really had won. And in fact, we have emerged victorious, and every additional Jew that comes to Uman and has the merit of saying the Tikun Haklali, and adds to the holiness of Am Yisrael, that person gives Hashem a most powerful victory in this world."*

"What's your name?" Nachman suddenly asked Ido, who was sitting on his right. Ido was a gentle soul who didn't stop smiling. I hadn't managed to chat with him yet, but I knew that he'd come with a friend of his from some yeshiva for *baal teshuvas* in Tel Aviv and another secular friend named Nadav, who'd decided to come along with them for the experience. Nadav was a musician, and we'd already discussed possibly playing together. He was a great guitar player, bordering on musical genius - I saw that from the two minutes he'd spent in my room playing my guitar before the *Chag* started, when he'd played a couple of guitar solos like a true virtuoso.

"Ido", he replied, through a mouthful of chicken.

"How did you come to be in Uman?" Nachman wanted to know.

"How did I get to Uman?" smiled Ido, furiously chewing the big piece of chicken that was still in his mouth.

I didn't want to believe it, but it looked like they were about to start another round of stories. My eyelids were already drooping, and they hadn't even got to me yet – at which point I'd have to invent some story to tell them about myself.

Nachman turned to me, and asked me: "Do you want to do a storytelling *zimun*, with me and Ido?"

"*Zimun*?" I was already dead on my feet from exhaustion. Motty saw what was going on, and stepped in to save the day.

"My brother, drink some coffee and sit with us for a little bit. Now, the real action is gonna start…"

Nachman went back to Ido, and asked him again: "*Nu,* so how did you get to Uman? Do you want to tell us how *Rabbeinu* brought you to him?"

Everyone's eyes turned to Ido, who was still smiling.

# The Stolen Light

## Chapter 7

*Let me tell you Ido the attorney's story, where he talks about Kobi and Aryeh, and also about Grandpa Natan*

I had overheard Ido telling my brother that he was studying law. He spoke very nicely, except for his habit of giving over a few too many minor and less than relevant details. What can you do, people are people.

*"The story starts a couple of months ago. Back then, I had no plans to travel to Uman, and I didn't even believe that I'd ever come here - not because I was necessarily opposed, but because the yeshiva that I was enrolled in was more interested in serious learning and less interested in trips to kivrei tzaddikim. The rabbi I was learning with never told us to go to Uman, so the idea was never really presented as an option for me to even consider. Until one day in the yeshiva's dorms, something happened that changed everything.*

*I'd been living in the yeshiva dorms for six months, ever since I'd left university. The yeshiva apartment was located on the first floor of an old building in Tel Aviv, on Balfour Street. On the four steps leading up to our dorm had been abandoned a pair of bikes and an old baby carriage with no wheels. The stairwell hadn't been properly cleaned or maintained for years, and it had a bit of a musty smell."*

Like I was saying, there were a lot of details. Who cares if there were bikes in the stairwell or if it smelled a bit funny? Stop with all the unnecessary information, and tell me the story already!

*"There were four of us yeshiva students staying there, all baalei teshuva who were studying at the yeshiva on Rashi Street. I'm Ido Sadeh, 25 years old, and until eight months ago, I was studying law at Tel Aviv University. My father is a well-known lawyer, and my mother is a very highly regarded doctor at Beilinson hospital."*

"How did you make *teshuva*?" my brother Motty asked him, and I had to hold myself back from giving him a congratulatory pat on the back for encouraging Ido to get on with his story already.

*"It's hard to explain exactly when it happened. As part of the curriculum for my law degree, we had to learn some Gemara, but the lecturer taught it in a very dry, narrow way. I'm not saying it's his fault; he was doing his job to the best of his abilities. But I was really lucky that there happened to be a chareidi guy in my Gemara class, and one day when I was sitting after class trying to understand the Gemara we'd just learnt, he came and sat next to me and started explaining it. He had a lot of additional knowledge about this particular tractate of Gemara, and could even explain what a few of the additional commentators were saying about it. The precise reasoning that we uncovered, much deeper than the dry way the lecturer had taught it, blew me away. I asked the chareidi guy if we could start learning the material together for the duration of the Gemara class.*

*I realized right away that my new friend was quite intelligent and also had a great sense of humour. He also did not conform to my previous notions of chareidim in any way. So that's how I found myself sitting with my chareidi learning partner twice a week, learning Gemara for an hour and a half - and I was really enjoying myself! I derived great satisfaction from my Gemara studies, more than I was getting out of studying law. I pushed my new friend to learn even more with me, and we ended up studying Gemara with the commentaries every day from 8:30 to 10:00am.*

*After a while, my friend asked me if I wanted to come and spend Shabbat with him at his parents' home. It wasn't because he wanted me to 'experience Shabbat' (at least, not at that point) - but more because we had a big Gemara exam on Sunday, and he wanted us to spend the whole of Shabbat together so we could study for it. He obviously couldn't come to me for Shabbat, nor did he want me to drive to his house in the middle of Bnei Brak on Shabbat. Thus, we came up with the idea that I stay with him at his home instead.*

*I was initially quite scared by the whole idea, but my drive to learn the material for the exam prevailed, and I agreed to come to him. I know that it's going to sound a bit hackneyed and stereotypical, but this is what happened as I arrived to his house:*

*His home was nothing like the big luxurious Rishon LeTzion villa I'd grown up in as a child. It was a four-room apartment, and seven kids were there to welcome me into their home. I felt a bit ill at ease, and I could see that they felt even more awkward then I did, although my friend had already told me to show up wearing a kippa. They showed me to a nicely prepared room, and it was only later that I realized that four of the kids were squashed together sleeping in the salon, so that I could have the luxury of my own private room.*

*As Shabbat came in, I went with my friend and his father and brothers to shul. That's not to say that I actually prayed, because even though each brother came up to me in turn to show me where we were in the siddur, I was still hopelessly lost. I was finding it really hard to concentrate, partially because I'd never been part of the prayer service in a synagogue before and partially because it felt like everyone was staring at me, trying to figure out how I was connected to the frum family they'd known for years.*

*In any case, when they came to singing 'Lecha Dodi', I recognized the tune and joined in with them. To my great surprise, with each additional verse, I started to feel more and more emotional. I didn't actually start sobbing, but I certainly felt a very pleasant, unfamiliar feeling. After the prayers concluded and the congregants wished each other 'Shabbat Shalom', I found myself shaking hands with dozens of friendly strangers whom I'd never met before. The atmosphere in the synagogue was wonderful. To put it differently, I felt very safe and secure there, like I'd somehow come home.*

*We merged out onto the street which was jam packed with people who'd also just left shul, and it goes without saying that all the shops on the street were closed. I don't think I heard even a single car driving around, a sensation which was quite wonderful and refreshing as well. We got home and the family started singing 'Shalom Aleichem'. I was completely hypnotized by the Shabbat candles that were burning beautifully over in the corner of the apartment. One of the children pointed to a candle and whispered in my ear that his mother had lit that one especially for me. At that point, I started tearing up again.*

*Next, they sang 'Eshet Chayil', and after that the father made Kiddush. Presently, the meal was served, and I ate with such gusto as if I'd never seen food before in my life, but I couldn't help it. This was the most delicious food I'd ever tasted. I'd been with my parents to plenty of expensive restaurants, but nothing ever came close to tasting as good as the meal I was served that Friday night.*

*Afterwards, we sang more Shabbat songs, and then the family started sharing divrei Torah. Each child had their own thing to say at the table, one after the other. Like I said, it's pretty soppy and stereotypical, but I was incredibly moved by what I was witnessing. It wasn't completely sterile - the kids were still having their fights and squabbles like any normal siblings, but I'd never experienced anything like what was happening around that Shabbat table. At home, we usually ate our meals together, but then everyone would go back to doing their own thing. Here, the warmth and the tranquillity completely conquered my heart, and I said to myself: 'regardless of whether I make teshuva or not, I want my home to be like this.'*

*After dinner, my friend and I went to one of the local study houses, which was full of fathers and sons learning together. Some light refreshments were laid out on the tables. We began studying, although really it would be more correct to say that we launched, and flew into worlds I'd never been before. Three hours passed before I'd even realized it. Of course, we weren't just studying the class material - we'd also opened up a Chumash with commentaries discussing Korach and his followers, or as my friend put it, 'the skeptic and his own opinion.' I suddenly realized how much I myself was a skeptic; I wasn't prepared to accept anything on faith, I had to analyze it all and bring everything within the purview of my own intellect. Like Korach, I also rejected other people's opinions on the grounds that I believed that they were false and stupid. Everything came back to what 'I' thought, and only me.*

*That night, I barely slept a wink. My mind was racing furiously, and I started to wonder if it was possible that my parents were wrong about what they believed in and what they'd taught me. Was it really possible to have a 'Jewish State' without paying attention to anything really Jewish? How could it be that the glorious history of the Jewish people and all our ancient profound wisdom only be found in a few enclaves of Bnei Brak and Jerusalem? What role did my family have to play in the ongoing saga of the Jewish people? Why weren't we actively participating in it?*

*I was overwhelmed with questions, and turned to my friend to help me find some answers. We sat there with his father, who was a very big talmid chacham, and before long we were surrounded by dozens of open books. The answers to all my unanswerable questions came from the pages of these volumes, and that's how I spent the rest of that Shabbat. On one hand, it passed in such a pleasant way, full of spiritual and earthly pleasures, and on the other, I experienced such a deep spiritual pain that even now I can't really put into words.*

*I left Bnei Brak a completely different person. I went home and I told my parents everything that had happened to me – and as I expected, they poured cold water on everything I was telling them, reacting to what I'd experienced with criticism and disdain. Strangely, their response gave me the strength to dig down even further into myself to find out what was really in there, and I discovered a whole new world to explore. I found disadvantages and deficiencies that I couldn't even name; and an internal pain and lack that only prayer and Torah learning seemed to be able to satisfy.*

*To my great sadness, once I discovered that there was a Creator of the world, my connection with my parents started to really fray, even though I considered myself to be a better person than I had previously been. Not that I was a bad person before or treated my parents in a particularly terrible way, but I was an average Israeli, and like most average Israelis, my parents were there to give me money and a five-star hotel experience whenever I felt like coming home.*

*From the moment I embarked on my teshuva process, I made a particular effort to visit them more than I had previously and to show them more honor than I had before. Objectively, I think that somewhere deep down, they truly did acknowledge that my attitude towards them was much better than it had been before I'd made teshuva, but it was really hard for them to absorb everything.*

*My father was a Holocaust survivor, but the Holocaust didn't only destroy his family - it also completely destroyed his belief in G-d's goodness. The bizarre thing is that he still really believed in G-d, but was just so angry at Him. My mother came from an intellectual-elitist family, and believed that religion was nothing more than an 'opiate of the masses'. But I, her son, wasn't 'the masses' - I'd been raised in the culture of the Israeli secular elite - so she found the change in me very hard to accept. She couldn't understand what would cause me to choose a path that was more suitable to creatures from the lower classes.*

*For the next three months, I was really only in touch with my parents via telephone, and it was always me calling them. Then one morning, my father paid me a surprise visit. I was in the middle of praying, which meant that I was wrapped in my tallit and crowned with my tefillin and just about to start saying\ 'Shema'. That same morning, I'd happened to have missed my regular minyan at the yeshiva and didn't have the energy to make the trip all the way over to Bnei Brak to find another one. So I decided to pray alone. I was there, in the upper worlds, when my father knocked on the door.*

*Initially, I didn't want to interrupt my prayers, but when I saw through the spy-hole in the door who it was, I nearly exploded with happiness. I opened the door, but of course I didn't say a word, because it was forbidden to speak in the middle of Shema. I mimed to him, as warmly and honorably as I could, that he should please sit at the table. The table was still rather messy, as the night before we'd had a celebration and hadn't yet gotten around to cleaning everything up. I felt a bit bad about that, because I knew that my father was used to my mom's ultra-hygienic environment, but I still offered him a drink. I signalled to my father that I'd be with him very shortly, and I continued to pray. In my head, I was trying to remember the relevant halachot as to whether or not I was permitted to cut my prayers short for honoring parents. It felt like the whole Mishna of Brachot was running around my head. I could sense that my dad was somewhat disappointed that I hadn't immediately started talking to him, but at the same time, I also wanted to show him that nothing was more important to me than praying to the Creator of the world.*

*(Incidentally, I spoke to my rav afterwards, and he told me that halachically, it would have been better to have just finished the Shema and then talk to my dad*

*right away, because honoring parents is a mitzvah de'oraita [directly from the Torah] - particularly when there's friction between the parent and child. But he also told me that I shouldn't dwell on the fact that I didn't do that. We baal teshuvas make a lot of mistakes out of ignorance and also out of our initial enthusiasm to do everything properly, especially in the first couple of months. We get so lit up and inspired at the beginning, for 'free', and then G-d takes the inspiration away from us, little by little, because He wants us to earn it back through our own efforts.)*

*My dad couldn't hide his impatience. He got up from where he was sitting and started riffling through the holy books and looking through some pages without really reading anything. I ignored this and smiled at him, then walked over to him and signalled that he should try and read a bit of the Mesillat Yesharim that he had in his hand. My dad threw the book down on the table with obvious contempt, but he nearly missed, and I held my breath waiting to see if the book was going to fall on the floor. I quickly managed to grab it just as it was about to slide off, and then gave it a kiss and placed it back on the table. It was really fortunate that I used to be the goalie for Maccabi Rishon LeTzion...*

*'Is this stupid ceremony ever going to end?' my dad asked me, and I could see that he was becoming impatient. I flashed some more hand signals telling him that I'd be with him very shortly. At that moment, someone opened the door to our apartment. It was Kobi, short for 'Yaacov', a short but confident young man at my yeshiva, with penetrating, lively eyes that darted about all over the place. He hadn't noticed that my father was there, and in a voice loud enough to raise the dead, he bellowed, 'My brother, I get a mazal tov!'*

*I came over to him, and pantomimed, 'Why?'*

*'I just got engaged!' he yelled, and then let out a joyous cry that must have sounded extremely abrasive to my father, whose sensitive ears were accustomed only to listening to classical music. What's more, we always spoke very quietly at home, barely more than a whisper, because my parents thought that was a dignified way of communicating. I saw from my father's expression that Kobi's rather coarse cry had unpleasantly jolted his 'musical ear'.*

*My father had no idea how much psychological damage I suffered from the music he used to force us to listen to. Every Friday night, it was the same story: he'd sit my sister and me down in the spacious living room of our home in Rishon, then force us to listen to classical music in hopes of influencing our musical taste for the better, so we'd develop a more 'cultured' musical ear and start to appreciate his higher quality music instead of the low-class, 'degenerate' music that we actually wanted to listen to. He would stuff it down our ears until we were dying for the musical torture to finish already.*

# The Stolen Light

*I gave Kobi a hug, and the two of us started to dance. At first, my dad looked at us as though we were developmentally disabled, but then his expression softened into simple abhorrence. Kobi was what you might call something of a shidduch expert. He'd lived in the yeshiva dorm for four years, and in that time he'd been out with literally dozens of girls. You could write a whole book about his funny experiences on the shidduch scene. So of course, I was overjoyed for him, and we started to enthusiastically sing the verse from sheva brachot, "Od yishama be'arei yehuda ibehutzot yerushalayim; kol sasson v'kol simcha." My father stood up, and Kobi tried to get him into our small dance circle. My dad didn't want to join, and was starting to get rather flustered.*

*I could see he was feeling increasingly uncomfortable, so I went over to him, hugged him, and said, 'My dear Abba, I love you so much, and I've missed you so much! It's so good to see you here!'*

*Never before in my life had I ever expressed my feelings to my father in such an open way, but that's how I felt, and I wasn't going to lie about it. My dad was obviously shocked because he's not a big hugger either, or particularly openly affectionate. I'd never once heard either of my parents tell me, 'I love you'. Maybe when I was still in my cradle they used to talk to me like that, but ever since, I'd gotten used to only hearing words of appreciation, disappointment, criticism, or commands. Saying 'I love you', or other words of love and warmth for no obvious reason was completely unheard of in my house.*

*'Instead of missing me, you could simply come back home,' said my father.*

*Kobi's a sensitive guy, and he instantly picked up on what was going on, not least because he was going through something very similar with his own parents. There's probably almost no Israeli baal teshuva these days that doesn't go through the same tikun with their parents. He came over to my father and stuck his hand out warmly, saying: 'Now that I've met the father, I can see why the son is such a high-caliber young man.'*

*My dad flashed him a super-fake grin. The last thing in the world that he ever thought he'd see was his oldest son becoming a baal teshuva. What had happened to me? What had I seen that would compel me to leave my home, my friends, my car, and my successful law studies, to hang out with this odd, short, dark-looking stranger? What had happened to me? How was it all going to end?*

*My father's inner dialogue was so clearly written all over his face that it was very easy for me to read his thoughts: how could an intelligent person do such lowly, infantile things? He used to have exactly the same expression when I was a child, and I'd bring home friends whom he thought were beneath me; kids from the other side of the city, usually Sephardim, who were outstanding students and completely devoted, loyal friends. But for my parents (and they should forgive me for saying this), these traits counted for nothing. And they didn't even feel the tiniest trace of guilt about treating 'lower-class' people like dirt, because their superior attitudes were ingrained in them, and had probably been passed down from generation to generation.*

*'You always told me that no matter what I was doing, the main thing was that I should just feel good, that I should feel happy,' I told him. 'And right now, I feel the happiest I've ever felt in my whole life.'*

*My father turned around and started heading for the door. He looked like he was terribly disappointed by what I'd just said, as though I'd made it clear that I was much happier in this dilapidated dorm than I'd ever been in the comfortable home of my parents.*

*'Are you leaving already?' I asked him, trying to salvage the situation.*

*'Your mother is waiting for me in the car.' He didn't even look at me as he spoke; he had his back turned towards me.*

*'Mom's here and she didn't come up? Call her and tell her that she should also come up and say hello.' I was certain that my father was going to tell me that there wasn't a chance in hell that my mother would want to come visit the dump I was staying in, and that he also wanted to protect her from seeing just how bad things had gotten.*

*Just then, Kobi's cell phone rang. He looked at the caller ID and told me, 'It's the Rav.' Grinning from ear to ear, he ran off to the kitchen to take the call. My father stared after him with a disgusted expression, not least because the kitchen really looked like an earthquake had hit it. The kitchen table was covered with dirty plates that still had old food stuck to them, as well as a tablecloth that used to be white in a previous reincarnation but was now a grubby grey.*

*'If your mother saw you like this - how you're living, where you're living, and with whom - if you can actually call this 'living' in any normal sense of the word - she'd die of a broken heart.' He said exactly what I thought he was going to say, almost word for word.*

*I started tidying up the apartment a bit. I took a load of books that were piled up on the table and put them back in the bookshelf that my father was standing in front of.*

*'What do you need so many books for?' he asked me.*

*'This is only a tiny fraction of all the books out there,' I told him. 'And take my word for it Abba, each book contains a world's worth of amazing ideas and*

*knowledge. The Torah's wisdom is truly 'a life-giving spring.'' I came closer to him, thinking that maybe he was giving it another chance.*

*'That all sounds wonderful, but let's keep the lecture for another time,' he cut me off mid-flow, without any patience to hear me out.*

*Kobi came back into the room grinning from ear to ear, which clearly displayed the decayed state of his teeth. 'The Rav will be here in half an hour,' he said. I knew that the whole subject of 'rabbis' was especially touchy for my dad.*

*'Abba, please stay a bit longer; I really want you to meet Rav Shlomo. I promise you, you've never met anyone as wise or sharp as him. He's a serious scholar and also very warm and friendly, and full of knowledge. He's really something very special.'*

*My father gave a tremor and seemed to be somewhat insulted, I guess because I'd never described him in such glowing terms. He turned to Kobi and casually barked at him, 'You know, it would be a really good idea for you to take care of your teeth. Do you know that they're rotting away?' Poor Kobi shrank visibly from my dad's insulting comment. I could see that my dad was feeling on the defensive and was trying to regain control of the situation by picking a fight, but that was no excuse for what he'd just said.*

*'Do you want to come down with me to say hello to Imma, and then maybe all three of us could go out to a café somewhere nearby?' he asked me.*

*I had no doubt that my father was expecting me to react to the incredibly wounding comment he'd just made to Kobi. He knew that all my life, I'd been a diehard humanist and committed to fighting against social injustice, attending every single demonstration for every single cause. Despite all this, I went over to him, gave him a lengthy bear hug, and just like in some schmaltzy, sweet Hollywood film, I whispered in his ear:*

*'Abba, do you know that I love you and Imma very, very much... more than anything else or anyone else in the world, and I will forever and ever?'*

*My father smiled at me and said: 'It's good to see that you still have a bit of your old intelligence, despite your newfound 'wisdom'. So now tell me, do you love Ima and me more than you do this so-called 'G-d' of yours?'*

*I thought to myself that it was probably better not to even try to answer him. Why should I destroy the first intimately warm moment that we'd shared after months of coldness, verbal sparring, fighting, blaming and aggression? He probably thought that with that one sentence, that one crushing blow, he'd severely damaged my religious faith, and who knows, maybe he'd even dealt it a knockout punch.*

*'Anyway, come down with me, son. Come, do it for your mother. Come with me.'*

*'Do it for your mother' - that line always got me. All my life, I'd been doing things for other people. I only studied law in the first place 'for my father'; I only behaved politely 'for my mother'; I'd only served in the army because of my conscience; I'd only done officer training because it looked good on my resume - and that was the first time I'd ever really done anything for myself. But how could I even begin to explain all this to my dad, particularly when he was so against it?*

*I'd already pretty much decided to just roll over and go with him to a café, when just then by some massive stroke of luck, Aryeh Blumenthal danced his way into the apartment holding an airplane ticket and singing "Uman, Uman, Rosh Hashana, Uman, Uman, Rosh Hashana" at the top of his lungs.*

*Aryeh didn't normally learn in our yeshiva. He was a Breslever who travelled all over the country distributing Rebbe Nachman's books and teachings, and he didn't regularly learn in any single yeshiva - wherever he happened to be giving out books, that's where he'd go and learn.*

*While on the road, he'd either just bunk down with friends or sleep in the local synagogue. Recently, he'd been sleeping in our dorm apartment and coming to a few classes at our yeshiva. Aryeh hated Tel Aviv for the simple reason that he used to be one of Tel Aviv's most popular bachelors. I understood his antipathy towards Tel Aviv; I also wasn't planning to stay there after I got married. Trying to raise kids in this city would be no easy task. But for now, my rabbi was here, so I was here with him. In the meantime, I was trying very hard to limit my excursions to yeshiva, dormitory, mikveh, and shul - and avoid going anywhere else.*

*Aryeh had come back to the apartment today to visit Shimshon, his childhood friend from Kibbutz Ayelet HaShachar, who was going to look after his passport and his plane ticket for Uman. Shimshon was a newly-minted baal teshuva who'd come to live at our dorm, and that's how Aryeh happened to be sleeping here. Aryeh was a very funny guy, who was constantly brimming over with great stories and jokes.*

*'Wow, what a miracle; really, open miracles! Uman, Uman Rosh Hashana - this is the ticket to the Garden of Eden!'*

*He noticed my father and before he even really knew what was going on, Aryeh came right over and gave him a big hug, like they were long-lost buddies. Aryeh said to him, 'Welcome, welcome! You came to the right place. You are standing on the threshold to the upper Garden of Eden...'*

*'This is the father of Ido the Tzaddik," Kobi told him, all the while trying to smile with his mouth shut, so that he wouldn't get another unprovoked attack about the state of his teeth. The great irony is that Kobi's dad is a dentist, and had been in the middle of doing some serious dental work to fix Kobi's problematic teeth when Kobi had made teshuva. His father had refused to continue with the treatment unless Kobi shaved off his newly grown beard and got rid of the big black kippa he'd started wearing.*

*'Wow, Ido's dad! Congratulations! How good is your heritage, and how wonderful is your lot! Wonder of wonders, that you have such a sweet, pleasant son! Really, Ido is as sweet as honey. You must have done something amazing to have a son like him, and Ido Natan, you must have done something amazing to have a dad like this! Your wisdom and understanding are mamash shining right out of your face!' My dad just gaped at him, shocked. He'd had one too many surprises for today.*

*'Ido Natan?'*

*My dad's face flushed red, and I worried that he was about to have a heart attack, G-d forbid. 'Where did the name 'Natan' come from, all of a sudden?'*

*He was staring at me, staring at Kobi, staring at Aryeh - and I noticed that he suddenly had tears in his eyes. Aryeh realized that his slip of the tongue might just have sparked off World War III, and clearly didn't know that I hadn't told my father anything about changing my name. He decided to try and change the subject to avert the pending disaster.*

*'Wow, what a day I've had today. Even the most exciting Hollywood thriller has got nothing on the rollercoaster ride that Rabbeinu organized for me today. Here's how the plot unfolded: It all started this morning, when I got up before dawn and prayed with the netz minyan, like I do pretty much every day. After prayers, I planned to go out and collect a bit of tzedaka money, to help me pay my way to Uman this year. There are a few carpenters in the Hatikva section of the city who help me every year, in addition to some buddies who also distribute Rabbeinu's books.*

*What usually happens is I get there, I dance with them, I tell them a few jokes, a few stories about holy people. You know, the working-class Sephardim, they are so pure and innocent - their hearts are chock-full of emuna. Even if they aren't obviously keeping Torah and mitzvot, they still have such a great love for our holy people. Anyway, at the end of our conversation, they usually give me a sum of money, and it's generally a very respectable sum, not the peanuts you get from the stingy Ashkenazim...'*

*Aryeh suddenly realized that my dad was Ashkenazi.*

*'Not that every Ashkenazi is stingy, G-d forbid, I don't want to generalize. I'm sure that Ido's dad, for example, is also going to give me at least a hundred dollars, once I've finished telling him my amazing story. Heheheh.'*

*Even Aryeh's lack of tact was endearing. But obviously not to everyone. I noticed that my dad was holding himself back from attacking him.*

*In any case, Derech Tzaddikim, the travel agency, called me this morning. I booked my ticket to Uman with them a while ago, and paid them $150 - just enough to secure the ticket. I should have paid them the rest a week ago already, and they told me that if I didn't pay them this week, they'd assign the ticket to someone else. Why? Because this year, the demand for Uman tickets is through the roof, yishtabach shemo, Am Yisrael chai v'kayam. Everyone wants to go and visit the holy Tzaddik Rebbe Nachman ben Faiga ben Simcha, the love of my life. But where am I supposed to find the other $650? It almost goes without saying that the first people I contacted were my parents, but I already knew that they weren't going to give me a penny. It's not that they don't have the money - they have bundles of cash - but they're currently of the view that I need to go and learn a profession, and stop spending my life collecting charity and distributing holy books.*

*Next, I called my uncle, my father's brother, who really loves me. He's a full-on kibbutznik; he lives, breathes and eats kibbutz life, and he's bought into the whole kibbutz philosophy 1000%. Cooperation! Self-sacrifice for a higher cause! etc, etc. Of course, it's all rubbish, because the only real kibbutz is the one happening by Rabbeinu in Uman.*

*Do you know, Abba of our sweet Ido, that they really did steal the word 'kibbutz' from Uman? One of the people who lived in Uman at the time that Rabbi Natan was organizing his gathering, or 'kibbutz', heard the word, and got very excited by it. He suggested it to some of the groups who were coming out to settle the land, they loved it, and the rest is history. All the bounty in the world comes down to us via the Tzaddik in revealed ways and hidden ways, whether we're aware of it or not.*

*Anyway, to make it quick because I'm really rushing, I called everyone I knew - friends, uncles, cousins, everyone - and having done that, I had a few shaky promises that didn't amount to more than $120. My last conversation with the travel agents gave me the impression that time was running out to pay for the* *ticket, and I was starting to feel a bit worried. Where was the help going to come from? How was I going to pay for the rest of the ticket?*

*On the way back to the apartment, I started thinking that I really needed to do more hitbodedut about my trip to Uman. Every single big Breslev rabbi tells us the same thing - without prayer, there simply isn't a trip to Uman. And Rabbeinu also tells us that if someone gets something without praying for it, he's in big trouble. It's like stealing from G-d. Even for small things like a cup of water or a slice of bread, we have to include G-d in everything.*

*Once, one of Rabbeinu's daughters was complaining to him about her housemaid, and all the problems the woman was making for her. Rabbeinu asked his daughter: 'Did you pray to have good servants when you were under your chuppah?' Rabbi Natan learnt from this just how important it is for us to talk to Hashem about every little thing. Of course, I'd already done a lot of hitbodedut about getting to Uman, but Rabbi Natan teaches us that if you're lacking something in your life, you should know it's either because you didn't pray for it, or you didn't pray for it enough. So I thought to myself that it seems like I hadn't prayed enough yet. I started to sing Psalm 121, 'Shir la'maalot; where is my help going to come from?' In my heart of hearts, I just knew I had to make it to Uman this year, come what may.*

*Anyway, to make a long story short because I'm really in a hurry, I got to your apartment, and everyone was still asleep. OK, it was 7am, so that's pretty normal, but Rabbeinu advises us that we should try to pray as early in the day as we can. No one knows if they're even going to live another day, so we should at least try to grab another opportunity to pray while we still can.*

*I grabbed one of the bikes - sorry, Kobi, I called you first to ask your permission, but your phone was switched off - anyway, I took one which wasn't locked (and incidentally, leaving a bike unlocked like that is a big sin, firstly because it's placing a stumbling block in front of the blind, and secondly because it's such a waste of money if someone steals it) - and I rode out to the Yarkon River.*

*For an hour and a half, I'm talking to G-d, I'm singing to G-d, I'm praising Him, I'm crying to Him, I'm pleading with Him, I'm trying to explain to Him every possible reason why I need to get to Uman this year, to the Tzaddik. I tell G-d I'm sick and that I desperately need my soul to be healed, and who better to do the job than our generation's premier Doctor of the Soul? I came up with so many rationales, so many convincing arguments, so many persuasive reasons. For an hour and a half, I only talked about Uman, and I didn't stop even for one second. I was talking a thousand words a minute.*

*At a certain point, I started to feel like I'd run out of energy and that I needed to take a breather. I lay on my back looking at the sky, and had the distinct impression that the clouds were smiling at me. Ido's father, you shouldn't think that I'm a lunatic or anything. My mom is a painter and a sculpturer, and she always used to tell us when we were kids that we should look at the clouds and see how they were smiling at us. And she wasn't religious at all. Quite the opposite.*

*I got my energy back, and I really felt like my prayers had made an impact in heaven. Sometimes, you pray and you just know that this particular prayer is going to be answered, but you can't explain why. Maybe it happens with the prayers that dafka come from such a weak place, that place of knowing that really, there is only G-d. The way things currently stood, I didn't have the money I needed, and I also didn't even have an idea of how I was going to get it.*

*I came back to the tree where I'd parked the bike and yishtabach shemo la'ad - it was gone! 'It's an atonement for my sins,' I told myself.*

*'They stole my bike?!' Kobi interrupted.*

*'It's an atonement for our sins, have a bit of patience. I don't know where I got the strength, but I started thanking G-d that they stole the bike.'*

*"You thanked G-d that they stole my bike?!' Kobi was making a super-human effort to keep his teeth covered.*

*'Yes!' Aryeh laughed, and continued. 'Everything that G-d gives us is for the good. Even this was for the best. After all, we're meant to happily bless Hashem for the bad, in exactly the same way we do for the good. And truthfully, I really did feel like it was a good thing. I did a little dance around the tree where I'd parked the bike, and then started enthusiastically walking back to the main road, where I'd hopefully be able to hitchhike back to the yeshiva and tell you the news about your bike in the hope that you'd also start thanking G-d about it.*

*Of course in my head, in addition to thinking about the money I needed for Uman, I was also now thinking about the money I needed to get a new bike for Kobi the Tzaddik. Don't get mad at me Kobi - in just a little while, you're going to be the proud owner of a new bike that's even better than the one that got stolen.*

*To make a long story short, I stood out in the burning hot sun for half an hour until the sweat was literally dripping off me. There was no shade anywhere, and I thought maybe I should just start walking back to the apartment even though it was miles away, because who was going to stop for me anyway, the way I looked? All the time, I'm still talking to Hashem: 'G-d, please help me out here, please do a kindness for me, and help me to get back to the yeshiva. I just want to learn some Torah and to sort out a new bike for Kobi. Please, G-d, I know I*

111

*don't deserve a thing, but I'm asking You to help me just because You are kind to all your creations.'*

*Maybe a second later, this car suddenly pulls up next to me, a luxury Peugeot 202 model. An older man who looks like he's a 'Big Boss' type, or at the very least, the Big Boss's right hand man gets out, and I realize that his back wheel's blown out. The man, who's clearly quite stressed, asks me:*

*'Is there a puncture repair place anywhere nearby here?' He then pulls out a pack of Parliament cigarettes and lights up.*

*'There isn't one here, but on the other side of this road, there's a place about a kilometer back.' As I'm talking, I wondered if I could ask him to give me a cigarette, even though I had decided to soon quit because Rabbeinu advises us not to smoke, as we already have enough lusts and vices and don't need to add more to the pile.*

*'You still need to change the tire now anyway, because you can't drive anywhere on that. If you want, I'm happy to help you do it.'*

*'Really? You'll really help me?' The Big Boss (or deputy Big Boss) sounded surprised, as he sucked in half his cigarette with one breath. Suddenly, I didn't feel like bumming a cigarette off him any more.*

*'Of course I want to help you! What sort of question is that? It's like they say, olam chesed yibaneh.' He was still looking at me kind of suspiciously, so I asked him to show me where the spare tire and jack were, and I got right to work. I asked him to give me the reflective visibility jacket that by law you're supposed to wear when your car breaks down in the middle of the road. 'Halachically, we have to respect the laws of the State,' I told him. I could see that by now, he was really confused.*

*I also asked him to put the reflective break-down triangle behind the car, and within five minutes I was done. As I changed the wheel, Big Boss explained that he on the way to a very important meeting, and that I really saved him just now. If he'd have had to turn around and drive a kilometer back to the garage in order to get the tire fixed, it would have taken him at least half an hour, which meant that he'd have arrived very late to the meeting.*

*We got into the car and I asked him to drop me somewhere on his way, but he wanted to take me to wherever I needed to go. I told him that the direction he was going in was already getting me very close to where I needed to get to. Then, he asked me if he could give me one or two hundred shekels to cover the tire change. I told him that I categorically refused to take any money for helping him out. I'd done it for the privilege of doing a mitzvah, and I wasn't about to sell the mitzvah that Hashem had sent me just to get a bit of cash.*

*He was surprised by my response, and asked me more about myself. During the couple of minutes that we were driving, I told him why I'd been standing there in the first place. I told him about hitbodedut, about the bike, about going to Uman. In another amazing 'coincidence', he told me that his father had come to Israel from a town that was very close to Uman. He told me the name of the place, but I forget what he said, it was some weird Russian-sounding name...*

*Anyway, a second before I got out of the car, I could see that he'd become serious and thoughtful. 'I want to make you happy, the way you've made me happy today,' he said. I told him that even just meeting him was enough to make me happy, but he leaned over to his glove compartment, took out an envelope, and put it in my hand. I didn't even have time to properly respond, because the next minute, he'd stepped on the gas and was off.*

*So I'm standing there holding the envelope deliberating whether to open it or not. In my head, I have some high hopes about what's inside, but I'm scared to open it in case I get really disappointed - the bigger the expectations, the harder you can be disappointed. I ended up opening the envelope, and start counting bill after bill: altogether, $900 in cash! I yelled with each bill: 'Thank You, G-d, thank You, Creator of the World! I love You!' Quite a few people on the sidewalk were watching me suspiciously - you don't usually get people screaming like that for nothing.*

*'$900?? You must be kidding me! Kobi burst out.*

*'No kidding!' Aryeh responded, smiling. 'I'm running so late today because I flew straight over to the branch of Derech Tzaddikim in Bnei Brak, slapped down $650 in cash on their desk, and here I am holding my ticket for Rosh Hashana in Uman!' Aryeh jumped up and started dancing a stormy dance, which swept me and Kobi up into its midst with him.*

*My father, the outsider, started muttering to himself: 'Uman? My Grandpa Natan was from Uman...'*

*Everything suddenly came to an abrupt stop, and there was complete silence in the apartment. Really, you couldn't hear a car beep, or a phone ring, or any voices from the street outside. I mamash felt like I was standing at Har Sinai.*

*'Who's 'Grandpa Natan from Uman'? Was that your grandfather?' I was flabbergasted.*

# The Stolen Light

*'Yes... My grandfather was called Natan, and he came from the town of Uman in Ukraine.'*

*My dad was looking a bit shivery, and I thought to myself that maybe he'd had more than enough excitement for one day. My dad has heart disease, and I became concerned that it had all been too much for him. I brought him a glass of water, then asked him as casually as I could:*

*'Grandpa Natan must have been one of the mitnagdim, right? The people who were anti-chassidut?'*

*'Not at all! He was a committed Breslever chassid.'*

*'Wow! How come you never told me that you had a Grandpa Natan who was a Breslever chassid?'*

*Aryeh practically jumped on me, and gave me a big hug. 'Now that we've discovered the truth about your Grandpa Natan, you have to come with me to Uman, Ido Natan, and no excuse can get you out of it. If you're not going to make the trip for Rabbeinu, you still have to go for your dad's grandfather.'*

*I wasn't really taking in what Aryeh was saying, and my father also still looked very pensive.*

*'There's a war going on there right now. What are you talking about, that Ido should go to Ukraine?' He said, in a weak voice.*

*'More than 30,000 people already go there from Israel every year, and a few thousand more join them from all over the world. People have been going there for years, and no one ever got even so much as a scratch,' Aryeh replied decisively, then turned to Kobi:*

*'Kobi, go and look at the bike I bought you. I hope you won't be disappointed...'*

*'You bought me a bike??' Kobi ran outside to look.*

*'I bought the bike for $200, which left me $50 to play around with. So, father of Ido Natan, what did you think about the story G-d arranged for me today?'*

*Kobi came back in, panting. 'I don't believe it! I'm telling you, it's completely crazy!' He was smiling from ear to ear, and really couldn't give a hoot about what anyone was going to tell him about his teeth.*

*'What? What's the problem? Don't you like the bike? It's no problem, we can take it back to the shop, and you can pick out the one that you like. When I was*

*buying it, I told the salesperson that I was buying it for someone else, and they agreed that you could bring it back and exchange it, if you didn't like it. I just didn't want to leave you stranded without a bike.'*

*'What are you talking about? I LOVE that bike! You have no idea about how much Divine Providence is going on here, you just won't believe it. For the last six months, every time I took the old bike that got stolen in for a repair, I used to look at that bike in the store. I would tell myself that, bli neder, one day, I was going to buy that bike, but so far I just haven't been able to do it. Every time I managed to save up a bit of money, I ended up spending it on something else that I needed. And now, you just bought me that bike! There's one chance in a million that you'd pick the exact bicycle I've been eyeing for half a year. Aryeh, you're unbelievable. You're really larger than life.'*

*Aryeh and Kobi gave each other a big hug. 'I'm larger than life? I don't think so; life is, for sure, so much larger than me. The person who sent you the bike was Hashem Yitbarach, and His messengers were the thief that stole your old one, and afterwards the Big Boss or his deputy, and when all's said and done, I was just the middleman between them all.'*

*Kobi went thoughtful for a minute, then said decisively:*

*'There's a halachik problem of taking interest here.'*

*'What? What interest?' Aryeh responded.*

*'How much did the new bike cost you?' Kobi wanted to know. He was now sitting at the table, wearing his best rabbinic expression.*

*'800 shekels,' responded Aryeh, and came to sit down next to him. All of us could feel the tension in the air.*

*'My bike wasn't worth anything more than 200 shekels,' said Kobi.*

*Aryeh touched him gently on the forehead: 'I forgive you, my brother, I happily forgive you the difference.'*

*My dad wasn't used to seeing things like this, and I could see that it was only with great difficulty that he managed to choke down another sarcastic comment.*

*Kobi wasn't mollified. 'I owe you 600 shekels, because otherwise I'm liable for the sin of being paid interest, and that's not a joke. That's a sin derived straight from the Torah.'*

## The Stolen Light

*'But I forgive the debt, and I'm giving you the bike as a present anyway!' Aryeh remonstrated.*

*'We need to ask the Rav,' said Kobi. 'Chas v'shalom, charging interest is worse than stealing. I'm going to call him now, and whatever he decides, I accept. Will you accept his ruling, Aryeh?'*

*'I'll accept it and a half; whatever the Rav says, that's the law. Now, I need to go and dip in the mikveh. Wow, what happened to me today requires another dunk, purely for the sake of Hashem. When I get back, I'd love a snack, because I haven't eaten anything since dinner last night, and my stomach is growling at me. Kobi, my friend, can I borrow your bike to get to the mikveh?'*

*Kobi happily gave permission. 'Until the Rav rules that it really does belong to me, it's your bike anyway.' Aryeh ran out of the door, and only narrowly avoided colliding with Nadav, who was standing behind it.*

*Nadav was a friend of Sharon, who lived in the apartment next to ours. Sharon was a young, but very promising, musician. Nadav was standing with his face shoved right up to the door, desperately yelling: 'Sharon! Open the door! Sharon! Sharon!' His face was right against the door hinge. He fumbled for his cell phone, clearly very stressed, and dialled Sharon's number. We could hear the phone ringing in Sharon's apartment, until someone apparently pulled the plug out of the wall. Next, Nadav dialled Sharon's cell phone, and after a long time, Sharon finally answered it: 'I'm sleeping. I'll get back to you in two or three hours. I only got to bed a couple of hours ago.'*

*'I'm standing outside your door! You have to let me in urgently, right now!'*

*But Sharon had already hung up, and apparently gone straight back to sleep. Nadav didn't have any other choice - he came and knocked at our door, the door of the yeshiva dorm.*

*'Who's there?' asked Kobi.*

*'It's a neighbor. Please open up. It's an emergency.'*

*Kobi opened the door, and Nadav burst through it: 'Sorry, I really need to use your toilet urgently.'*

*Meanwhile, I was still trying to process the shocking piece of information that my great-grandfather was a Breslever chassid. I went over to my dad and hugged him.*

*'Abba, did you really just say that your grandfather was a Breslever chassid?"*

*'Yes. I have a couple of his letters that he wrote to his brothers.'*

*'I have to read them, Abba. I just have to... And I also can't believe that he was called 'Natan'. It's really spooky, all the coincidences that have being going on today, don't you think so? For two months, I was trying to decide what additional name to take. Initially, I really wanted to go for 'Moshe' or 'Avraham', but my rav, Rav Shlomo, I promise you, Dad, I think he has ruach hakodesh or something. He advised me to take the name 'Natan', and I didn't argue with him. I simply agreed to take the name, and from the moment I started using it, I felt like I'd somehow been reborn a completely different person. Now, I understand what must have happened: it seems that the soul of your grandfather must have somehow got reincarnated in me.'*

*My father looked at me in shock: 'Reincarnated?!'*

*To my great fortune, just at that moment, Nadav came out of the bathroom and saved the day. I felt that maybe some of the things I'd just said to my dad had been a bit too extreme, or 'out there', and I was worried that he might react by getting antagonistic again. I was sorry that I'd said so much. Nadav came out of the bathroom, obviously feeling a bit embarrassed, and started to apologize profusely: 'I didn't have any choice, sorry. My friend was sleeping, and didn't open the door. So I'm really sorry to disturb you all, and thanks so much for helping me out.'*

*Kobi went over to him, and grabbed his shoulder. 'If you came here, it seems that you have something you need to fix, or do tikun on, here. You didn't just land up here by chance, everything is being guided by very precise Divine Providence.'*

*Nadav continued walking and apologizing all the way to the door, but in the meantime, we all noticed that he smelled funny, and that in particular, he smelled very strongly of air freshener.*

*Nadav realized that we were all wrinkling our noses, and visibly became even more awkward. He explained that he'd wanted to spray air freshener, but that he'd somehow managed to spray it all over his shirt instead. Initially, he'd become really angry at the people who made the toilet spray - 'why couldn't they do the holes clearer, so when someone needed to use the spray they could see exactly which way it was pointing?!' He was already composing the letter of complaint in his head when he suddenly realized he could take his idea to another company, patent it, and make a couple of million.*

*It's not like it couldn't happen - he'd heard a story where some guy had gone to a drinks manufacturer and sold them the idea of making the holes in their cans bigger so that they'd be easier to drink from.. The company had followed his advice, and their sales had really taken off. The guy had received a nice percentage of the additional profits as a result. After that, he'd taken the same idea to the people who made toothpaste, and he'd come away from them with another fat stack of cash...*

*On an 'off' day, Nadav still came up with at least one invention every 24 hours; when he was on point, he could easily invent six or seven things. He'd already opened up dozens of businesses - in his head - and earned millions of dollars. In his head, he was a bona fide billionaire. Not one of his ideas had actually ever made it out into the real world, but the potential was definitely there.*

*Nadav didn't stop talking. He was telling us about a bunch of his latest projects of the mind, and the truth is that some of them actually sounded pretty interesting. In the meantime, Aryeh came back from the mikveh and let himself back into the apartment.*

*'Aryeh? I don't believe it! Is that really you? What are you doing here??'*

*Aryeh and Nadav gave each other a big hug. I was still in shock about my great-grandfather who'd turned out to be a Breslever chassid. My dad was over in a corner muttering to himself about Uman, Grandpa Natan, and taking interest. Kobi was busy handing out cups of tea and coffee and passing around cookies for breakfast. He also offered people a shot of something a bit stronger, should they be in the mood.*

*'Don't forget with all this Uman / Grandpa Natan stuff that I got engaged today!' he said. We sat there for a whole hour, Aryeh, Kobi, Nadav, me, and my father - who'd called my mother and told her to go on to the mall without him for now, and do whatever she needed to do there. He'd meet up with her later. I felt so incredibly happy that my dad had decided to spend a bit more time with us. I thought that maybe all the truth and miracles in the room were starting to affect him in a good way.*

*In the meantime, we found out that Aryeh and Nadav had grown up together in the same part of Haifa - Neve Sha'anan. Aryeh's dad owned a very successful butchery which specialized in selling non-kosher meat, while Nadav's parents were both gifted classical musicians. They'd grown up together, gone to the same high school, and even formed a band, with Nadav on guitar and Aryeh on keyboards. They'd lost touch with each other three years ago when Aryeh had left for an extended trip to India and Nadav had gone off to study wind-power at university - not because he really wanted to, but because that had been his parents' condition for continuing to support him financially.*

*'You know what Areleh, you are the last person from our chevra that I would've ever dreamed of making teshuva. How an earth did you come to do something like that, something so unexpected, Areleh?'*

*'Believe me, I didn't do anything,' replied Aryeh. 'G-d is the one who helped me make teshuva. As you know, I went off on my trip to India, and then I went on to Thailand, and I hung out there for a couple of months just like all the rest of the Israelis. There were all sorts of parties with lots of drugs, and all the other garbage that goes on there. When you're in the middle of it all, you don't really have the time to think about what you're doing or why you're doing it. Even though there's a lot spirituality there, and a lot of people do start thinking more about their souls there, I wasn't one of them. The meaning of life just didn't really figure into my equation.*

*I was not a soul-seeker; in fact initially, I was the opposite - I wanted to get away from all the rules and all the authority - to just be free. You know, father of Ido Natan, I grew up in a family of intellectuals, where everyone was very highly educated. Even though my father owned a butcher shop, he was still an intellectual, and my mother was an author and poet. She never actually got anything published, but still regarded herself as something of a 'Nachmana Bialika'. When kids grow up in a home like that, they usually come out feeling pretty frustrated, because they're living life for their parents and not really for themselves.*

*For the first couple of months in India, when I saw the sea, and the huge open spaces, and the desert-like landscape on one side and the jungle on the other, and all the simple, poor people there, I felt like I was going to stay there for the rest of my life. But after I'd been there for around six months, I started getting bored and restless with my routine. Every morning I'd swim in the sea, and every night I'd go to a party. I'd spend most of my time sitting with a few of the chevra, playing some music and just sitting there quietly - but how much time can a person really spend with their head completely empty and their heart sealed up, looking at the most breath-taking scenery?*

*So I started to do a bit of the 'searching for meaning' thing, and looked into a bit of the 'spirituality' there, as people like to say. I attended a couple of workshops run by Thai spiritual types, and one of the gurus recommended that I spend some time in a particular monastery, where he said everyone came out feeling stronger and wiser and more relaxed. What can I tell you, Nadavi? I signed up to stay at the monastery for a while, and for the next two months all I did was stare silently at a wall. I barely ate, I barely spoke to anyone, and I thought I was seriously going to go crazy. Walking into the monastery had been a breeze; walking out was something else entirely.*

# The Stolen Light

*I won't bore you with all the details, but let's just say I had a massive stroke of luck when one of my army buddies, Shmuelik, showed up completely by coincidence. I say 'by coincidence', but today I know it was G-d's Divine Providence at work. Shmuelik was also keen to check out the monastery and spend some time there. That day, I happened to have felt pretty unwell, so I was in the monastery head's office, and that's where I met Shmuelik. I told him to forget about signing up for a stint in this prison, and that he had to help me to get out of here, the sooner the better.*

*That same evening, Shmuelik showed up at the monastery with another two guys, former paratroopers from the army, who pulled some crazy stunt to somehow get me out of there. The day I escaped from there, I went straight back to Goa to try to relax a bit from all the torturous 'relaxation' I'd received at the hands of the silent monks.*

*That night, I was walking on the beachfront when I suddenly had this overpoweringly strong feeling that this place was hell. At that point in my life, I still had no connection whatsoever to religion; I hated anything to do with it, especially after my traumatic experience at the horrible monastery. So I had no idea why that idea suddenly popped into my head, but I suddenly looked around and could see that everything was only about lust, drugs and money. The whole place only existed to fulfill people's most base desires, and money was the only thing that really mattered there. Goa completely disgusted me, to the point that I felt like I was going to throw up. I decided that I had to get back to Israel.*

*I had a friend there, Nir, a great guy from Tel Aviv, with whom I'd been hanging out for most of the last six months. I told him I was leaving, and I knew he was sad to see me go, but he was still enamoured with life there in Goa. He'd met some Dutch non-Jewish girl, and was planning to marry her and stay there a while longer.*

*In the meantime, I was still feeling seriously panicked and had no idea why, but I decided I had to get out of there that night. I had no idea where I was going to end up, but one thing was clear to me: I had to get out of there ASAP. I got all my stuff together in a big rush, and got onto the next bus headed out. An hour and a half after I left, the tsunami hit. The bus driver heard the news and immediately turned the bus around, because his entire family was still there.*

*We rushed back to Goa, and I just don't have the words to describe the scene of devastation and destruction that greeted us. Even today, whenever I remember what I saw, I just start crying. Whatever you saw in the media was a joke compared to the death and destruction that really took place there. I was shocked to the core of my being. I started looking for Nir, but to my great sorrow I found out that he'd been killed in the disaster, together with his Dutch girlfriend.*

*Two days later, I touched down in Eretz Yisrael.*

*The first month, I didn't leave my parents' house. I was completely shattered by Nir's death and the pointlessness of my own life. I had no idea where I was going or what I should do with myself. I didn't even feel like playing my keyboard. Friends came to visit, but they didn't know how to deal with me or what to say. I argued with all of them, especially about how meaningless our lives were. They tried to tell me that the only point of being alive was simply to be alive: 'eat, drink and be merry, for tomorrow we may die.'*

*I felt like no one understood me. Even my parents had no idea what had happened to me, although at that point they were happy to do anything to help. They offered to rent me my own place, to pay for me to go back to school, to buy me a new computer, to pay for some new musical instruments... But none of it interested me. The despair I felt was corroding my heart. I was crying out for help, but I had no idea where it was going to come from. My parents sent me to a shrink, but after our first two meetings, he decided he couldn't help me. I'd driven him crazy with all my questions about the meaning of life that he simply couldn't answer. The only way I could get to sleep at night was if I took sleeping pills, so I made sure to always have a full bottle.*

*To make a long story short because I'm in a rush, one day I woke up with this crazy idea in my head that there was no point being alive any more, G-d have mercy on me. I'd lost interest in everything, and I didn't want to continue living. I wrote a letter to my parents explaining why I couldn't continue on like this, and that they shouldn't wait up for me because I wouldn't be coming back. Then I set out for the sea.*

*I was sitting on the sand looking at the waves, when suddenly - and I have really no idea where he came from - this frummie appeared out of nowhere. It was like a scene in a movie or something. He was a plump man with crazy side curls down to his shoulders, and as he gives me a leaflet, he tells me: 'Rebbe Nachman says there is no such thing as despair.'*

*I looked down at the leaflet he'd given me, and looked back up - and he was gone. Initially, I just wanted to rip the leaflet up, but instead I put it on the sand next to me. A little while later, I glanced over at it and noticed that the title was, "Why are you full of despair?" I felt like I was dreaming. What was going on here? How had that guy guessed what I was planning to do? Did I have some sign written on my forehead?*

*I opened it up and started reading, and couldn't believe my eyes. It's like someone had written me a personal letter and then gone to all the trouble of printing it out as a leaflet. It was talking about things I'd never heard of before, like Divine Providence, that there was a Creator of the world, and a purpose to every creation. I felt so full of joy when I finished, there are no words to explain how I felt.*

*I got out of there, and flew back to my house as fast as I could, so that I could rip up my suicide note before my parents read it. I got to my house and my parents were sitting there in the salon with the suicide note in their hands. They were crying hysterically. My mother was on the phone to the police when suddenly she caught sight of me. They dropped everything and ran over to me, and started hugging and kissing me, their only child.*

*To cut a long story short because I'm really in a hurry now, from that moment on my life completely changed. I went to visit the address that was written on the back of the leaflet, and hooked up with a whole new chevra. Before long, I started distributing the leaflets myself. At the beginning, my parents didn't know how to react to the big changes that I made in my life, but soon enough they saw it was actually a very positive thing.*

*You won't believe this, but my father decided to close down his traif butchery and renovate it. Today, it's the most successful kosher l'mehadrin meat place in the whole of Haifa. But that's not all - after a while, my dad became the gabbai of his local synagogue! My mother became a charity activist, and now helps a whole bunch of organizations including Lev L'Achim and a few other charities that do things for sick people in hospitals. They're really pleased to have her on board, and she's finally putting her writing talents to good use.*

*So what I can tell you is that my parents went from being very demanding people who were obsessed with money, politics, and pointless intellectualism, to becoming very spiritual people. Today when I go home, I sit with my father and study Gemara, or some Mishnayot, or a bit of Likutey Moharan. Last year, my dad even came with me to Uman, which was really something else. My parents are so happy today. And when I get married, that'll be the cherry on the cake for them.'*

*My father listened to Aryeh's story intently, and I could see that something had really changed in him. Just as Aryeh finished, my mom called to tell him that she'd done everything she needed to get done, and was going to be outside any second. My dad asked me to come with him, and I readily agreed. On the way out, he asked me if I really was thinking about going to Uman. I told him that I wasn't a Breslever chassid, and that the thought hadn't really crossed my mind before - but the whole story with Grandpa Natan was really making me think.*

*I asked him if he could lend me some money to buy a pair of tefillin, because at that moment, I was using a pair of tefillin that was borrowed from a gemach. I was sure he'd make some excuse and refuse, so I was overjoyed when he took his checkbook out of his bag and asked me how much I needed. I told him I needed 1500 shekels, and promised that as soon as my savings plan came through in another two months, I'd pay him back. Who knows, but I think that Aryeh's story must have really penetrated his heart, because he wrote me out a check for 6,000 shekels - and asked me to promise that I wouldn't breathe a word about it to Imma.*

*Just as I put the check in my pocket, my mom drove up. I ran over to her and gave her a big hug, and then we drove off to a 'neutral' café. We sat there and talked for more than two hours, and I could see that their whole attitude towards me had really softened. They opened their hearts to me, I opened my heart to them, and that's really that. I bought myself a plane ticket, and here I am."*

"Did you manage to find the grave of your Grandpa Natan yet?" my brother Motty wanted to know.

"Yes," said Ido Natan, "I found it, and cleaned the headstone, which was in a really neglected, awful state. I called my father to tell him, and he was so emotional he started sobbing. He asked me to take a picture of the grave. I also found out a few more details about Grandpa Natan. It seems as though he was one of the students of Shimshon Barski, one of Breslev's 'big guns' in Uman."

Nachman corrected him, "Shimshon Barski was one of *Rabbeinu's* grandsons, and truthfully, he left a very powerful mark on Breslev *chassidut*. He was a real servant of *Hashem*, in a way that you just don't see these days."

These people certainly know how to tell a tale. If you didn't know better, you might think there was some sort of competition going on, to tell the most interesting story. From the moment I got to the airport, I was surrounded by hundreds, maybe even thousands of people telling each other stories called 'Divine Providence'. Me? I call them fairy stories, fantasy stories. It just can't be that everything they're telling me actually happened in real life. And everyone here seems to have a story! Apparently no one got here in a nice, normal way.

Even before the holiday started, I managed to grab a few minutes of conversation with a few of the other people I'm with, even though everyone here is always on the run, trying to spend every spare moment they have at the *Tzion*. Me, on the other hand, I haven't set foot there. Not even once. Not even for a minute.

But there was another 'exception to the rule' in the apartment, someone who was very similar to me in a lot of ways: Nadav. Aryeh managed to convince him to join Ido and come with them to Uman. The truth is that Nadav, like me, was not really cut out for the whole 'Uman Rosh Hashana' thing. But then, just when Aryeh was trying to convince him to come, his life in Israel suddenly got a bit complicated, and he realized he didn't want to spend the New Year with his parents. Aryeh promised him that he'd raise all the money to pay for the flight and accommodations, and bingo! Nadav decided to come along, just for the experience.

On the first night, after we'd settled in to the apartment and the rest of the *chevra* had run off to go and visit the *Tzion*, Nadav and I found ourselves there alone, and we talked a while about music, soccer, and a few of our favorite TV shows. I played him one of my recently composed songs, he joined in with his own musical refrain, and we realized we had some great musical chemistry. We talked about maybe starting a band together when we got back to Israel.

Discovering Nadav was better than winning the lottery, because the rest of the *chevra* were usually just busy reading books by Rabbeinu HaKadosh, and after every couple of lines you'd hear a 'pssssshhh!' about how great it all was. So I was gratified that there was at least one other normal person here, and if the holiday atmosphere got too much for me, maybe he'd sneak out with me to a local pub or something. The point was, I wasn't alone. And I was certain of that right up until the eve of the *Chag*, when something happened to Nadav which resulted in him too being stolen away from me.

Chapter 8

## Chapter 8

*Let me tell you about Nadav, who got stolen away during Tikun Haklali on the eve of the holiday.*

Aryeh, he should live and be well, had the sort of convincing gift of gab that you'd usually only find in the most talented insurance-type salesmen. He'd managed to convince Nadav to come with him to the communal recitation of the *Tikun Haklali* that was organized every year for exactly 12 noon, on the eve of Rosh Hashana. At that time, everyone crowded in together around the *Tzion*, and yelled out the *Tikun Haklali* together.

As part of his salesman's patter, he'd told Nadav and me that *Rabbeinu* had taken two kosher witnesses – close students of his and big holy *tzaddikim* in their own right - named Rabbi Aaron and Rabbi Naftali, and sworn a tremendous oath in front of them and on the Torah. He swore that a person could fall in whichever way they fell, but if they came to his grave and said the *Tikun Haklali* and then gave a penny to charity, then Rebbe Nachman would do everything in his power to pull them out of the depths of *Gehinnom.*

I have to tell you, I didn't understand a word of what he was talking about. After all, Rebbe Nachman died more than 200 years ago. How was the dude supposed to help *me*? Of course, these guys have an answer to every question, and apparently *tzaddikim* are more active after their deaths than when they're actually alive... I try to avoid getting into discussions about all their theories, but I obviously didn't buy anything Aryeh was trying to tell me.

That's not to say I mocked him or made fun of him, *chas v'shalom*, because he really was a wonderful clever guy, and I found him really interesting. But still, I just didn't buy all his *emuna and tzaddik* stuff.

He told us a story to try and help us 'get' who Rebbe Nachman really was, and who his students really were. He really wanted us to understand just how saintly

125

# The Stolen Light

the Rebbe was. According to the story, one day, the Rebbe and Rabbi Leib Yitzhak, one of his students, were out walking in a forest, when Rebbe Nachman decided that he really wanted to dip in a *mikveh* - but there was no *mikveh* in the middle of the forest. So Rabbi Leib asked Rabbeinu for permission to create a mikveh for him, and Rebbe Nachman gave it.

Rabbi Leib then took a container of water, drew a circle on the floor, said the name of some angel who apparently was known for digging holes in forests, and a couple of seconds later, shazam! There was a *mikveh*. Rebbe Nachman used the *mikveh*, but he forbade Rabbi Leib from using it even though Rabbi Leib had actually made it, and was in actuality much, much older than he was. I had no idea what to make of all that.

Anyway, I decided to go and check out the mass *Tikun HaKlali* thing to see what Aryeh was talking about. But when I saw thousands of people packed together, I realized immediately that it just wasn't for me. For a kilometer around the grave, all you could see were *chassidim* with their little prayer books swaying all over the place like a bunch of *lulavs*. Some of them were sobbing, some were yelling, some were just whispering intensely to themselves - but I decided there and then to turn right back around and head back to the apartment, where I took a nice snooze.

It's actually really weird how tired I felt in Uman. By nature, I'm usually a night owl, and don't need a lot of sleep. From the moment I wake up, drink my coffee and have my first cigarette, I'm usually wired until at least midnight. But here, I just felt exhausted all the time. I'd sleep two hours, wake up for a few minutes, then sleep another two hours - and this continued until two in the afternoon. My brother told me afterwards that apparently, the sleepiness is a common phenomenon here. It was my body kind of shutting down as a result of not being able to handle all the holiness of the place.

At 2pm I woke up, and what did I see? I see Nadav, sitting on his bed, crying his eyes out. But he wasn't crying like a normal person, he was crying like the whole world had just died, and he was the only person left alive.

"What's going on, Nadav?" I asked. He didn't reply, so I went over to him, but I realized he was basically looking right through me even though I was right up in front of his face. I tried to shake him, but he didn't seem to feel it, and just went on sobbing.

I left the bedroom and went out to the salon, looking for someone who could tell me what on earth had happened to Nadav. Ido and Aryeh were there, sitting together and talking enthusiastically about something or another. Ido in particular was talking very passionately. Usually, he spoke in a very measured, quiet tone, and threw in far too many specific details in that precise way of his.

But now, he was throwing his hands all over the place, and his eyes were so lit up they looked like two small projectors.

"Listen, it was incredible, once in a lifetime. It was really amazing... Wowwww. I felt like I standing at Mount Sinai! Did you?"

Aryeh had a huge grin on his face that stretched from ear to ear. Ido continued: "What a crowd! What an experience! I tell you, I've been in a lot of crowds and a lot of celebrations, but I've never seen anything like it! I was on cloud nine; *mamash*, it was like I wasn't even here anymore. I just kind of completely melted into all the *kedusha*. It's the 'hidden light'; I'm telling you, what I experienced just now was the 'hidden light'.

I wanted to tell him that he'd gotten it wrong, and that it was the 'stolen light', but just then I noticed that Ido was crying. What had happened to them that they were all crying like babies? Was someone cutting up onions for dinner? What was going on?

Aryeh stood up. "It's the *achdut*, the feeling of unity here. That's what G-d wants from us. Do you know what happened the last and only time that *Am Yisrael* were together, completely unified? We got the Torah given to us, on Mount Sinai. Are you starting to understand the enormous power of unity? Just think for a minute, what would happen if all of *Am Yisrael* took ten minutes out of their day and stopped all the business of their lives to get together and cry out the *Tikun HaKlali* at precisely the same amazing moment? Do you know what that would do in the world, and all the upper worlds as well? We'd shake up the whole world order; *Moshiach* and *geula* would literally be running after us, trying to catch up."

"So why aren't we doing that already?" Ido asked, in a tone of immense frustration.

"You know why? Because the *Sitra Achra* would never let it happen. Believe me, if I thought there was even a small chance of pulling it off, I'd jump in and get the ball rolling immediately. But the *Sitra Achra* would just throw up all sorts of obstacles and arguments, and the whole thing would get buried under feuds and politics. He'd throw everything at it, just to prevent the Jews from uniting as one people."

"Do it anyway! G-d is the one running the show, not us or the *Sitra Achra*. We just have to do our *hishtadlut*, and make our effort, and then it's up to G-d how it turns out. I'm happy to help you, and I'll do anything you tell me. I'll be the second-in-command. Or maybe I should say, the third-in-command, after *Rabbeinu*."

# The Stolen Light

Wow. Ido had completely changed. Now he was talking like a Breslever, with fire and enthusiasm, and in short sentences!

"Ido, you got lit up with the fire of *Rabbeinu, chaval al ha-zman*! I wish that I had as much light coming out of me as you do right now. For sure, you are giving your great-grandpa Natan so much *nachas* right now. But you should know that *Rabbeinu*'s wisdom doesn't just give us the vessels and the tools we need to ride the spiritual highs; he also helps us navigate the spiritual depths. Why am I telling you this? Because right now, you are completely filled up with light. When we're filled up with light like this, *Rabbeinu* tells us that Heaven doesn't give us the permission to act on it. Why not? Because this light is so powerful, it could burn the whole world to a crisp, like what happened with Rabbi Shimon Bar Yochai and his son. They'd been hiding in a cave to escape the Romans for 12 years, and the whole time they were learning Torah with *Eliyahu Hanavi*. When they left the cave, they saw all these people plowing their fields and carrying out their normal, everyday lives, and got so heated up about it that everywhere they gazed became burnt it to ash.

"*Hashem* took them both to task, and said to them: 'Did you only come out of your cave to destroy My world? Back you go for another year, until you calm down a bit.' G-d wanted them to build the world and help people get closer to Him, and not just return it to chaos and destruction.

"You know, when *Rabbeinu* told Rabbi Natan about the secret of doing *hitbodedut* every day, Rabbi Natan immediately felt like he'd just been told the answer to all of the world's problems. He knew that that piece of advice could bring *geula,* redemption, and he wanted to run out into the street and start screaming at the top of his lungs that a Jew was fooling himself if he believed that he could really be a Jew without *hitbodedut!* But *Rabbeinu* grabbed hold of him, and told him that he'd just look like a mad man if he ran outside shouting. 'You do your part, and you try to wake up the people who are around you, and then each person needs to make an effort to share their light with someone else, with each student creating their own students in kind… and that's how we'll bring *geula.* "

Ido and Aryeh hugged each other joyfully, and started to dance and to sing… what else? "*Ashreinu, ashreinu, she zachinu lehitkarev le Rabbeinu.*[6]"

They got me to join in with their dancing, even though I still hadn't recovered from having my sleep so dramatically disturbed, not to mention the back ache I'd gotten from lying down on the rickety Russian mattress. By the fifth round I was pooped, and secretly impressed with these guys that they were physically fit enough to dance for hours on end.

---

[6] Literally: 'Fortunate are we, that we merited coming close to Rabbeinu'.

"What happened to Nadav?" I asked them, feeling like any minute now, I was going to pass out from all the exertion.

"He had an epiphany - a really massive one," laughed Aryeh, and then he called out to me over his shoulder, "It's a real shame that you didn't make it to the *Tikun Haklali*. You'd have gotten the same present Nadav received."

"I hate presents like that," I retorted. I knew that Aryeh was talking about making *teshuva*. Ido started laughing hysterically, then ran off in Nadav's direction. In the meantime, Aryeh asked me if I wanted a cup of coffee, and I said yes.

"Where's my brother Motty?" I was sitting on the only armchair in the passageway between the rooms.

"Your brother Mordechai is pouring out his heart in the *Tzion*; everyone else left already, but he's still there, ripping the Heavens open with his prayers. Believe me, your brother is a real *tzaddik*. I haven't seen that sort of sweet simplicity and strong *emuna* for a long time. Much credit to him and your family."

Aryeh brought me the coffee and I took a sip and realized that it wasn't as strong as I liked it. I couldn't bring myself to drink any more of it, and started to think to myself, 'I've woken up to a bona fide nightmare. This one's crying hysterically, that one's screaming maniacally, I'm feeling completely exhausted, and even the coffee doesn't work here.' I wished that I could have a couple of hours of normal sleep in my normal bed back home, where I could wake up in peace and quiet with the music I liked... But the reality was that I was stuck in Uman, seven hours before the *Chag* was to begin.

Just then the *chevra*'s cook, Pinchas Bardogo, came into the room. His eyes were also red, and it looked to me like he'd also been crying. OK, gentle Ido I could kind of understand. Sensitive Nadav? Also fine. But Bardogo!? The man was built like King Kong. Why on earth was *he* crying? It looked like I'd signed up to spend Rosh Hashana with a bunch of crybabies, who were going to be leaking tears the whole holiday.

"Who's going to help me finish the cooking and get the kitchen tidied up?" he asked, looking straight at me. "Avi, my sweet brother. Will you come and help me?"

Cooking is not exactly my strong point. "Give me a bit of time, I need to drink my coffee first. I only woke up a couple of minutes ago." I felt really stiff, like my back had just seized up because of the horrible beds. I think they deliberately brought them here from some medieval torture chamber somewhere.

# The Stolen Light

Bardogo let out a low whistle, and put his massive hands behind his even more massive head. "You only woke up now? What time did you go to sleep? Please don't tell me that you missed out on the *Tikun HaKlali*..." Bardogo came over to me. "I don't believe it! Avi, you weren't at *Tikun HaKlali?* Do you know what sort of global rectification you just missed out on? Do you know what tremendous light there is when you stand there fixing the mess you made the whole year? Man, what a pity. What a pity you missed out on that! Why didn't you come? I don't understand why you'd come all the way here just to go to sleep. Did you think you were coming to a hotel or something?"

He spoke loudly, and was circling around me like a caged lion. I felt a bit under attack.

"You'd have to be crazy to think this was a hotel!" I snorted. "The fold-up beds I used to sleep on in the army are more comfortable. I think I aged fifty years from sleeping in that bed," I said, grinning. I noticed that even the muscular man-mountain that was Bardogo was apparently still crying. "It's such a shame you weren't there. Your soul is really so, so sad it missed out." I don't know if he was crying for me, or crying for him, or just crying because everyone seemed to have come out of the *Tikun HaKlali* crying. I'll never know, because just then, we heard an ear-splitting shriek from the room where Nadav and Ido were. We both ran over.

I was sure something really serious and terrible had just happened, because the shriek had been so blood-curdling and had obviously come from a very deep, primal place. We entered the room fearing the worst. Nadav was standing on his bed, jumping around all over the place like some sort of deranged ballerina, and yelling at the top of his lungs: "Oyyyyyy! I'm living a complete lie! It's all just one massive lie! I've been living a lie for 15 years.... Oyyyyyy!" He didn't stop sobbing or jumping around for a second. "They stole all my life away; all my life, they just told me lies... They deceived me; they must have hated me so much to do that to me. Why did they lie to me? Why did they tell us so many lies?

"Aryeh, you should know that if we'd never met, and if you'd never persuaded me to come here, I could have continued living those lies for decades, and to even think that I was living a good, honest life. I always used to look at them, at the charedim, like some sort of unfortunate thorn in Israel's side. I always thought they were so primitive, and that they didn't develop or embrace the modern world because they didn't want to come out of the dark ages. But now I see that you guys really are living the truth. You're really alive; you're really feeling things. All we do is chase after 'progress', but what progress is there, really? How are things really better for us, in our modern world?

"Ok, maybe here and there they invented a couple of interesting things that helped us to do some stuff faster than in the past. But who's to say that's even a good thing? Who can really say that all these inventions are really good for us? Now that we have cars, a trip that used to take 10 hours has been shortened to an hour. But how many lives are cut short every day because of car accidents? How many people have died because of them? All the material bounty we have today is just making everything cloudy, confused and contaminated. Everything today is a competition, or even a war. Today, there are a hundred movie channels and everyone's constantly plugged into the Internet, which is fundamentally corrupting our minds and our humanity. Keep busy doing a million things a day, but don't you dare ever stop to think about what it's all for! Don't start looking at what's really going on inside of you, inside your heart. I felt more alive, more emotional, in the half hour while I was doing the *Tikun* than I've ever felt in my life. It's like my heart cracked open, and I suddenly just filled up with this indescribable feeling of inner happiness."

What was the man talking about?? Who was lying to him? What were they telling him? I'd kind of gotten my hopes up that Nadav would be my secular partner in crime in Uman, and that we could do some fun stuff together while everyone else was off being crazy and religious. Now I realized that he'd also been stolen away from me. Evidently, the 'light of *Rabbeinu*' really was capable of kidnapping everyone that came near it, but *Baruch Hashem,* it hadn't nabbed me yet.

Ido jumped on to the bed next to Nadav and gave him a hug. Next, Aryeh jumped on to the bed, agile as a panther, and hugged Ido, who was busy hugging Nadav. Bardogo didn't wait to be asked twice, and he also jumped on to the bed, like some sort of huge mountain bear, and gave the whole group a squeezing hug. They lost their balance, fell off the bed into a big heap on the floor, and then started laughing hysterically as they tried to untangle themselves. Even I couldn't help but crack up too, and laughed the most I ever laughed in my whole life.

We were all rolling around holding our sides for a quarter of an hour, and then some people started crying again, some started laughing again, and some were laughing and crying both at the same time. Nadav was groaning: "I caaaan't stoppppp cryyyyyyyying. What's happening to meeeeee? Why can't I stopppp cryyyyyyinggggg?"

Bardogo called across to him: "Keep on crying! Why do you need to stop? The Hebrew word for crying, *'bechi',* has the same *gematria* as *'lev',* heart. Your heart is actually starting to work properly. It's no coincidence that *Rabbeinu* is called 'Rebbe Nachman of *Breslev'.* If you rearrange the letters of Breslev, you get *'lev basar',* which means 'heart of flesh'. That's the whole job that we got sent down here to do - we need to work on ourselves until we develop a heart of flesh, a heart that really feels, and a good heart that empathises with the pain of other people - whether they be friends, parents, or simply the pain of every Jew."

Nadav tried to tell me what he'd gone through (or to be more precise, what had gone through him), but the words seemed to get stuck in his throat. He just kept breaking down, crying and letting out another soul-rending cry, while mumbling things that none of us could understand.

"Maybe he had something a bit too strong to drink?" I whispered to Bardogo. "Don't you think he's acting a bit too weird for just a 'spiritual' experience?" Bardogo shot me a mischievous grin, and there was something very knowing in his smile. Although it came packaged together with a big dose of love and warmth, I still felt like somehow I was being told off. I blushed, but luckily I'm practically black, so no one else noticed.

"All that happened to him is that he got intoxicated by the pure, holy air around *Rabbeinu*'s tomb, which is the same as the holy air of *Eretz Yisrael,* except that here, next to the head of *Am Yisrael*'s household, next to this angel of *emuna* and joy, next to this Doctor of the Soul, it's all super-concentrated. *Rabbeinu* opens the heart of anyone who comes to him seeking the truth. Anyone who really wants to change, anyone who really understands just how little they actually know about their own life or anything else for that matter, *that* person can admit that they really are completely clueless, and that they need a guide to show them their path in life. And then *Rabbeinu* opens their heart."

Bardogo hugged me and gave me a kiss on my forehead, and I suddenly felt panicky and worried. OK, I still wasn't really feeling anything; I was still exactly the same person I'd been when I'd left Israel, albeit much more tired than usual. So far so good, because I hadn't changed, and I didn't feel at all like I wanted to. On the other hand, so many apparently sane, normal, successful people - and we weren't talking about the screwed-up crazy people here - seemed to come away from Uman feeling unusually emotionally lofty about all sorts of things.

Maybe there was some sort of witchcraft or black magic going on around here. Maybe, they'd created this *'teshuva* virus' and let it loose on the unsuspecting crowd. I wouldn't put anything past these *frummies.*

Bardogo could clearly see on my face that I was having some sort of inner struggle, so he picked that moment to drag me off to the kitchen and start giving orders: "We need 10 potatoes peeled! We need a few onions finely chopped! We need to boil some vegetables!" And I did it all like a robot, on automatic pilot, half spaced-out and half hypnotized, without even speaking. In truth, I found all the monotonous chores rather calming.

## Chapter 9

*Let me tell you the story of the shortcut that Bardogo the Mafioso took to get to the Upper Worlds.*

Bardogo was jumping around the kitchen with the skill and agility of a French chef, cutting up fish and meat. As he was cooking, we started to chat, and Bardogo told me a story that was amazing by anyone's standards, while chain-smoking his way through a pack of cigarettes.

*"You have no idea what sort of life I had before I got religious - although today, I understand just how much I actually gained from turning my back on that so-called 'great' life that was actually so miserable. Yes, I had a ton of money, Baruch Hashem: I was earning the sort of sums that even the most successful managing directors don't bring home. You have no idea how over-the-top my standard of living was, before I met Rabbeinu... yishtabach shemo la'ad.*

*I drove the latest model BMW, and I'd upgrade it every year. I lived in a two story villa on its own estate, and I lived there like a king, without any family ties weighing me down. I had money pouring through my hands like water; whatever I wanted, I got, even things that I had absolutely no need of whatsoever. Right up to the end, I was hooked on the money, and I loved the high-rolling lifestyle.*

*If I woke up in the middle of the night wanting to go gambling in Las Vegas, I'd make one call to arrange it and then be on my way. If I wanted to go yachting and sail around the Caribbean for a few days, one call and I'd be on the high seas. I did whatever I wanted, with whomever I wanted, whenever I wanted to, if you get my drift. And to this day, I have no idea how I had the zchut of escaping from that world and entering the world of Torah and mitzvot. I have no idea how I merited to be the person you see before you today, with a beard and tzitzit, who sits learning Gemara, Mishna and the Torah of Rebbe Nachman and his student Rabbi Natan at the kollel every day.*

# The Stolen Light

*Until seven years ago, I was second-in-command of one of Israel's biggest mafias, which operates in quite a few places around the world. I don't want to tell you all the gory details about the sort of 'business deals' I was involved in, not least because you're not supposed to remind a person of their past sins, but you're a sharp guy, and I'm sure you can paint your own picture of the sort of things I'm talking about.*

*When I remember the cruel tactics I used against people to extort money out of them, or to force them to respect me, I feel so mortified. And I'm not talking about reasonable measures; I'm talking about things that were unreasonably bad in the extreme. I stopped at nothing, may G-d have mercy on me, and also on them."*

Now that he mentioned it, if you took away his beard and tzitzit, he really did look quite scary. I realized his face actually looked pretty similar to the way gangsters always looked in the movies - and this whole conversation was going on in a tiny kitchen that measured about two square meters. We were surrounded by dozens of plastic food containers stacked on top of each other and by two refrigerators that were stuffed full of food, and the place simply smelled like *Gan Eden*. See, I'm starting to talk in their ridiculous jargon. *'Gan Eden'*. What I really meant to say is that it smelled wonderful. Bardogo continued to tell his story…

*"Baruch Hashem, I have no idea how I merited it, but in the ten years that I was involved with all that underworld stuff, I never actually killed anybody. Not that I wasn't involved in many murders and beatings, but luckily, no one ever died as a direct result of my actions. I was always just standing next to them, or occasionally, I'd give the order to do it. But I never actually killed anyone with my own two hands, Hashem should have mercy on my miserable soul. If it wasn't for Rebbe Nachman, who else would have given me the chance to escape from the hell I found myself trapped in?*

*Not that I felt that way then, you understand. Quite the opposite - I felt like I'd really hit the big time. You know, all my life I'd lived in poverty and my parents were destitute. We lived in a poor, run-down neighborhood, and most of the kids there were getting into trouble most of the time. It was almost the natural next step for me to become a criminal. That's not to say I didn't try to change my destiny, because I did. I stopped all the petty thieving and tried to go 'straight' by hanging out with the more clean-cut kids from the higher class neighborhoods - but they wouldn't let me forget my past, and kept telling me things like 'once a criminal, always a criminal'.*

*So to tell you the truth, I didn't so much pick my career, as my career picked me. Every fat, rich kid in the neighborhood would come to me to help them arrange a little bag of something to help them 'concentrate on their studies' and completely mess up their brains. But me? I never once even touched the stuff, because I'd had a nephew who'd gotten seriously addicted to drugs, and I'd seen what it had done to him. There was almost no level he wouldn't stoop to in order to get his fix, so I made a promise to myself that come what may, I was never going to touch that garbage.*

*But then, my so-called new friends started asking me to act as their go between. I was so desperate to be accepted by the 'good' chevra and be treated by them with a little respect that I agreed to become the middleman between them and the dealers, most of whom happened to be my neighbors. They'd give me the money, and I'd bring them their substances.*

*It goes without saying that the principal and teachers in school had no idea what was really going on. Whenever we got lectured about drugs, they'd always say that it was a problem in my sort of poor neighbourhood - but where they lived, with the higher-class people and the higher-class kids, everyone was clean as a whistle. This went on for a while, until one day, the whole dirty business exploded in their faces. Thirty teenaged boys and girls were busted having a party at one of the more expensive villas in the affluent town of Savyon. In addition to the party, they also discovered a massive quantity of hard drugs on the premises.*

*As the main supply man for the party, I'd also been invited to attend, and when the police showed up, all the 'good' crew who'd been using me to fuel their addictions decided to blame me for everything. They made out like I'd somehow convinced them to use the drugs against their will, and the police believed them. Thanks to all their lies, they got away scot-free, while I sat in prison for two years for being their dealer.*

*When I saw how they'd hung me out to dry in order to get themselves off the hook, I made a solemn oath to myself that I was going to make them pay for what they'd done to me. When I got out of prison, I began my payback campaign in earnest. I didn't hurt or injure anyone physically, but I used to follow them around and slash their tires or break their car windshields (Not that they owned the cars they were driving, of course; everything belonged to their parents). After that, I started stealing their car stereos, being really careful to keep a very low profile. I started selling the car stereos on the black market, and after some time, I came to the attention of one of the local mafia bosses, who decided he could use someone like me on his staff.*

*I'm not going to bore you with all the details of the criminal activities and the terrible sins that I got mixed up in after that. But suffice it to say that I was his right-hand man for the next 15 years.*

# The Stolen Light

*My connection with Rebbe Nachman started exactly seven years ago, when the boss and I arranged a meeting with one of the heads of the Russian mob, here in Ukraine, in Kiev. By the way, I've spotted quite a few of the Russian gangsters I used to know driving around here in exactly the same sorts of flashy cars that I used to drive, way back when. They haven't recognized me of course, and that's the way I want to keep it.*

*Anyway, I won't burden you with all the details, but my boss was a criminal genius who had the most finely tuned animal instincts. As soon as we landed in Kiev, he sensed someone was following us. He immediately called up the mobster head we were to meet with and told him that we were being tailed through the terminal. They agreed to switch the meeting place to somewhere outside of Kiev instead, and it goes without saying that a car was already there waiting to take us to our destination as soon as we left the airport building. We were supposed to just get in and drive off, but my boss decided that he wanted to rent a car instead, to try and evade the people who were following us. To this day, I have no idea if anyone was really tailing us or not.*

*When you're in that line of work, you are permanently paranoid about everything and everyone. You're convinced that you're always being followed, or that someone's always out to kill you. You need nerves of steel just to stay sane when you live that sort of life, and there are many people who just can't take all the stress and fear. Anyway, we're finally on our way, with the Russian boss giving us directions where to go. We were there to attend to a deal on the table worth millions of euros.*

*The Russian mobster told us to turn off the highway and follow the signs to Uman, explaining that we'd meet at the grave of Rebbe Nachman, where we'd just mingle with all the other people praying there without having to worry about anyone following us or bothering us. That was the first time in my life that I ever heard the words 'Uman' or 'Rebbe Nachman'. Of course, I'd seen all the 'Na Na Nachma Nachman M'Uman' graffiti on the walls in Israel, but why would anyone pay any attention to that?*

*So we got there, and there were a couple hundred people praying by the grave. My boss stuck a kippa on his head and so did the Russian mafia boss, and we all entered the building around the tomb and started pretending to be absorbed in looking at the place and doing whatever we saw everyone else doing around us.*

*At some point, I saw the two of them find a bench and sit down together, and then I knew I had at least five or six hours to myself. Here in Ukraine, the grave of Rebbe Nachman is as famous as the Western Wall is back home in Israel. This place is one of the country's most popular tourism sites, and they make a lot of money from all the tourists that come to visit. An awful lot of money.*

*I got in the car and drove off in the direction of the city, to see what fun things I could find to pass the time. I didn't even set foot in the kever, but as I was driving away, I called out, 'See you later, Rebbe Nachman!' and that was it. I only came here to help my boss hopefully seal a good business deal, and once he'd settled in, I took off. Five hours later, my boss called me on the cell to tell me he'd finished his meeting, and that I needed to come pick him up. He was in fine spirits because the meeting had gone well and they'd come to an agreement. That same day, we flew out of Kiev back to Israel to start planning all the next steps needed to move the business arrangement forward (it had something to do with gasoline).*

*A few days later, Hashem should have mercy on me, I was on my way down to Eilat to collect some money from a few businesses, and afterwards was planning to spend the rest of the week there relaxing. On the way down, I pulled into a gas station just before Beer Sheva to fill up the brand new car I'd just upgraded the week before. It was a convertible BMW that I'd taken in lieu of cash from one of my clients. It was the guy's own car that he agreed to give me; well, which he agreed I should take. Kind of. After I'd 'persuaded' him.*

*While the car was filling up, I got out and start walking towards the convenient store at the gas station to pick up some more cigarettes and a few other things. I have no idea where the guy came from - he was riding a motorbike and I had my back to him and didn't suspect a thing. He came up alongside me, shot me at point-blank range in the head, and then drove off at high speed. To this day, they still haven't caught him. Avi, tzaddik, please turn the fish down a bit, because otherwise the sauce will burn."*

You had to give the man some respect! Between the cooking and the story telling, I was truly enjoying this conversation with Bardogo. He was a really sweet guy, former Mafioso or not.

*"The bullet entered my head and stopped a millimeter short of severing my brain stem. I lost consciousness, and after a second or two, I actually died. Wow, is it two o'clock already? Where did the time go? I'll tell you the rest another time, my brother, because I want to go and use the mikveh in honor of the Chag, and maybe also grab a few winks. What can I tell you, my brother? Going to the mikveh once before Rosh Hashana is equivalent to going to the mikveh every day the whole rest of the year... If you'd have told me a few years ago that I'd be dunking in a pool of chlorinated water with 30 other guys and getting a huge spiritual kick out of the experience, I'd have said you were crazy. Do you know what sort of clarity you have after using the mikveh? It's like all your thoughts are zooming around your head, but everything is exactly where it should be..."*

"Why are you telling me all this stuff about the *mikveh*? What happened to you after the motorcycle assassin shot you in the head, and you died?"

# The Stolen Light

Bardogo started guffawing.

*"You want to know what happened next, eh? OK, so like I said, I was dead. I was kind of floating on top of my body, and was looking at it from some distance away. I can't really put this into words, but I was feeling this intense mix of incredible pleasure, and also the most profound fear. So I'm up there, watching all these people rushing around my dead body, and someone was unsuccessfully trying to revive me for a few minutes, before the ambulance came to collect me. As I watched all this, I was rising higher and higher, like I was being pulled up at a very fast speed towards a beautiful source of light that was kind of wrapping me up and pulling me towards it.*

*Now you're really going to think I was imagining things, but there were thousands of 'beings' around me that I'd never seen before, some of which looked human, and some of which looked like hideous monsters. These beings started coming closer to me, and then would run away from me, and I felt so scared and helpless I just started yelling at the top of my lungs - but no one could hear my screams.*

*What I'm about to tell you now is going to sound incredibly weird, and amazingly wonderful, and also very, very heavy. I suddenly found myself in an extraordinary building that was the most beautiful place I'd ever seen in my life. It was like the palaces you read about in fairy tales. It was full of the most beautiful fountains, with water the color of molten silver. The whole place was built from gold and diamonds, and the overall affect was absolutely stunning - really something completely out of this world.*

*Looking around, I got this thought that I wanted to take some of the treasures on display here for myself, and started looking around for a sack or something similar to use. It's the most bizarre thing, but even though I was dead, I didn't actually feel like I was dead. Old habits, eh?*

*I wasn't alone in the palace; there were thousands of other people there, and everyone was running from place to place. It was like being on the front line of a battle. Suddenly, this transparent person came over and said to me, 'Pinchas Bardogo?' I told him, 'Yes, that's me,' and he beckoned me to follow him. So I started following behind him, but the whole time I couldn't actually see him; I just kind of knew he was there.*

*We went up stairs, then down into tunnels, then jumped over buildings, and everything was made of the most sparkling precious metals - gold, silver and copper. It was like being in the most amazing sci-fi movie. Finally, we got to a really long corridor filled with a very strong, dazzling light. The being in front of me stopped and told me: 'Wait here. They'll call you inside shortly.' I asked him,*

*'Who's calling me in? To where?' But he'd already disappeared. So I sat down there, alone. Part of me was absolutely petrified, and part of me was feeling a sublime sense of calm and inner peace that I simply can't even begin to put into words.*

*The door swung open and I went inside. I found myself standing in front of three figures. On the right was a frightening creature that definitely wasn't human, on the left was the shining face of a kind looking rabbi, and the one who sat between them looked like another sort of angelic rabbi. The angelic-looking figure turned to the hideous creature, and said to him, 'Speak!' The hideous creature began reading out of a book that contained a record of every single bad thing I'd ever done since the day I was born.*

*As he recounted each negative deed, another hideous creature would suddenly appear out of nowhere, and before long, the whole chamber was filled with these terrible creatures - each one scarier than the last. All these creatures were looking at me with murderous hatred on their faces, like they wanted to kill me. At some point they began screaming and screeching in unison at me, in a voice that went straight through me and pierced me to the deepest recesses of my inner being: 'Why did you create us?' they wailed. I was thinking that I was already dead, and what could these terrible things want from me? It dawned on me that I'd been creating these terrible creatures every time I did something wrong.*

*I was shocked at how many horrible things I'd actually done in my life. While I was there listening to it all being read out, I felt like the most evil person on the planet. First came the lighter stuff: I beat someone up, I stole something, I insulted someone, I lied, and so on. That took us up to the time I was ten years old. After the age of ten I was already completely out of control, and the prosecuting creature spent a few good hours detailing every terrible thing I'd done. At least, that's how it felt - but the truth is that it could have taken just a minute or even just a second. I could see that the rabbis were looking at me with tender pity on their faces, because they clearly knew what sort of punishment was awaiting me once the proceedings were over.*

*When the horrible creature finally finished detailing all my sins, it was the nice rabbi's turn, and he started to read out all the good things I'd done while I was still alive. He held a single sheet of paper in his hand, and I could already tell where things were heading: the horrible creature had been reading out of an encyclopedia, and this guy had one small page. He recounted all the good things I'd tried to do to help my brother and how I'd helped my parents. Each time he mentioned a good deed, a beautiful, sweet-faced creature suddenly appeared, dressed in white. Each of these new beings in turn thanked me for creating them. If only I'd known that every good deed I did created a fabulous creature like that, I'd have been doing mitzvot morning, noon and night.*

# The Stolen Light

*Unfortunately, the kind rabbi didn't have a lot to say, and there weren't a lot of the beautiful creatures in the room with us. The panel conferred amongst themselves, and then the middle rabbi turned to me and summed up my life in one very brief sentence: 'you missed the entire point.'*

*Suddenly, a gigantic video screen appeared in front of me, and the angelic-looking rabbi said, 'Now, look what you could have achieved with your life, if you'd decided to walk on the straight path.' What can I tell you? I couldn't stop sobbing. I cried like a baby when I saw what an essentially good soul I had, and what an amazing person I could have been. What sensitivity I could have displayed; what degree of Torah learning I could have achieved! I saw the ten beautiful, holy children I was meant to have fathered, all the books I was meant to have written, the thousands of people I was supposed to have helped. I was wealthy in that other, holy life - and the biggest irony of all was that there, my boss was supposed to have been my subordinate, and not the other way round. I really had missed the boat. There was nothing more to say.*

*The judges asked me if I had anything I wanted to add, but I just sobbed, and told them, 'I'm sorry. I'm so sorry...' They got ready to hand down their ominous verdict, and at precisely that moment, another rabbi suddenly appeared in the room. He was very striking and elegant, and was radiating a light that I couldn't even begin to describe. He went over to speak with the panel, and at the end of the discussion, he said to the middle judge: 'He's one of my people. Leave him to me.'*

*The whole room disappeared, and the only people left were me and the newcomer who'd somehow managed to rescue. He turned towards me, looked me straight in the eyes, and I burst into tears again. He then said to me: 'In the merit of coming to visit me in Uman that one time in your life, even though you didn't even enter the building or pray, and even though you didn't even have any intention of specifically coming to visit me... Despite all this, I'm giving you another chance to come back to life. But remember, if you go back to the lifestyle you had before, within a month you'll be back here.*

*'I'm giving you a sign by which you'll know that everything you've experienced here is real, and the sign is this: the bullet that entered your head will stay there for the rest of your life. Under no circumstances are you to give the doctors permission to try and remove it. They'll want to operate, but don't let them.' And then, he too disappeared.*

*I woke up and found myself in the hospital, laying on a bed that was being wheeled somewhere by an Arab nurse who was casually smoking a cigarette. I asked him where he was taking me, and before he realized what was going on, he answered, 'The morgue.' Then the penny dropped, and he realized he was talking to someone who was supposed to be dead. Needless to say he completely lost it, and half a minute later the whole hospital was milling around us.*

*They whisked me off to the operating room, where already a bunch of newspaper photographers were waiting to take the picture of the man who'd miraculously come back to life. It was a complete circus. They X-rayed my head, and one of the doctors came to tell me that I'd taken a bullet a millemeter away from my brain stem and needed an urgent operation to remove it. 'Over my dead body', I told him. 'I don't want any operation.' He told me that it was very dangerous to leave it there, and I told him that it would be much more dangerous for me if they tried to take it out. He actually ended up agreeing with me, and asked me if I was a doctor or something, and how did I know that? I told him that I'd consulted with the best doctor in the world up in shamayim, and after that he left me alone. I got out of bed and stood up while the doctors looked on in shock, unable to believe their eyes. I moved my head right and left, then took a few steps over to the water fountain, and drank. They could see that apparently I was just fine, and could not even begin to fathom this. They began arguing with each other about what was really going on.*

*I wasn't even going to start trying to explain to them what had just happened to me; they'd just take me out the operating ward and stick me in the loony bin. I asked them to discharge me, but they told me that they wanted to keep me in for observation for a couple more days, and also to sew up the bullet hole so that it would heal faster.*

*But I didn't have patience for observation time. The minute they finished sewing up my head, I was out of there. The first thing I realized was that the shirt I was wearing was drenched with blood, so I headed to the nearest clothing store, which happened to be right next to the hospital. I stopped at an ATM to take out some money and then bought myself a new shirt and pair of trousers. Next, I found a taxi and I told the driver to take me to Jerusalem, straight to the Kotel.*

*On the way I was talking to the driver telling him what had just happened to me, but I could see that he didn't really believe me. He dropped me off by the Kotel, and I went and stood beside its ancient stones. Once again, I wept my eyes out. There was a young chareidi man standing next to me with long side-curls and a white kippa on his head. He could see I needed some help, so he came over and started to chat. I told him everything that had just happened to me, and he told me I had to come with him and tell my story to his rabbi.*

*I had no idea what my next move was anyway, so I agreed to come with him to his rav. We had to wait half an hour until he could see us, and then were told to go in. The moment I saw him, I passed out from shock. I'd never died before, and I'd never fainted before, but now I'd done both in less than 24 hours. This rabbi looked exactly the same as one of the judges of the heavenly panel I'd appeared*

## The Stolen Light

*before in my vision moments before the glowing rabbi, Rabbi Nachman, brought me back to life. And in case you think that I was just imagining things, even before I'd said a word to him, the rabbi told me: 'It could be that I look like the judge, but you should know that it wasn't me...' How did he even know to tell me that?*

*Anyway, the Rabbi spoke with me for a while, and told me which yeshiva he thought would be good for me. I didn't argue with him, I didn't ask any questions, I just did exactly what he told me to do. Only that morning, I'd been on my way to Eilat to extort a few thousand shekels out of a couple of clients who needed to pay me 'protekzia'. Three hours later, I was a 38 year old man who'd just been assassinated, officially pronounced dead, came back to life, and now sat with some avreich in a yeshiva in Jerusalem, learning about the morning blessings.*

*My phone rang, and I realized that my boss - or should I say, my former boss - was trying to get ahold of me. Should I answer the call? Should I tell him what just happened to me? I went to find the rav of the yeshiva, and asked him what to do about my boss. He told me: 'You're a new man now. You don't have any connection to anyone from your past. Throw your phone in the garbage and buy a new one.' He told me that I should sit and learn at the yeshiva full time for a year, and after that I'd have a better idea of what to do next.*

*My near-death experience was still so fresh and so firmly imprinted on my psyche that I didn't say a word, even when I found out I'd be sharing a room with five other guys, all baal teshuvas, and all a good 10-15 years younger than me. They'd already been studying in yeshiva for a while, and would talk all the time about visiting the graves of dead tzaddikim and about their Torah and their prayers. It was such a change from the life I was used to, chaval al hazman.*

*I'm telling you this now seven years down the road. The bullet is still in my head and is still a millimeter away from my brain stem, but everything else has changed. Now, I'm married with three beautiful kids, Nachman, Natan and Faige, and there's a fourth on the way, be'zrat Hashem. My wife is due to be giving birth to him or her - or maybe 'them', who knows? - around Sukkot. Hashem gave me my wife as a gift, and we live in an apartment in Jerusalem which is small, but very cozy, Baruch Hashem, yishtabach shemo la'ad, the King of the entire universe, the Holy One, blessed be He... Well, I'm heading off to the mikveh now. You're welcome to join me."*

## Chapter 10

*Now I'll tell you about Zevik the outstanding soldier, and his missions in Syria and Lebanon, and how he ultimately got captured by Rebbe Nachman.*

We'd just finished singing the song "You chose us from all the peoples", and finally, f-i-n-a-l-l-y, Nachman was indicating that it was time to say *birkat hamazon*, the blessing after the meal.

This made me happy as a clam. Finally, we'd finished the meal and I could get to bed. With the little bit of strength I still had, I read a couple of paragraphs from a blessing text that someone put in front of me. I was already half asleep when my somehow well-meaning brother suggested that we all read the *Tikun Chatzot* together before bed.

Nachman smiled his very big smile, which meant the suggestion had clearly met with his approval. Luckily, Aaron the unwilling realtor piped up with a counter-suggestion that anyone who wanted to say *Tikun Chatzot* should say it, and anyone who didn't could go straight to sleep. What a great idea! But I noticed that we were in a minority - apart from the two of us, everyone else just dove straight into the *Tikun Chatzot,* apparently forgetting that it was Rosh Hashana, and we'd be spending nearly the whole day praying tomorrow as well.

I somehow managed to stagger off to bed - but not before practically the whole *chevra* got in their last word. This one told me, *"ashrecha, tzaddik!"* That one said, "the light of *Rabbeinu* is *mamash* shining straight out of you!" All I could think about was my lumpy pillow, and the bonanza that was waiting for me tomorrow morning.

I crept under the duvet still wearing all my clothes, even though usually I'm a real stickler for pajamas. It didn't matter where I was - even in the army, when I was in the Golani Brigade, we could have just finished an insane march or a three day exercise with barely any sleep, and I'd still put my jimby jambies on before I hit the sack.

Anyway, this time I collapsed on the bed fully clothed, and then a red flag went up in my head: why had I changed my usual *minhag* tonight, and not put on my pajamas? Could it be that maybe I was starting to change? Could it be that all their talk and funny ideas were starting to influence me after all?

I conked out, exhausted. After an indeterminate amount of time, I was abruptly woken by a series of frightening screams. I don't know where I found the strength to get up, but I ran off in the direction of the screams and what did I find? Nachman, my brother Motty, Aryeh, Ido, Nadav and Baruch, a young Ethiopian guy, were all sitting on the floor screaming their heads off. And the Ethiopian was louder than the rest of them put together.

"Oyyy! Oy, that the light of the *tzaddik*'s eyes dimmed!"

"What's going on?" I asked them. "What happened?"

Nachman yelled out: "Oy, that our holy house was destroyed!" and then everyone started up after him, with another round of 'oyyyys'.

"Oy, that the *Shechina* is in exile!" And everyone yelled out more oyys and started crying. I looked out the window to see if I could spot which house they were talking about, but apparently the action had ended by then. I regardless, they carried on 'oyying' anyway, seemingly completely obsessed with a random act of anti-Semitic vandalism.

I staggered out to the balcony and nearly lit up a cigarette, until I remembered just in time that it was FORBIDDEN to smoke today, because it was also *Shabbat*. All I could think about was the comfortable bed that was waiting for me at my parents' house.

Zevik, another one of Rebbe Nachman's prisoners, sat on the balcony floor mumbling to himself. I peeked over the edge and saw that the street below was as full with people as it had been earlier in the day, and the crowd was still giving off a crazy amount of energy.

"Do you have any idea how much the *Shechina* is suffering?" Zevik asked me.

"Who's Shina?" These Russians had the oddest names.

"The holy *Shechina*," he told me. "Do you know how much She's suffering?"

I obviously had no idea who he was talking about, and really wasn't that interested. Life was tough in Russia, what'd they expect? I only had one thought in my head: sleeeeeep.

"All the souls of *Am Yisrael* are collectively called the *Shechina*," he told me. Great, I'd run away from all the wailing just to get stuck here in a lecture...

"It's like this: *Rabbeinu* taught us that *Hashem Yitbarach* is waiting and yearning to come back to us, but we, *Am Yisrael*, keep pushing Him away from us, so to speak. Our sins caused the destruction of the *Beit HaMikdash*, our holy Temple. And it's taught that every generation that doesn't rebuild the holy Temple is considered as if they themselves destroyed it. How? Because we are continuing to commit the sins of that previous generation. And not only that, we actually *were* that generation in a previous lifetime, and now we need to fix the sins that caused the destruction of the Temple."

"Do you really believe in reincarnation?" I asked him, mostly because I had to keep up appearances and pretend to be at least a little bit interested.

"Of course! You can even prove it scientifically. Do you really think that the 30 million people who have had a 'near death experience' and all describe almost exactly the same experience are all lying? But that's not all, there are also big *tzaddikim* you can go to, and they'll tell you exactly who or what you were in a previous incarnation. Even in our lowly generation, you can still find *tzaddikim* like that. But whether you believe in reincarnation or not, *Rabbeinu* still told us that we had to get up at midnight every night, to cry and mourn for the destruction of the temple, and that if we did this it would be as though we were rebuilding it.

"You can't even begin to describe how highly a person is regarded in Heaven when he gets up to say the midnight lament every night to bewail and mourn the destruction of the Temple. Because he's not just crying about the Temple, he's also mourning the fact that his soul is still in exile, and that *Am Yisrael* is still so beset by suffering. Saying *Tikun Chatzot* is the single best way for us to rescue our Lost Princess."

I have no idea what 'lost princess' this Zevik was talking about. The last I checked, Israel didn't have a royal family. The last time we had a king was thousands of years ago. I thought maybe Zevik had been reading his Bible and got a bit too into it, like these guys can do, and that he was tragically still stuck in the wrong time period. He continued:

"It's like *Rabbeinu* explained in his famous story 'Tale of the Lost Princess'. The Lost Princess is really our own holy soul which has been captured by the forces of darkness. The Royal House of Israel is meant to be ruling over the whole world. It isn't, because the *Erev Rav* have taken over, and there is no level they won't stoop to cover up, hide and ignore the reality that G-d exists and is running the world. That's the real fight going on today, that's the real war, the war for *Am Yisrael*'s soul. We think our worst enemies are physical countries and Arabs, but really, our worst enemies are purely spiritual.

"My brother, do you realize what sort of *zchut* you had to get out from underneath all the *klipot* and actually start doing what you're meant to be doing in life? *Ashrecha*, my brother, *ashrecha!* There should be many more like you in the Nation of Israel. And the most important thing of all is that *Rabbeinu* should reveal even more things to us, or rather, that we should have the merit of learning more of his teachings via his sweet, holy student Rabbi Natan. There's nothing quite like his *Likutey Halachot* in the whole wide world, is there brother? Whenever I read it, my soul feels like it's going to explode."

"Yeah, man, me too!" I tell him, and Zevik seems pretty satisfied by that response, presumably because he thinks I know what I'm talking about.

"Rebbe Nachman tells us that the biggest thing we need to cry about is the fact that the true *Tzaddikim* who worked so hard to help us make some space for G-d in our souls, have been taken from us, leaving us an orphaned generation without anyone to turn to. We need to work so hard to uncover a true Tzaddik, who can bring himself down to help even the people like us, who are stuck on our tremendously low level."

And at that point in the conversation, Zevik also decided to start bawling. In the meantime, the guys inside were still crying and wailing, and you could hear that it really was hurting them that we didn't have a Temple any more - and in truth, at this point it was really hurting me too, because all their pain violently woke me up and was still preventing me from getting to bed. So now you tell me, who's the normal one here?

In the meantime, Zevik was continuing to add to my pain by telling me more and more details about the Temple, and about *Rabbeinu*, and then finally, he asked me the question of questions: "Tell me, how did you get close to *Rabbeinu?*"

I was so wiped, I couldn't even speak. I said to him, "It's a long story, for another time. But how did *you* get close to *Rabbeinu?*" I was on automatic pilot, but as soon as the words left my mouth, I regretted it. I hoped he was going to tell me that he also really needed to go to sleep now, and that he'd fill me in tomorrow or something, but I was wrong. Zevik apparently had all the energy in the world, and immediately started telling me his story:

*"My story starts four years ago, when I was still in the army. Firstly, you should know that I grew up in a house that was glatt chiloni - my dad used to make a*

*special effort every Yom Kippur to organize a big meal for us, with pork and shrimps, Hashem should have mercy on him. Thank G-d, these days he's less 'anti' than he used to be, not because he made teshuva or anything, but maybe because I'm still living at home (although I'm getting married next month). But in the meantime, I've managed to convince them to kasher the kitchen and to stop bringing traif into the house, as well as a few other things.*

*Anyway, I grew up in the lap of the Israeli academic elite. My dad is a card-carrying 'intellectual' and a senior lecturer of philosophy at Tel Aviv University, while my mother is a famous television presenter. Do you know how my family celebrated my bar mitzvah? They arranged a family trip to Disneyland. Forget about buying me a pair of tefillin or calling me up to read the Torah in shul. Instead, my parents, little sister, and I were off to spend a fortnight with Mickey Mouse.*

*These days, my sister is a hardcore chabadnikit. She married a really sweet guy who spends most of his time learning Torah, and they live in Tzfat with their four kids. In the end, she really outdid me... So you can start to understand a bit about the sort of environment I grew up in.*

*When I reached the age of 18, I went against my father's wishes and joined the army. My dad was really upset with me, because he isn't just a run-of-the-mill intellectual, he's also a full-on pacifist and leftist who is against war and violence of any kind, even when it comes to trying to defend yourself. He tried to persuade me to get out of doing the army, but I was stubborn and deliberately signed up for the most dangerous, high-risk special forces unit I could find. After I enlisted, my father didn't talk to me for six months. He was very embarrassed about what I'd done, and his embarrassment gave me even more motivation to be the most successful soldier I could be.*

*Baruch Hashem, I was an outstanding soldier. I finished my induction with top marks, and began to be sent out on top secret missions. I could write a whole book about the things I went through in Lebanon, Jordan and Egypt. Even though I look pretty Ashkenazi, that didn't stop me from sitting in cafes in all these places, making small talk in Arabic with Lebanese informers in Cairo.*

*One day, they got all the guys in my unit together and they told us that we needed to infiltrate some enemy intelligence bases located in a Syrian village and plant a few spy cameras and recording devices there. It was a really tough mission. Ten guys from the unit were chosen for it, including me. We trained for that mission for six months down in the Negev, using an exact replica of the enemy bases specially built for us, right down to the barbed-wire fences and guards. The army had been observing the main base for some time, and they had very precise information about how it operated and who went in and out. To give you some idea of how detailed our intelligence was, for example, I even knew when the base commander usually went to the bathroom.*

*So every couple of days for six months, we'd drill infiltrating the mock bases, hiding the recording devices and cameras, and getting out of there safely. We must have successfully practiced the mission at least 40 times, until we finally got the order to go to Syria and do it for real.*

*The big day finally came, and we were all feeling somewhat scared but completely pumped up on adrenalin. We boarded the plane that was to fly us over the Syrian border in the middle of the night and drop us three kilometers away from our target destination. We were supposed to parachute out somewhere over the desert and then make our way towards the base. The whole operation was to take less than three and a quarter hours, which meant we had to move at basically the speed of light. We had three hours before the rendezvous back at the helicopter which was going to bring us back home, bezrat Hashem, once we'd successfully completed our mission. Obviously, I wasn't saying things like 'bezrat Hashem' back then; I was completely relying on my own strength, cunning, and intelligence, and that of my team. We all felt like we were the kings of the world, and that no one else called the shots.*

*So we parachuted out over the desert and started moving towards the base. Even that desert hike was an experience for me. It was a freezing cold night, and the moon was starting to wax big in the sky. The stars were so bright and twinkly, they looked like huge candles that someone had put there to light up the otherwise pitch-black sky.*

*Poetry aside, when we were a kilometer and a half from the enemy base, we were suddenly surrounded by a massive flock of sheep, and in the distance could see the Arab shepherd guiding the sheep along the exact route that we were supposed to take. We immediately halted and went to ground, while our unit commanders had a quick discussion about what to do next. They radioed back to headquarters and got their instructions: we had exactly five minutes to dispatch the shepherd together with his 200 sheep, and then hide the evidence.*

*Nobody from my unit so much as asked a single question about the orders we'd just been given. We removed our standard issue combat knives and got on with the job. Half of us did the actual killing while the other half got busy digging the shallow grave where we buried the bodies. It's hard to really describe the scene, but within a few minutes, there were no sheep, no shepherd, just a big but barely-discernible mound of freshly turned earth. After that we continued on with our mission as though nothing had happened. I didn't even have time to wash all the blood off my hands. I was in a state of shock, but couldn't really think about anything too deeply just then, because very shortly afterwards we reached the enemy base. Baruch Hashem, we got to work and safely completed our mission - and then were back on the helicopter bringing us back to our own base.*

*Laying on my bunk a little later that same day, I started to think about what had happened. If we'd needed to take out 10 guards, that wouldn't have bothered me in the least, because when all was said and done, we were at war with these guys, and soldiers kill and get killed. If it wasn't me killing them, it could just have easily have been them killing me, had we been discovered during the mission. But I couldn't say the same about the dead shepherd and his sheep, and disturbingly, it appeared to be a huge miscarriage of justice.*

*It was killing me, thinking about how 'Ahmed the Shepherd' had woken up that day to take his sheep out to graze like he did every night, oblivious to any war that might be going on around him, and that we'd cut him down in the prime of his life. It was bad enough that he'd had to die, but I kept picturing his family trying to figure out what had happened to their husband, their father, who'd gone out with the sheep one day and would never come back. How would that family eat, now that their breadwinner and flock of sheep had disappeared? In three minutes, we'd completely destroyed the life of that shepherd and his family, and for what? Just so we'd stick to our schedule and complete the mission in the time we'd been allotted for it. They told us to eliminate him, and we'd done it, no questions asked.*

*As I lay in the bed, I started trembling. I started thinking to myself that just as his life had been unexpectedly destroyed in a minute, the same thing could happen to anyone, including myself. It was like all the fundamental beliefs I'd based my life on until that point, including my own invincibility, suddenly came crashing down.*

*The next morning, I couldn't get out of bed, and I couldn't even talk enough to explain to anyone what was happening to me. I was violently shaking like the proverbial leaf in the wind, and was consumed by feelings of guilt and sorrow. They took me to the doctor who diagnosed me as suffering from post-traumatic shock, but I knew it was the wrong diagnosis. Today, I'd call what happened to me hashgacha pratit, or Divine Providence, but then, all I knew is that I'd suddenly become aware that a Higher Power was running the world. People could not just simply die like that, so apparently randomly, all by some enormous coincidence. There had to be a Higher Power guiding things, and deciding who would live and who would die.*

*In any case, I was given a two week leave to get over the trauma, so I went home to my parents. They were very happy to see me because now they thought I'd swap active duty for a more 'backroom' role, or that I'd quit the army altogether. But something in me wasn't quite ready to come around 100% to their worldview, and I became stubborn again and decided that I was going to continue with my army career, albeit in a different capacity.*

*I put in a request to be transferred over to Golani Brigade, and very quickly, I developed a reputation as an excellent, high-caliber soldier, thanks in no small part to my previous experiences. Always, when a soldier from a more elite unit joins a less elite unit, he gets a reputation for being something special. But without trying to boast, I was also a born soldier, and whatever job I was asked to do, I always did with the utmost efficiency and commitment. So very quickly, my superiors sent me for officer training, where I received a commendation for excellence and was appointed Platoon Commander for a Golani Brigade stationed in the north of Israel.*

*I got a bit more active in the area of overseeing the soldiers' training; in particular, defining the regulations about how to act in combat situations. I worked hard to clarify these moral guidelines, which was an almost impossible task. My revised guidelines were adapted by the army, and the Chief of Staff even wrote the introduction to my work.*

*Around that time, the officer I directly reported to received an order to plan an assault on an enemy village, and he asked me if I wanted to act as his deputy. My superior knew all about the traumatic experience I'd had in Syria, so he made it clear that if I wasn't up to it, it was fine to opt out. I refused to opt out however, and so begins my 'hero's tale' where I was wounded in action, and subsequently discovered Hashem Yitbarach.*

*The operation was meant to be a reprisal raid by the army, coming hot on the heels of a series of missile and Katyusha rocket attacks that had recently been fired at villages in the north of Israel. We were given orders to enter a Lebanese village which contained a Hizbullah stronghold. The plan was to hit the stronghold and capture one of the most high-profile and well-known leaders of the terrorists operating in South Lebanon, a man named Dr Mahmoud Asawiya. The operation was supposed to kill two birds with one stone: firstly, it would be payback for the recent rocket attacks that Hizbullah had launched from Lebanese territory, and secondly, we were hoping that taking a senior Hizbullah man captive would ultimately give us more of a bargaining chip to find out what had happened to Ron Arad, the Israeli pilot who was shot down over Lebanese territory over three decades prior.*

*Tragically, the terrorists, yemach shemam, somehow knew we were coming and were waiting for us. They attacked us en route to the stronghold, and two of my soldiers, Udi and Shlomi, were mortally wounded and died right in front of me. It was the most traumatic experience I've ever had, and it's impossible to accurately describe it to you. It was so painful to see my soldiers die like that, but there was no time to give the pain expression because we were in the middle of a fight for our lives, and had to continue trying to extricate ourselves from the deadly ambush we found ourselves in. The terrorists threw a couple of grenades towards us, and one of the grenades rolled very close to where we stood. I had a split-second to decide what to do: either I could risk trying to kick the grenade away and hope it would explode far away from us; or, I could order everyone to immediately lie down on the ground and hope for a miracle. It was clear to me that if I took the last course of action, a sizeable number of my men would probably sustain serious injury, so I decided - or really, I should say that Heaven decided for me - to try kicking the grenade away.*

*At the moment I kicked it, the grenade exploded, and shattered my leg. But by a massive stroke of 'luck', apart from the massive injury to my leg, no one else in my unit sustained even so much as a scratch. And the fact that it was only my leg that was injured was an even bigger miracle, because according to the laws of nature, I should have died on the spot. G-d had mercy on me and protected the rest of my body by arranging that the rest of the grenade should explode far off to the side. If I hadn't seen what happened with my own eyes, I simply wouldn't have believed the magnitude of the miracle that was done for me and my guys.*

*As you might expect, my brave act of heroism earned me a medal, and a lengthy stay at the Rambam hospital in Haifa where I underwent a number of lengthy and complicated operations to try saving my shattered leg. The doctors prepared me and my parents for the worst possible scenario, because they were sure they'd have to amputate my leg from the knee down, it was in such a bad state. There was almost no flesh left on my leg, and I had multiple fractures along its whole length. But Heaven had mercy on me, and what do you know? The operations were successful beyond anyone's wildest dreams, and even the doctors admitted that some sort of medical miracle had occurred.*

*At that point, I was transferred to the rehabilitation ward of the hospital, where I spent the next six months. Over that period, I was taking stock of myself and my life every single day. Everything in my life seemed so unclear and so mixed up; I couldn't really understand why I was still alive. Why hadn't the explosion killed me? I felt like I was some sort of puppet, and that someone else was pulling my strings. One day, I was being made to fight; another day, I was being laid up in hospital, having to see so many people suffering around me. I was on a ward with a lot of other injured soldiers, but there were also a lot of sick civilians there - kids, old people, you name it, all waiting to be delivered from their own particular brand of suffering. Every night, the whole ward would be woken up by the pain-wracked cries of a different patient, and the doctors and nurses on call would mamash do everything they could to try helping them.*

*My parents had no idea how to handle the situation, so they tried to bury me in presents. They bought me an mp3 player, books, movies, they gave me anything I wanted. Anything, that is, except for their love and affection. I'm not blaming them, the poor souls. They also grew up in an environment where materialism and superficial values weren't just the main game in town, they were the only game in town. And all that unbridled materialism simply kills our inner dimension, and our humanity, and our ability to really connect to others, even the people we love. Anyway, I don't want to keep you up. You look really tired. Do you want to go to bed?"*

Tired? I couldn't even remember what tired felt like any more, I was so far gone. But it didn't seem nice to leave him hanging like that, in the middle of telling me his life history.

"Tired? Me? I'm like the Energizer Bunny; I can keep going all night..." I thought maybe I dreamt saying that, but he seemed to have heard me anyway, and continued with his story.

*"It was the morning of Rosh Chodesh Elul; I'd just come back from yet another round of physiotherapy to find a group of five chareidi guys walking around the halls. They had big white kippas and long, thick, rope-like side curls dangling from by their ears. They'd come to the ward to try and cheer up the injured soldiers and other patients and give out some small presents. They sang loudly, they danced crazily, and they really did manage to cheer a lot of us up.*

*I was observing them from a little way off, and I had very mixed feelings. On one hand, they looked like absurd, nutty people, but on the other hand, they really seemed to be filling the ward with a genuine sense of joy - and that was no small achievement. They were singing songs about 'Nachman, Nachman, Me'Uman' and other songs that I hadn't really heard before. I'd heard the name 'Nachman' previously from people's conversations and also from the 'Na Nach' graffiti that's all over the walls in Eretz Yisrael. But I'd never stopped before to think about who this Nachman actually was, because when you're healthy, you rush around living life and you don't stop to think about anything. But when you're laid up in hospital you're not going anywhere, and you have all the time in the world. So for the first time, I had a bit of space in my heart and in my head to start thinking deeply about things, and I was very curious to find out more about this 'Rebbe Nachman from Uman', who had followers who liked to sing about him.*

*I managed to get over my embarrassment enough to call one of the chareidi guys over, the one who looked like he was the leader of the group. I asked him what his name was, and he told me 'Nachman'. I asked him: 'Are all these guys singing about you?' and he started laughing hysterically. 'You think they're singing about me? That's hilarious! I should be so lucky to even get to the level of being the dirt under Rebbe Nachman's fingernails! I'm just named after him. The original Nachman is Rebbe Nachman of Breslev, who's buried in Uman.'*

*I wanted to know more, even though I had no idea why I was finding the whole idea of this 'Rebbe Nachman' quite so fascinating. Nachman the chassid told me that if I was really serious about learning more about Rebbe Nachman, I should come with him to Uman for Rosh Hashana, where I'd get lit up with such a big spiritual light that it would completely change my whole life.*

*It was such an unexpected answer that instead of satisfying my curiosity about Rebbe Nachman, it ignited it. Even though I had no idea why I'd want to go and what I'd even do in Uman or what the whole thing was really about, something about what Nachman said really appealed to me. I kept talking to Nachman (and here I'm getting ahead of myself and telling you how the story ends already), but by the end of our conversation, I'd made a firm decision that come what may, I was going to do everything in my power to go to Uman for Rosh Hashana. My soul was crying out for some answers, and the thought of going to Uman somehow gave me great comfort.*

*Of course, I knew that the biggest battle I'd have to fight to get there would be against my parents, who naturally would be completely opposed to the whole insane idea. I could hear them already, accusing me of having been brainwashed by religious people who'd just been telling me a bunch of superstitious nonsense and lying to me, like all the frummies do... And anyway, what sort of crazy person would want to go and visit the tomb of some dead rabbi who'd passed away more than 200 years ago anyway? The whole idea was preposterous!*

*You know, let's rewind a bit. After that initial meeting, Nachman the chassid came back to the hospital the next day with a book in his hand, and we ended up having another long conversation. He told me he wanted to read me a few of the stories about Rebbe Nachman's life. I was surprised he'd come back just to visit me, but what was even more surprising was that my sister Yael turned up on the ward at around the same time.*

*When I realized what was happening I started to feel somewhat anxious, because my sister (to put it mildly) hated all religious people with a passion, and she hated the black-hatted chareidim most of all. It wasn't so long ago that I'd been in exactly the same headspace, thinking that all these chareidim were rude, boorish parasites who fed off the State, were obsessed with maintaining the primitive lifestyle of their grandparents at any cost, and would stop at nothing to curtail the modern development of Israeli society. So I got ready for World War Three to explode around my bed.*

*As soon as she saw Nachman sitting there, she bristled, and the battle began. I didn't know what to do - should I ask my sister to come back and visit me another time, or should I ask Nachman to come back a bit later? In the end, I decided to let go and let the situation develop however it was going to, without getting too involved.*

# The Stolen Light

*Nachman immediately realized what was going on. He paused for a split second, but then just continued on doing what he'd been doing anyway, namely reading out an excerpt about the life of Rebbe Nachman: 'Rebbe Nachman of Breslev, z"l, was born in 5532 on Rosh Chodesh Nissan, on the holy Sabbath, in the Ukrainian city of Medhzibozh, to his holy father Rabbi Simcha, and his holy mother, the saintly Faige, the daughter of Udel, the daughter of the holy Baal Shem Tov, may the memory of the holy Tzaddik be for a blessing.'*

*My sister wasn't about to take that lying down. She immediately came back with her own biographical sketch: 'Binyamin Ze'ev Herzl was born more than 150 years ago, in the city of Kovno, to his mother Sarah and his father Rahamim, who was the son of Gershon the cobbler.'*

*Nachman smiled, and continued: 'Very nice! May all his merits serve to protect him. As I was saying, Rabbeinu was named after his holy grandfather, Rabbi Nachman Horodenker, z"l, who was one of the main students of the Baal Shem Tov, may the memory of the holy Tzaddik be for a blessing. When the time came for Rebbe Nachman to have his brit mila and receive his holy name, his saintly uncle Rabbi Baruch of Medhzibozh, the brother of Faige, read out the famous biblical passage: 'This one will comfort us'. And truly, anyone who walks along the path that Rabbeinu set out and learns his holy books and tries to live his teachings, really does feel comforted in the depth of their soul. Our battle-weary hearts are so tired from all the suffering we experience and all the apparently sweet but ultimately bitter illusions that fill our lives. But they really are soothed and comforted by Rebbe Nachman's Torah and advice.'*

*My sister fired right back: 'When Herzl was born and was given his name, his uncle announced that 'this one will build us a Jewish State, and in his merit, the Jewish people will be revived, and will become the nation of Israel.''*

*I tried to get my sister to calm down a bit, but it was very hard to get her to stop. And Nachman also didn't seem to be ready to call a cease-fire. He shot back with: 'Herzl in Hebrew spells out 'Tzel Har', the shadow of the mountain'. The mountain refers to our holy Patriarchs, who were really the ones that earned Eretz Yisrael for their descendants by virtue of their holiness and their hard spiritual work. It's in their merit that we have the land of Israel. But then Herzl came along and tried to overshadow all the holy achievements of our forefathers with his completely unholy nonsense about creating 'a modern state for a modern people'.*

*'Incidentally, do you know that Herzl has no living Jewish descendants, Israeli or otherwise? All his children converted out of the faith and completely assimilated. By contrast, and it really is like comparing light to darkness and life to death, Rabbeinu HaKadosh has hundreds of descendants living in Israel*

*today. He lived for 38 and a half holy years, and in that time he married two wives. His first holy wife was called Sashia the daughter of Rabbi Ephraim from Ossatin, and they were married in the Ukrainian city of Medvedevka. Rebbe Nachman had four daughters and two sons with his first wife. His first son was named Yaakov and his second Shlomo Ephraim, and both of them unfortunately died at a very young age. Rabbeinu, may the memory of the tzaddik be for a blessing, was completely devastated by the death of Shlomo Ephraim, and would tell his followers the most amazing things about his son's lofty potential, had he lived.'*

*'What, he wasn't 'devastated' when his first son Yaakov died as well? Only about the second one?' my sister was still bristling with antagonism.*

*'Rabbeinu was all heart; he used to say that when a Jew came to him in pain, he would feel that pain even more acutely than the person who was experiencing it firsthand. So it goes without saying that he also mourned the death of his first son Yaakov very, very deeply. A man who feels the suffering of every single one of his fellow Jews is of course going to feel the suffering of his own children incredibly deeply. His daughters were called Adel, Sarah, Chaya and Miriam. Two of his daughters also died at a young age. Rabbeinu held all of his offspring in the highest esteem, but he particularly praised the offspring of his daughter Sarah. And Sarah's offspring continue to be held in very high esteem even today, because Rabbeinu told his followers that our Holy Redeemer, the Moshiach, would come from his loins, and he implied that it would be one of her descendants.'*

*Yael couldn't hold herself back: 'He must have been completely in love with himself, to say things like that about himself and his descendants!'*

*At this point, I was convinced Nachman was going to let my sister have it, but instead, in his quiet, modest way he said, 'I can't really do justice to what I'm about to tell you, because it's an idea that contains the most profound depths. But there's a concept called 'Tzaddik yesod olam', or 'the Tzaddik, the foundation of the world.' The basic idea is that there is a tzaddik who is the spiritual pipeline for bringing every type of abundance into the world, both for the Jewish people and for everyone else. Moshe Rabbeinu had that job when he was alive, and in our generation, the Tzaddik yesod olam is Rebbe Nachman.'*

*'Nice idea, but he's been dead 200 years already!' My sister was clearly furious, and was making no effort to hide how angry she felt.*

*'Even when the Tzaddikim are dead, it's as though they're still alive. In fact, they can actually do more once they're no longer constrained by their physical bodies, when they just continue rising to higher and higher levels in the spiritual worlds.'*

# The Stolen Light

*'How do you even know all this stuff you're telling me is true?' my sister wanted to know. 'Did you ever meet someone that experienced all this stuff for themselves? Did any of these 'tzaddikim' ever show up here after they'd died to tell you all this? You people have such nerve - I don't understand how you can dare to give out your books full of your stupid theories, when all you're doing is stealing people's lives away! You're robbing children of their childhoods, you're oppressing women, and you just destroy everything you come into contact with!*

*'One of my friends, her husband made teshuva, and the next thing she knew, she was given an ultimatum: 'either you get religious, or we get divorced.' So they got divorced, and every time I see her with her two sad-looking kids, my heart breaks. And why did it happen? Because her moronic husband got the idiotic idea in his head that there's a 'Creator of the world' and that we all have to run around doing things to keep Him happy.'*

*I was rather embarrassed by my sister's rant, and I felt that she'd completely crossed the line in the way she'd spoken to Nachman. After all, the guy was only here because he was trying to help me recover some of my will to live. What gave her the right to come here and make me feel even more down than I already was? If she'd have bothered to look at me even once when she was trying to verbally rip Nachman apart, she would have seen that the things she was doing and saying were pulling me lower and lower. I didn't want to insult her so I couldn't tell her what I really felt, namely that she was acting like an egotistical maniac who was willing to completely trash the truths of other people just to try and prove herself right.*

*I mumbled something I'd recently heard, that one of the prophets said that: 'A man will live by his faith'. I had a great internal battle raging as I tried to calm my sister down again. On the one hand, I was worrying that Nachman the chassid would give up on me and stop telling me all the fascinating stuff about Rebbe Nachman that was like cool water on my parched soul; on the other hand, I didn't want to fight with my sister, especially as up until two days ago, we'd had exactly the same opinions. I couldn't tell her that something seemed to have changed in my thought process now, and that I was yearning for something different.*

*Luckily, Nachman didn't seem to be too fazed by my sister's brutal outburst, and he just picked up where he left off. He said: 'It's not that 'a man will live by his faith'; rather, it's a 'tzaddik, a righteous individual, will live by his faith', and that's something completely different. A lot of people think that they can wake up one morning and decide that they are now a person of truth and a person of faith, and that they now have the right to start dictating things to other people based on their own warped notions of what's right. When a person is really straight, when they're really a tzaddik, there is no 'them' in the picture; it's only what G-d wants, what G-d says.*

*'G-d is truth, and there can only be one truth. But once a person is distanced from G-d, they can tell as many lies as they want. Even the Nazis, yemach shemam, thought that their ideas were true and right. I can see you're genuinely upset about your friend. I want you to know that I was really listening to all your complaints and questions, and not only that, but with G-d's help, I'd like to try and address them, to the best of my ability. If you're really interested in getting some profoundly deep answers to the questions you raised, I'd be more than happy to arrange a meeting with you and a few of your friends, where you can ask me any questions you have and I'll do my best to answer them. I won't preach anything at you, I'll just do my best to respond to whatever questions you throw at me.*

*'Asking questions, particularly hard questions, is an essential part of our Yiddishkeit, and it's normally a very good thing. If a person didn't have any questions about G-d, then there'd be real reason to worry, because either it would mean they were living completely superficial lives, or that they believed themselves to be on a par with the Al-mighty. If a person believes they can perfectly fit G-d into their very limited human understanding and intellect, then they're really in trouble.*

*'Throughout Jewish history, there have always been difficult questions and difficult times, and there have always been ups and downs. That doesn't faze us. It's much better to be passionately angry about what's happening to us and around us than to be completely indifferent to it.'*

*It looked like Nachman's answer had completely blown my sister away. She sat there silently while Nachman opened his book and continued reading about the life of Rebbe Nachman:*

*'While he was still a child, he decided to separate from the world and to break his lust for eating. Already at the age of six, he would eat without tasting the food. He would make his food into a ball and swallow it straight down, without chewing. This sort of sacred devotion was usually only for older tzaddikim, but little Nachman was not scared of anything, and all he ever wanted to do was to fulfill the verse 'I place Hashem before me always'.*

*He was very diligent in his Torah studies. In addition to the wage that his father paid his Torah teacher, Nachman would give his teacher additional money for each extra page of Gemara they learnt together, to encourage the teacher to cover many pages of Gemara every day. He was very modest about his learning and learned in purity and simplicity. He testified about himself that he did not have a particularly sharp or quick mind in his youth; rather, he would cry to*

# The Stolen Light

*Hashem for hours on end that He would open his heart to the Torah. He would cry buckets of tears over every Mishna and over every page of Gemara, and only once he understood the simple meaning of the words would he continue on to the next page or next Mishna.*

*He always put a lot of effort into everything he did, and even though he had a number of ups and downs, he strengthened himself very much in order to continue doing his avodat Hashem. After every setback, he would simply begin anew without despairing, and in this way he made a number of new beginnings every day.*

*Rabbeinu spoke a great deal about bitul and about the importance of acting with humility and holy self-abasement, which are both required in order to reduce the ego. Bitul is a fundamental principle in the process of coming closer to the ultimate purpose, because you need to lower yourself in order to merit this revelation. A holy spark of Hashem exists in each of us, and this part is only revealed when we succeed in nullifying our individual self, or ego. So it was that he invested a great deal of effort in his own self-nullification.*

*In addition to Mishna and Gemara, he also learned the halachic decisors, the Tanach, the Ein Yaacov, the Zohar and other kabbalistic works, and all the writings of the Arizal. He said that he learned the book 'Reishit Chochmah', the Beginning of Wisdom[7], countless times. And further more, he would also undertake many fasts, and often would fast from just after the holy Shabbat until the next Shabbat.*

*He undertook all these things when he was still a youth, growing up amidst physical comfort, pleasures and games. But even so, he didn't have mercy on himself and in just one year, he fasted from Shabbat to Shabbat 18 times."*

'*So basically, you're telling us that Rebbe Nachman was a Buddhist, just like all the other truth-seekers wandering around India.*' Like I said, my sister wasn't going to go down without a fight. She'd keep it going until her very last breath.

'*The difference between the Jewish people and the idol-worshipping sects you're referring to is that when we do something, it's the real deal. If we're fasting or meditating, that's because it really is the way for us to connect to G-d, and to cleave to Him. With these other sects and religious cults, it's just an 'experience' in and of itself, or a way to try to attain some spiritual peace and quiet, but it's all rooted in vanity and nothingness.*

'*What's more, Jews don't believe in completely nullifying our physical nature; rather, we want to elevate and sanctify it. We use the material world to achieve*

---

[7] Authored by Rabbi Eliyahu Davidas

*very lofty spiritual levels. Do you want me to read you a bit more about Rabbeinu, or shall I stop here, and we'll do some more another time?' Nachman asked me. As you'd probably expect, I was keen to hear more. I was finding Nachman's personality and responses just as intriguing as the stuff he was reading about. So Nachman continued:*

*'Rabbeinu also told us that in his youth, he put a lot of effort into working on his avodat Hashem. Already at the age of six, he would wait for his parents to go to sleep, and then at midnight he would go out of the house to tovel in a mikveh. He would immerse himself in the icy waters of the lake even on the harshest winter days, and then from there he would run to the grave of his holy great-grandfather, the Baal Shem Tov, the founder of chassidut, who also had many books written about him, due to his immense holiness.*

*There, he would do hitbodedut until just before the morning, and then would return to his house a few minutes before his family woke up and creep into bed as though he'd been asleep the whole time. When his mother came to wake him up, she'd be mildly surprised that his payot were wet. And thus, he continued his secret holy devotions for years, without even one person knowing about his great efforts.*

*Once, he wanted Hashem to show him a sign in order to strengthen his emuna. He prayed a lot to Hashem about this, and three miracles were done for him.*

*The first miracle: it's known that Rabbeinu did a lot of hitbodedut, and in the place where he used to go to pray and try to totally cleave to G-d, there was a crucifix by the side of the road which he found very disturbing. He asked Hashem to do a miracle for him and uproot the cross from its place. His request was fulfilled, and suddenly, the cross was uprooted and fell to the ground.*

*The second miracle: when he was walking next to the river, he asked Hashem to arrange it that the fish would come into his hand without him having to use a fishing rod or net. And also here, his request was fulfilled, and the fish swam into his hand without him having to do anything.*

*The third miracle: he asked to see the soul of a dead person. He convinced Hashem to fulfill this request too, and suddenly, the soul of a dead person came to him. Rabbeinu was terrified because he was still just a youth, and this was the first time he'd seen a dead person. In addition to this, the dead soul that came to him had been a wicked person in his lifetime.*

*After this, Rabbeinu saw thousands more dead people, because it was known that Rabbeinu worked a lot to rectify the souls of the dead. There are many souls that wander around the world without a tikun, and their suffering is very great. Only the greatest tzaddikim know how to fix them, and how to help them rise up to Gan Eden, to the Garden of Souls, where they grow.'*

*My sister interrupted him: 'It really seems to me like you live in some sort of fantastic imaginary world! Where on earth do you get all these fairy tales from?' She was clearly just trying to get Nachman all riled up.*

*'I can't explain everything in one go, but there are seminars you can go to and plenty of Torah classes you can listen to that go into great detail and explain everything. You're correct that a lot of the phenomena Rebbe Nachman talks about sound fantastic, and once you've studied them in more depth you'll probably find them even more amazing, but for very different reasons. I'd be very happy to recommend some good classes, or even a couple of excellent Rabbis you could go to who are very learned about these topics and excellent speakers. After you hear them speak about the world to come, what happens to our souls after we die, and other interesting and amazing things like that, all the grey disappears, and you really start to understand the stark reality about our existence on this planet. Not everyone has the merit to really understand what's going on down here, because it's Hashem's will that only the people who really want the truth ever attain it.'*

*Yael liked to represent herself as the quintessential 'seeker of truth', and Nachman, in his gentle way, had just hinted to her that perhaps she wasn't as committed to finding the real truth as she liked to believe. Having dropped his quiet bombshell, Nachman returned to the book:*

*'In the year 5558, on the eve of Pesach, our holy teacher came out of the mikveh. Sometimes, Rabbeinu would spend an hour or even two in the freezing mikveh, despite being thin and physically weak. But he would go to any length in order to reveal truth, and so it was that he came out of the mikveh, and said to one of the chassidim with him that this year, he was definitely going to be in Eretz Yisrael. "Every part of my soul yearns to be there, and even though there will be many tremendous obstacles in the way, Hashem will do what is good in His eyes.'*

*And so it was that in the month of Iyar of that same year, he started his journey to Eretz Yisrael, which is a long and fascinating story in and of itself. Every single step that Rabbeinu took involved the most profound mysteries and secrets, which only he knew about. Once, he said, 'If the people of the world really knew what each one of my journeys was accomplishing, they would completely nullify themselves to me, and cheer my every step." But Rabbeinu wasn't at all interested in having fame and honor; his only motivation was ahavat Yisrael and love of G-d.*

*'Two days before Rosh Hashana, Rabbeinu, may the memory of the tzaddik be for a blessing, took his first step on the holy soil of Eretz Yisrael. Nobody can*

*even begin to imagine just how joyous Rabbeinu was to finally arrive in Israel and stand on its holy soil. At each moment, he would turn to his attendant and say: 'Ashrecha, that you merited to be here with me.'*

*My sister asked me if I wanted to eat something. I was completely hypnotized by the story of Rebbe Nachman's life, and I told her no. She got up to leave, and as she was walking off down the corridor, she threw over her shoulder: 'I really hope that when I come back in a few minutes, you'll still be exactly the same person that you are now, and not sitting there with a kippa and payot...'*

*Nachman continued to read: 'As soon as word got out that Rabbeinu had arrived in Eretz Yisrael, all the tzaddikim and Torah giants who lived in Eretz Yisrael sent messengers to Rabbeinu Hakadosh, asking him to come and reside with them. Then some messengers from Tiberias arrived, bearing a letter from that city's tzaddikim and community leaders, asking him to come and spend the festival of Sukkot there.*

*'First, Rabbeinu travelled to Haifa, where he spent some time in the cave of Elijah the Prophet, z"l, and then afterwards, he set out for Tiberias. There, he met the famous holy Rabbi Avraham Kalisker, and decided to stay with him. Afterwards, Rabbeinu Hakadosh went to visit the grave of his grandfather, Rabbi Nachman Horodenker. From there, he travelled on to visit the grave of Rashbi in Meron, and also the graves of Hillel the Elder and Shammai. From there, he went to the grave of Rabbi Kruspedai, and then on to Tzfat.*

*'There's a whole book that describes all his journeys in Eretz Yisrael in detail, and it's well worth reading. Anyway, he returned to Ukraine having made peace between many tzaddikim, and having helped a great many of the self-sacrificing Jews who lived in Israel amidst tremendous poverty and pressing need, solely in order to fulfill the mitzvah of living in the Holy Land.*

*'In the year 5562 in the month of Elul, Rabbeinu came to live in the city of Breslev, where his holy books were printed. Rabbeinu also wrote another two awesomely holy books that were lost to us, and he said that when the Mashiach came, he'd write a whole commentary on one of them. Moranu Rabbi Natan, his chief disciple and student, is buried in Breslev. Rabbeinu used to say about him that if he'd only come to live in Breslev in order to have Rabbi Natan as his student, that would have been enough of a reason by itself.*

*'Rabbeinu's time in Breslev passed relatively peacefully. It's told that upon his arrival in Breslev, he poured some Kiddush wine, and then repeatedly spilled some of it on to the ground. Then he said: 'Today, we are planting the name of the Breslever chassidim, and it will never be forgotten, for our people will always be called 'Breslevers', and this will continue for all generations.' Rabbeinu also set the three fixed times when his followers should travel to be*

*with him: Rosh Hashana, the Shabbat that falls in the middle of Chanuka, and on the holiday of Shavuot.*

*'Rabbeinu, may his memory be blessed, set it as a firm principle for all generations that his followers should travel to be with him for Rosh Hashana, and he told them on many occasions that 'nothing was bigger' than his Rosh Hashana. That's why every year, his chassidim gather together to spend Rosh Hashana at his holy burial place in Uman, in Ukraine. There are some amazing stories about how in the past, some Jews were willing to sacrifice everything they had to fulfill their Rebbe's request to be at his grave for Rosh Hashana. It's not like today, when you can get to Uman relatively easily just by jumping on a plane.*

*'Rabbeinu lived in Uman for less than three years, and he knew from the beginning that he was destined to be buried there. At the end of his life, Rabbeinu, may the memory of the tzaddik be for a blessing, was terminally ill with tuberculosis, and when he was sick, he used to cough incessantly, until he'd cough up massive quantities of blood.'*

Nachman paused for a second, and I could see a couple of tears glistening in his eyes. *'He was in a very bad way, physically, and none of his followers wanted to believe that the day of his death was drawing near. One day, Rabbeinu said to the shamash who was standing next to him, 'Behold, I don't fear death at all."*

*'Around the same time, Rabbeinu made a promise that was witnessed by two kosher witnesses, that when a person would come to his grave in Uman, whomever that person might be, and give a coin to charity and say the ten chapters of Psalms called the Tikun HaKlali, then Rabbeinu would do his utmost to span the breadth and depth of the heavens to help the person in question. It didn't matter what that person might have done, even if he'd committed the worst sins in the world. All he asked in return is that the person would undertake to not commit the sin again.*

*'Another thing Rabbeinu said was that his Rosh Hashana was an unparalleled spiritual innovation, and that Hashem Yitbarach knew that he hadn't acquired it because of his forefathers' merits, but only because Hashem had given him the present of really understanding what Rosh Hashana was all about.*

*'He said: 'It goes without saying that you, my followers, are of course all completely dependent on my Rosh Hashana; but even more than that, the whole world in its entirety is also dependent on my Rosh Hashana.'*

*'Rabbeinu, may his holy memory be blessed, departed this world peacefully on Tuesday afternoon, the 18<sup>th</sup> of Tishrei, 5571, in the middle of the festival of Sukkot. A few minutes before he died, Rabbi Natan held his holy hand and*

*hugged him, and bound himself to him. Then, Rabbeinu whispered to Rabbi Shimon, another one of his followers, to close the buttons on the cuffs of his shirt sleeves, and to comb out and clean his beard, which had some blood on it as a result of his last severe coughing fit.*

*'When the people around him saw that he was approaching the end, they started to murmur 'Crossing the Yabok', which are the passages you say about the tzaddikim. And our Rabbi and teacher Rabbi Natan, may his memory be blessed, cried out: 'Rebbe, Rebbe, why are you abandoning us?' and Rabbeinu HaKadosh turned his holy head and awesome face towards us, as if to say, 'I'm abandoning you?! Chas v'shalom.' And so, he returned his clean, pure, clear soul to his Maker, with enormous holiness and clarity of mind.*

*'When the people around him saw his holy body lying there, it seemed as though he was smiling, and his face was bathed in an amazingly graceful and wonderful light. He looked so beautiful that there aren't the words for those who witnessed this awesome sight to even try to describe it. He also recounted the supernatural circumstances surrounding his burial: blinding lights covered the area of the grave and then those who were responsible for burying him found that Rabbeinu was already lying on the ground, in the grave, without them putting him there. From this they understood that those who had actually buried him, and who had involved themselves in his holy burial, had been ministering angels. May his merit always protect us, and all of Am Yisrael, Amen, v'Amen.'*

*I hadn't noticed at the time, but while Nachman was telling Rabbeinu's life story, a sizeable group of people had gathered around him, including some of the ward's medical personnel. They were all hanging on to every word of Nachman the chassid's story, told in his quiet, hypnotic, passionate way, where every so often he'd wipe away a tear. I felt that something profound had stirred in my soul, and I asked him to tell me more. Even then, I could clearly tell that some Divine Providence, or hashgacha, was pushing me towards Rebbe Nachman, although at that point I still didn't know enough to call it 'hashgacha'.*

*Even though I didn't grow up with any real Jewish foundation, I still had my secular, leftist, pacifist values until I'd joined the army. But once I went into active army service, I'd even had to let go of those, and I felt an aching void inside of me. I had the weird feeling that Nachman was some sort of holy conduit to help me fill that void with G-d and Torah and mitzvot. As he spoke, powerful feelings of wanting to return to G-d redoubled themselves in my heart, and it was clear to me that I was turning a page in my life, and that it was the beginning of something awesomely different and new.*

*Nachman closed his book and looked like he was getting ready to leave. Without exception, everybody who'd been listening to him speak begged him to continue a little bit more. Desolation, distress and fear of death were regular visitors on our ward, and the chassidim had a way of softening up even the toughest characters. Even the people who had reputations for being as hard as nails and appeared to have no emotions in their normal life were completely hypnotized by Nachman.*

*There was a chareidi guy on the ward who had made a big show of not listening to a word that Nachman said. But as the crowd around grew bigger and bigger, this guy had ended up joining it. He said, 'But you know, there's a lot of controversy around Rabbi Nachman, and not everyone agreed with his teachings or his practices. Even today, not everyone agrees with his teachings.'*

*'It's very interesting that people seem to know so much about all the controversy around Rabbeinu, but that very few people talk about all the big rabbis who fully supported him,' replied Nachman the chassid, and he started to read out passages that described what some of the Gedolei HaDor had said about Rebbe Nachman.*

*'Rabbi Levi Yitzhak of Berditchev, who was the undisputed spiritual leader of his generation, told his students: 'Believe me, if I thought the world would listen to me, I would scream out in a loud voice from one end of the world to the other, that whoever truly wanted to be a sincere, kosher Jew and sincerely serve Hashem, should make every effort to get close to the holy Rabbi, Rebbe Nachman of Breslev.'*

*Nachman the chassid continued to read out other things that famous rabbis had written or said in praise of Rebbe Nachman and his holy teachings. He started to recount the very well known story involving Rabbi Yehuda Tzedaka, the respected rosh yeshiva of Yeshiva Porat Yosef, who heard the university friend of some of his students making fun of something they'd just read in Rebbe Nachman's writings. He told him, 'Anyone who approaches this book in sincerity and truth will certainly open up all the pathways of their heart, and will completely repent and return to G-d.'*

*This same student then went and told his friends that even if he studied all of Rebbe Nachman's works in depth, he could guarantee them that he'd still never make teshuva.*

*And so it was that this student started diligently studying Rabbeinu's works and exploring the depth of Rebbe Nachman's approach to life. Slowly, slowly, he started to change. Eventually, he became a baal teshuva and ended up leaving the university completely. Rabbi Tzedaka summed it up when he said: 'You see what amazing power is contained in the teachings of Rebbe Nachman of Breslev.'*

*Nachman the chassid continued teaching, and told us some of the amazing, incredible things that Rebbe Nachman had said about himself, for example: 'I don't have any of my own spiritual work to do in this world at all... I only came to the world in order to bring Jewish souls closer to Hashem Yitbarach,' or 'The world has barely had a taste of me yet. If people would hear just one of my Torah teachings from my lips together with its tune and dance, the whole world would become completely nullified in spiritual bliss, including all the animals and plants and everything else that exists in the world, from the incomparably great joy that they would feel.'*

*Everyone who was gathered around my bed - the patients, nurses, and even some of the other visitors - all thanked Nachman for telling us his interesting stories, and a few of them even asked him for his number so they could get in touch with him afterwards. Nachman was so happy that telling over Rabbeinu's life story had seemed to touch so many people, and I could see that even my sister seemed to be less antagonistic than before. That's not to say that she said anything nice to Nachman, because she hadn't, but I knew her well enough to see that something had started to soften up inside of her.*

*The crowd began to disperse, but many of the people continued to discuss the fascinating ideas they'd just heard from Nachman, and some of them continued to gather around him, asking him more questions. Once everyone had gone, Nachman turned to me and said, 'Now that I've told you more about Rabbeinu, and now that we've already discussed you coming with me to Uman for Rosh Hashana, I'd like you to tell me a bit more about yourself, including how you ended up here, and how you got injured.'*

*With that question, all sorts of different emotions started to flood in, and I began to feel somewhat vulnerable. All of a sudden, my brain was overwhelmed with questions: what was I doing here? How was I going to cope with all my new feelings, including the nascent emuna that had just started circulating around my heart? My injured leg throbbed very painfully; in the distance, I could see the doctors starting on their rounds, so I asked Nachman if he could come back again tomorrow, because usually after the doctors did their rounds, I'd try to go to sleep straight afterwards to help me cope with the newly-aroused pain.*

*We parted on very good terms, almost like brothers. Nachman gave me a big hug, and it was the first time in my life that anyone had ever done that to me. Even my parents had never hugged me, and to this day, I can still remember how amazing it felt..."*

Zevik suddenly broke off from his story to ask me: "Do you maybe want to go to bed? You look really tired."

Honestly, I was completely wasted. I'd been 'tired' around four hours ago and now, at three in the morning, I was something approaching dead. But what could

# The Stolen Light

I do? I'd gotten hooked on his story, and now I just had to find out what happened next. So despite my exhaustion, I asked him to continue.

*"That whole night, I tossed and turned in my bed. I kept trying to imagine what Rebbe Nachman must have looked like, and my admiration for him just kept growing. It was like he'd somehow morphed into the hero of all the stories I'd loved as a child, and I couldn't wait for Nachman the chassid to come back again the next day. We'd agreed that he'd come and visit me in the morning, but the next day, morning came and went - and there was no Nachman. The day continued, and I started to feel uneasy; my stomach started flipping over, and I had the weird sense that maybe something had happened to him. I got even more worried as the evening visiting hours came and went, and Nachman still hadn't shown up.*

*But even though Nachman didn't come back, I had other visitors, namely my parents, who'd been filled in on all the gory details about the 'missionary' who'd been 'trying to brainwash me' yesterday by my sister. They'd come to conduct some brainwashing of their own, to make sure that I wouldn't fall for any of the 'lies' those black-hatted ghetto Jews (who were only interested in bleeding the State dry) were telling me.*

*I completely switched off. I didn't even try to get into it with them, because in my heart I knew that the new path I wanted to go down was for sure more sensible and more correct than the path I'd been going down for many years already with my parents. That night, once again, I was tossing and turning in bed and yearning for it to be morning already, because I was really hoping that Nachman would come visit me. I couldn't believe I hadn't taken his phone number.*

*Morning came, and the hospital was in a frenzy of activity because of a serious terrorist attack that had just happened in Haifa. A suicide bomber wearing an explosive belt had just detonated himself in Haifa's central bus station. By some miracle, the only person who died in the attack was the terrorist himself, yemach shemo, and dozens of first responders and ambulances were quickly despatched to the scene to help the injured and get them to hospital quickly.*

*The wounded people were brought to the Rambam hospital, ranging from the seriously injured to people who had sustained medium or light injuries. The whole hospital was put on high alert to deal with the emergency situation caused by the terrible terrorist attack. I lay on my bed in the ward trying to fight off all the feelings of worry and unease that were crowding into my head, both for the people who'd just been injured in the suicide bombing, and also for Nachman, whom I was still desperately hoping would show up. The hours ticked by, until once again the evening visiting time was over, and Nachman still hadn't come.*

*In my heart, I started to fear that maybe Nachman had lost interest in me, or gotten too caught up with his own life to give me any more time and attention. It's not like he'd known me before he visited the hospital that first time, and whatever time we'd already had together was the extent of our connection. Just as I started to think that I was never going to see Nachman again, I remembered one of the things he'd told me: 'Ein shum ye'oush ba'olam klal! There is no despair in the world!' I felt a wave of joy burst into my heart, and I buzzed the nurse who was assigned to look after me and asked her to please bring me a siddur, a book of Psalms, and a kippa from the hospital synagogue.*

*She brought me the things I'd asked for and then asked me in a worried tone, 'Did that guy manage to catch you in his net?' I didn't respond. I just got busy with the siddur she'd brought me, and afterwards, I decided to read a few chapters of Psalms - and that in particular did me a world of good. It didn't make any sense, logically, but I felt like the words I was reading were somehow helping my wounds to heal - and then I just couldn't stop myself from continuing. I think I read the whole book of Psalms; then prayed the morning, afternoon and evening prayers, and everything in between - but even that wasn't enough for me. I felt like I was swimming in the most wonderfully sweet waters, and experiencing the most beautiful things I'd ever experienced in my life in that sea of Torah and prayer.*

*I felt such a deep inner contentment and happiness about the process I seemed to be going through. I asked the nurse if she could arrange for someone to assist me to get to the hospital's synagogue at least once a day so I could pray with a minyan, and also hear the hospital's rabbi give his daily Torah class. But at the same time, I also took my kippa off my head, because I didn't want to wear it until and unless I was really committed to being a sincerely observant Jew.*

*Rosh Chodesh Elul had only been a few short days ago, and now here I was already, going to synagogue to pray for the first time ever. When I got there, some avreich appeared out of nowhere, and asked me if I'd liked to lay tefillin. That was the real turning point for me. As soon as the guy finished arranging the tefillin boxes on my head and my arm, I was overwhelmed by the most intense feeling of joy I'd ever experienced in my life - it was a thousand times stronger than any other pleasurable experience I'd ever had. I could suddenly see so clearly how so many people were wasting their lives chasing after rubbish and false promises of pretend happiness and fulfillment.*

*It struck me how empty my life had been up until now, without this connection to the Creator of the world, my Abba in shamayim. That was the very first time I'd ever laid tefillin, because remember, I'd spent my bar mitzvah in Disneyland with my family and grandparents. On the very day that I should have been embracing the yoke of Torah and mitzvot for the first time, I was walking along with a bunch of man-sized puppets, going up and down on roller-coasters and stuffing my face with American ice-cream and traif burgers from McDonalds, Hashem should have mercy on me.*

*I finished praying the Amidah prayer, and then turned around - and who did I see in the back corner of the synagogue, but Nachman the chassid! But now, he was in a wheelchair, and was covered in bandages from head to foot. Shocked, I looked him up and down, blinking my eyes in disbelief. It really was him! Now it was Nachman's turn to look at me half-disbelievingly. My heart filled with joy, and I felt the happiest I'd ever felt to see another human being, albeit one that I actually barely knew. I couldn't stop hugging and kissing him, because it was like a hole in my soul had just filled up. Nachman asked me to stay behind once the morning prayers were finished, so that we could speak."*

## Chapter 11

*Zevik the brave soldier tells us the story of Nachman the chassid, and about Yaacov, and about the Army Liaison Officer's sister, Vered... and also a little bit about hitbodedut.*

I was already basically hallucinating; I was so exhausted, I thought maybe I was dreaming the whole thing. But what could I do? Zevik had already offered to stop and let me go to bed a few times already, and I'd refused, so now I was backed into a corner. But on top of that, his story was so fascinating that I really wanted to know how it ended. So Zevik paused for breath, and then continued:

*"After prayers, I sat down next to Nachman and asked him why he hadn't shown up for our meeting. It sounds a bit strange, but I was so happy to see him that it didn't really cross my mind to ask him why he was sitting in a wheelchair covered in bandages.*

*Nachman started telling me his story: 'The second I left your bedside, I was rushing to get to my regular learning session that I'd arranged with my study partner in the kollel. As I was making my way over there, I decided to swing past my house first, to pick up a couple of interesting books that I wanted us to look at. If I'd been thinking straight, I'd have just gone straight to my meeting with my chavruta because I was already running late, but something clicked in my brain, and almost without meaning to, I found myself walking towards my home.*

*I was almost there when I spotted my neighbor Yaacov, who just that day had been released on parole from prison. He was the oldest son of my neighbors, who were a good family who kept mitzvot and had a lot of yirat shamayim. Yaacov had simply fallen in with a bad crowd from our neighborhood, a bunch of hotshots who slowly pulled Yaacov away from his family and into a lot of trouble. Ultimately, Yaacov decided to leave home and go live with his irresponsible friends.*

# The Stolen Light

*One night, they decided to break into a jewellery store in one of the more upscale areas of Haifa - but what they didn't realize was that the whole area was full of security cameras. It didn't really matter that they'd manage to successfully pull off their heist, because their faces had been clearly captured on the security videos and it was simply a matter of time until the law caught up with them. After a few days of intensive investigation, the police managed to track down Yaacov and most of his partners in crime, but not before the 'brains' behind the robbery had already left town, together with all the stolen goods.*

*Yaacov didn't want to make a bad situation worse, so he confessed to the crime in the hope that they would go a bit easier on him when it came to sentencing. They didn't, and Yaacov and his friends were sentenced to four years in prison for their part in the robbery.*

*While he was sitting in prison, Yaacov had plenty of time to think about the circumstances that had gotten him there, not least that he'd left his parents' home to follow his 'friends' into a life of vice, crime, and debauchery. Now, there was a Breslev chassid in Yaacov's cell, who'd been incarcerated for a few days for failing to pay his ex-wife's alimony. The chassid spent hours talking to him about what he himself had done wrong, and how he needed to fix things. Yaacov soaked up all his words of teshuva, until he also was moved to start looking at the sins he'd committed in his past.*

*After a short time, Yaacov submitted a request to the prison guards to be moved to the shomer Shabbat block of the prison, which would take him far away from the bad friends who had already gotten him into so much trouble. Yaacov told me that the prison guards could see that he wasn't cut from the same cloth as the rest of the crew, so they decided to help him come up with a ruse to leave his existing block without raising the ire of the prison management, who usually tried to stop prisoners from moving around unless there was a very good reason for it. The guards advised Yaacov to pretend he felt unwell, then they'd take him along to the hospital infirmary for a check-up. From there, it would be fairly straightforward to transfer him over to the shomer Shabbat wing.*

*So that's what happened. Yaacov got transferred to the new wing and very quickly struck up a close relationship with the prison rabbi, who would sit with him for hours discussing the pointlessness and emptiness of a life of crime. They also had some very deep discussions about how to deal with the feelings of regret that were starting to bubble up in Yaacov's heart; regrets about what he'd done, about turning his back on his faith, and how he'd hurt his parents. When he started talking about his family, Yaacov burst into tears, and begged the rabbi to help him arrange some sort of meeting with his mother and father so that he could ask for their forgiveness.*

*The prison Rabbi agreed to act as the middle man, and sent Yaacov's parents a heartfelt letter, where he described their son's great remorse for what he'd done and for all the embarrassment, pain and shame his actions had caused them, because Yaacov really had gotten himself involved in a lot of bad things.'*

*Nachman told me that by the time he happened to meet Yaacov on the street, he was already well on his way to making complete teshuva, and had even grown a little beard. He'd appeared to Nachman like a completely different person.*

*Nachman continued: 'Yaacov asked me how I was doing, and then he asked me if I had a bit of time to talk because there was something important bothering him that he needed to discuss with someone. We went over to sit in the local park, which was a relatively calm, peaceful spot full of trees and bushes, and Yaacov started to speak. I could see that he looked somewhat depressed, so I tried to give over some words from Rebbe Nachman to encourage him.*

*I told him how important it was to try to be happy, and that it didn't matter what a person had done in his life, he still needed to make every effort to be happy. I told him what the Rambam wrote, that if someone committed a sin, the way to make teshuva for it was to firstly regret what they'd done, then confess what they'd done, then take it upon themselves not to repeat their sin again in the future - and that was it. There was nothing in there that said a person needed to fall into despair, or that they should feel sad and depressed, or that they should beat themselves up about what a terrible person they were. Remember, Rebbe Nachman taught us Ein ye'oush ba'olam klal! There is no despair in the world! The whole point is to not feel afraid, and to believe with all our hearts that everything can and will be turned around for the good. A mere human can't understand what G-d's doing, but we can and must believe that it's all for the best.*

*Yaacov responded that it was very hard for him to really believe what I'd just told him, and started talking about the concept of reward and punishment, asking why so many apparently random things, both good and bad, happen to people. So we got into a serious discussion about all these things, which are big questions, but also pretty standard questions that are addressed and answered by our holy sages and Rabbis in their writings.*

*For example, the Gemara talks in depth about the idea of 'a tzaddik, and things are bad for him, and a rasha, or evil person, and things are good for him.' Of course, not everyone needs a very deep answer to their questions; sometimes it's just enough to give them the chance to talk and to sort through what they're really feeling. In any case, I said to Yaacov, 'Come, let me tell you the amazing story from the Gemara about Rabbi Yehoshua ben Levi and Elijah the Prophet'. And this is what I told him:*

# The Stolen Light

*The great Rabbi Yehoshua ben Levi decided that he wanted to meet Elijah the Prophet. Rabbi Yehoshua prayed to Hashem that He should answer his prayers and fulfill his request to have Elijah the Prophet revealed before him. Hashem obliged, and Elijah the Prophet suddenly appeared before Rabbi Yehoshua, and asked him, 'What do you want?' Rabbi Yehoshua replied: 'I want to see what you do in the world.' The Prophet said. 'I cannot give you what you ask for.' Rabbi Yehoshua asked him why, and Elijah the Prophet answered him, 'Because you are going to see things that you aren't going to be able to stand.' Rabbi Yehoshua replied. 'Even so, I still want to come with you and see.' The Prophet relented and agreed.*

*And so, the two of them set off together. As night fell, they turned toward the hovel of a very poor couple, and asked them if they could stay the night. The only thing this poor couple owned in the world was a small cow. The poor man gave them a very warm welcome, generously gave them whatever they wanted to eat and to drink, and treated them throughout their stay with tremendous honor and respect. When the clock struck midnight, Elijah the Prophet got up and struck the couple's cow a fatal blow on its head. When Rabbi Yehoshua saw this, he exclaimed, 'G-d forbid, that Elijah the Prophet should have done such a thing! Even the most wicked person in the world wouldn't have done something like that! How could you have done such a terrible thing, when you knew full well that the cow was this poor couple's only asset? Is this how you reward them for all the kindness and hospitality they showed us?'*

*Elijah the Prophet replied, 'If you ask me any more questions, I'm going to leave you behind and you won't be able to come with me any more. So if you want to continue our journey, keep quiet and don't ask me any more questions about what I'm doing!'*

*The second night, the two lodged at the home of a very rich man, who was so selfish and self-absorbed that he didn't even nod a greeting in their direction or get up from his place to help them find a place to sleep. Nor did he offer them any food or drink. At the stroke of midnight, Elijah the Prophet got up, as did Rabbi Yehoshua. Elijah said to him, 'Take a bit of this sand, and help me,' and together, they built the wealthy man a fabulous castle, with 180 rooms.*

*Rabbi Yehoshua wondered out loud: 'The first person we stayed with, the poor man, welcomed us to his house, served us food and drink, and heaped honor upon us. In the night, you got up and killed his cow - his sole source of income. Now for this rich man who barely acknowledged us and certainly hasn't troubled himself to do even the smallest thing for us, you got up and built him a splendid castle overnight! If this man had tried to build this castle himself, it would have taken him months, or even years to complete it.'*

*Next, the pair travelled on to a new location where everyone was rich, and so incredibly arrogant that they didn't even want to look at this pair of wise men who had arrived in their town, much less offer them anything to eat or drink. The next day, Elijah the Prophet prayed for the people of the town that G-d should make them all successful leaders. They travelled on and came to a place where everyone was poor. As soon as the townspeople spotted the two wise men, they came running up to offer them help and hospitality. They gave them food and drink, and accorded the pair great honor. The following day, Elijah prayed for them that G-d should have compassion on them and grant them just one successful leader.*

*Rabbi Yehoshua ben Levi had had enough, and he said to Elijah the Prophet, 'I can't stand what you're doing anymore! I insist that you tell me what's going on.' Elijah said to him: 'If I explain everything to you, you won't be allowed to come with me any more.' Rabbi Yehoshua agreed, but insisted that Elijah tell him why he killed the cow of the first poor couple, who were relying on it to put food on the table. Elijah the Prophet responded, 'You should know that on that fateful night, there was a decree that the poor man's wife should die, and she was dearer to him than many thousands of gold coins. So I got up and killed the cow in her stead, so that it should be a kapara for the poor man's wife, a soul in place of a soul.'*

*Then Rabbi Yehoshua ben Levi said to him: 'Why then did you build that tremendous palace for the rich man who didn't so much as look at us, let alone offer us anything to eat or drink?' Elijah the Prophet replied, 'Know that if that rich man had managed to dig three amot down on that piece of land, he would have found an enormous treasure. I didn't want that to happen, so I girded my loins and built him a castle on that exact spot. That castle won't last very long, because it's made of miracles, and soon, it's going to collapse back into dust.'*

*Rabbi Yehoshua asked him: 'What about the blessing you gave to those rich misers we passed, that they should all become leaders?' Elijah replied, 'That wasn't a bracha, it was a curse! When you have a large number of leaders, it always ends very badly. Everyone knows that 'too many cooks spoil the broth'. That's why when we met that village of poor people who treated us so kindly, I blessed them that they should only have one leader, because when there's only one person in charge, a town can make a lot of progress.'*

*Nachman the chassid continued: 'Yaacov really cheered up when he heard that story, and started to realize that we really don't understand what's going on - which is why we need to accept everything that happens to us with love. We continued talking for a long time after that, until we agreed that Yaacov would come with me to a shul in town where I could introduce him to one of the rabbis I knew there whom I felt could really help him.*

# The Stolen Light

*On the bus there I told Yaacov a few more gems from Rebbe Nachman, like some of his advice about making parnassa. Rebbe Nachman teaches that whenever someone finds themselves in a situation that's making them angry, they should know that they are being tested from Above. Heaven wants to send that person a lot of money or the particular salvation they need, but before that happens, they first send them the test of anger. If the person doesn't get angry, then they get the bounty that's been earmarked for them, but if they do get mad, they lose it all.*

*The trip really wasn't going too well. We were stuck in a traffic jam for ages, along with thousands of other people. We heard over the radio that the police had set up a number of roadblocks to try and catch a terrorist that they'd been alerted was making his way into the city. Almost every crossroads was swarming with army and police people, and they were pulling tons of vehicles over to the side of the road to check them.*

*With busses, they were ordering all the passengers off and checking each and every one of them before letting them back on. The whole time, Yaacov and I were sharing our life stories. He was telling me all about what had happened to him up until that point, and about his family and his parents who'd been completely broken when their son had been sent to prison. Yaacov was obsessed with finding some way of compensating his parents for all the pain he'd caused them when he'd left their home and got mixed up with his bad friends.*

*He told me that only now, four years later, had he sobered up enough from his past to really be able to look at what had happened to him and start absorbing how his actions had wrecked his life and left an indelible stain on his character and prospects that was going to be very hard to clean off.*

*We were so engrossed in our conversation that we weren't really paying attention to the scene going on around us or really looking at what was happening with all the soldiers and police. We were in the middle of a profound conversation from the heart. I'm also a baal teshuva, so I could really get where he was coming from, and I was telling him about all the doubts and problems and barriers I'd had to overcome when I started to make teshuva.*

*Suddenly, we heard an incredibly loud explosion, which literally tore us out of our seats, ripped the seats themselves out of their places, and shattered all the windows, covering us with shards of glass.*

*There was a moment of silence, and then the air was filled with the most appalling cries and screams, as the injured passengers started crying for help. The stench of roasted flesh hung in the air, and as the smoke started to clear, a terrible scene of carnage and devastation emerged.*

*I started to check myself, and felt that my whole body was hot and sticky. I looked down, and saw that I was completely covered with blood. That's when I realized that I'd been injured in the blast. Thanks to my body's inbuilt coping mechanism, the pain didn't start immediately then, only a little while later.*

*I couldn't see very well because my eyes were very blurry, but I still tried to find Yaacov. I spotted him lying on his stomach on the left side of the bus. He'd sustained some very serious injuries to his back, arms and legs, and it was so hard to see him mangled like that. I called his name, but he didn't answer. Right next to me, there was a man who'd been killed in the explosion, and I was gripped with a tremendous fear that Yaacov was also dead. I tried to call his name again even louder, but no sound came out of my mouth, I think because I was in shock.*

*I could hear the sound of the ambulance sirens rushing to the scene, and the thought that help was on the way revived me somewhat. With my last ounce of strength, I dragged myself over to Yaacov, and pretty much collapsed when I got next to him. I called his name again, and this time, I heard something like a sigh escape from his lips. I thanked G-d that Yaacov wasn't dead, and I started to recite some prayers and some chapters of Psalms until I think I must have passed out, because the next thing I knew I woke up in the trauma wing of the hospital, here. I was completely blind and could barely move. It was only with the greatest difficulty that I could even turn my head a little bit from side to side.*

*I could hear that my family members were standing next to my bed praying, and the doctors were rushing around me hooking me up to all kinds of machines. I heard one doctor telling my wife that they had to urgently get me into surgery if they wanted to save my eyesight. He said that it was too early to tell for sure, but it was very possible that I'd been permanently blinded because the force of the blast had dislodged the optical nerve in my brain. Not only that, but the injury I'd sustained to my nervous system could also leave my whole body permanently paralyzed.*

*It took me a moment to absorb that as well as potentially losing my sight, I could also be permanently crippled for life. I tried to speak, but couldn't get a single sound to come out of my mouth. I started rapidly blinking my eyes, hoping that someone would notice that I was awake, and luckily, my youngest son Benny saw me and screamed to my wife and the doctors: 'Abba opened his eyes! Abba opened his eyes!'*

*My wife came over to me sobbing, and told me that the doctors wanted me to have an operation to try and save my sight. I don't know why I reacted like this, but I suddenly had this very strong gut reaction that I didn't want the operation. Somehow, I managed to signal to my wife that I didn't consent to the surgery.*

# The Stolen Light

*Of course, the doctors didn't want to let it go at that, so they started telling my wife that we were taking an enormous gamble by not operating. Once again, I signalled to my wife that I was completely against having the operation - period.*

*The whole time this was going on, I didn't stop praying. I was pouring out one prayer after another to G-d, and then also started appealing to Rabbeinu to help me. I promised him that if he would help me get out of the terrible circumstances I found myself in, every year I would try to bring 10 new people to Uman for Rosh Hashana. For the next few hours, I kept pleading my case before G-d and reiterating my promise to bring 10 people to Uman, if I'd get the miracle I so desperately needed.*

*I could hear that my family was under an incredible amount of pressure from the doctors to reverse their decision. Literally every couple of minutes, some doctor would come into the room to tell them that time was of the essence, and each minute that passed made it less and less likely that they could save my vision.*

*'The optical nerve is central to the whole nervous system, and if you don't act soon, your husband is going to be blinded and paralyzed for life! This is not the time to be an extremist; your husband's whole life is hanging in the balance. It's completely irresponsible of you to delay the surgery.'*

*My family started discussing among themselves the possibility that maybe it was too big a decision for me to have made by myself, and that they should talk to a rav to find out what to do. The doctors brought in the hospital rabbi, who also tried to persuade my wife to agree to the operation. 'Give the doctors permission to heal!' he told her, paraphrasing the famous quote from the Talmud. I could see that my wife was starting to waiver and lose faith that I'd made the right decision for myself. But I wasn't relying on myself, but on Rabbeinu, who always told his students to stay away from doctors as much as possible.*

*Still, I was praying intensely with the last drop of my strength until I fell into a very deep sleep. I started dreaming, and in my dream, I saw Rabbeinu walk over to my bed. He was smiling at me, and his smile made me feel so good and so full of joy. In a soft, beautiful voice he said to me, 'Get up and stand on your feet!' I replied, "Rabbeinu, I can't! I can't feel my legs, and I'm also blind!" Rebbe Nachman gently gave me his hand to hold, and said to me, 'Do you believe me, or your own eyes and legs? Take my hand, and stand up.'*

*So I grabbed his hand, and the instant I did, I felt this amazing sensation, like electrical currents zooming all over my body. I got up and stood next to my hospital bed as if absolutely nothing had just happened to me. 'Start walking,' he told me, and it's simply impossible for me to tell you how pleasant and warm Rabbeinu's voice sounded in my dream. I started walking, and he kept pace with me at my side. Suddenly, I heard an amazing niggun that I'd never heard before, like thousands of people were playing and singing this incredible tune of d'vekut and joy. Rabbeinu started dancing with me - probably only for a minute - but that minute felt like it lasted for all eternity. I can't begin to describe how beautiful that dance was.*

*Rabbeinu stopped dancing, turned to me, and said: 'Don't forget to bring lots of people to me in Uman every year for Rosh Hashana, like you promised. The whole redemption of Am Yisrael depends on us making more and more houses[8] there. Don't forget that my Rosh Hashana is greater than anything else!' and with that, he disappeared.*

*I woke up back in my hospital bed. My wife was asleep on one of the armchairs and the place was quiet. I could see a few lights turned on, so I realized that it must have been the middle of the night. I can see! I thought to myself. What are these doctors talking about, 'permanently blinded?' They are the ones with the sight problems! But I didn't let myself get too excited yet, because the thought crossed my mind that perhaps I was still dreaming.*

*Next, I decided to try to get out of bed - and I did. I still didn't quite believe that my legs were working, because still I worried that I was dreaming. I started calling to my wife: 'Batya! Batya!' My wife woke up with a look of utter shock on her face. 'What are you doing?!' she asked me. 'I'm going to the bathroom,' I told her. 'You can't! You're blind and paralyzed! You can't stand up!' She called after me, but I was already off to the toilet.*

*My wife started screaming, 'He can see, and he can walk around!' In less than a minute, the on call doctor, three nurses and a few other patients who'd heard the commotion arrived at my bedside. Everyone looked panicked. 'What's going on here?' the doctor asked my wife. 'My husband can walk!' she told him. She started calling up the entire family to tell them the amazing news. 'It's a miracle, a complete miracle! Nachman can walk!'*

*I couldn't stop smiling; I was grinning this huge grin, from ear to ear. 'I'm starving hungry,' I told one of the nurses. 'Is there anything to eat?' The nurses took my request to the doctor, and I couldn't understand why they needed the doctor's permission to give me a sandwich. The doctor came over to me and said, 'Don't move! Every single step you take could seriously endanger your vision.' I told him: 'I just saw Rabbeinu, and if I saw Rabbeinu, my eyesight is just fine! I'm standing on the two legs that my Creator gave me back as a present, looking out the two eyes that the Creator gave me back as a present, and everything is fine. I'm not endangering anything. It's time to dance, not get all stressed out.' The doctor looked completely shocked, but I felt on top of the world.*

---

[8] See Likutey Moharan II, 8:6

# The Stolen Light

*'You are blind and paralyzed! It's impossible for you to walk, I saw that clearly from your x-rays!' he shouted at me. I was laughing hysterically. 'The x-rays can show whatever they want, but you can see with your own eyes that I'm OK, and that I'm walking around in front of you. Do you want me to stay blind and paralyzed, G-d forbid, just so you can say the x-rays were right?' The doctor was in unchartered waters, and he had no idea what to do next. He was so agitated that he was almost hysterical. 'We have to get you x-rayed right now!' he started shouting at me again. 'Save the film,' I told him, but he wouldn't hear of it, and took me off to be x-rayed.*

*There was another expert doctor there, and the two of them spent ages poring over the new x-rays, and comparing them with the previous ones. 'The optical nerve has moved back to its place,' one whispered to the other. 'But that simply can't be!' replied the second. 'It's impossible for nerves to do that by themselves, unless someone opened his head up and moved them back without us knowing...'*

*If that doctor would have only known that Rebbe Nachman was the one who'd opened up my head, he'd have fainted on the spot. I chuckled to myself. The second doctor was saying, 'He must have made some sort of weird movement in his sleep, which jolted the nerve back into place.' The guy really had no idea what he was talking about, but doctors are supposed to know the reasons for everything, so he kept going regardless. 'No, that's impossible,' replied the other doctor. 'This is an interior nerve. It can't be jolted from the outside, only invasive surgery can get to it.' At that point I decided to come clean, and told them: 'Rabbeinu put my optical nerve back into its right place.'*

*'While it appears that your sight has been fixed, your brain functions are clearly still damaged,' opined the big expert doctor. I wasn't going to take that lying down. 'You can give me a check-up, and you'll see that my brain has never functioned better,' I told him. 'You believe in all your x-rays, and in all your operations and your medical knowledge, but I believe in the Creator of the world, and in his tzaddikim. Rebbe Nachman came to me in a dream and healed me. The reality is, I'm healed, and even you can't argue with that.'*

*Nachman finished his tale by telling me that now, he just had a small leg wound that needed a few more days to heal up, with G-d's help, and that after that, he was being discharged from the hospital. 'And then, you can come with me to Uman, to thank Hashem Yitbarach and Rebbe Nachman for all the miracles they did for me,' he told me.*

*What an amazing story! I told Nachman that he had to tell as many people as possible about what had happened to him. As for me, after I heard about all the miracles that had been done for him, my desire to go to Uman only intensified. Nachman got a very thoughtful look on his face. 'There's one thing, though, that is still giving me a lot of heartache; I have no idea what happened to my good friend Yaacov. I don't know if he survived the attack - and if he did, where they took him.'*

*I was still feeling very weak, but I could see the sincere determination and caring in Nachman's eyes as he spoke, and that gave me the strength to try and help him. I took Yaacov's details from Nachman, and then I went off to start making inquiries. My first stop was with the army clerk assigned to help wounded soldiers with all their needs while they were in recovery. I asked her to help me with my latest mission, because I knew from previous experience that she had a lot more determination to get to the bottom of things than most other people.*

*She took Yaacov's details, and after just a few hours came back to me with an answer: the guy we were looking for was under observation in intensive care, here in the hospital. He'd sustained a serious head injury from the bombing when a piece of metal shrapnel had been blasted into his head, and the doctors were very concerned that he might have fallen into a deep coma.*

*I went to find Nachman and told him that Yaacov had been admitted here to our hospital, and described the state he was in. He immediately asked me to help him back into his wheelchair and take him to intensive care. I was limping from being involved in an army operation, Nachman was wheelchair-bound from being caught in a terror attack, and now the two of us were off to visit a third casualty. We both felt that there were absolutely no coincidences in the world, and that it was no accident that Hashem had caused us to meet when we did. It seemed we had a lot of things we were meant to be doing together. I decided then and there that once I got out of the hospital, I was going to continue learning and spending time with Nachman.*

*We got to the intensive care ward where Yaacov had been hospitalized and found out what room he was in. As soon as we set foot in the room, Nachman started reciting the Tikun HaKlali, and I joined in with him. We just kept repeating it over and over again, like we were in some kind of trance. We continued to do that over the next few days whenever we came to visit Yaacov, interspersing our recitation of the Tikun HaKlali with a bit of learning from Sichot HaRan (the conversations of Rebbe Nachman), Likutey Moharan, and also some Likutey Tefilot.*

*But Nachman wasn't just content with that; the next day he showed up with 'reinforcements' - 10 yeshiva guys who sat around Yaacov's bed and recited, sung and shouted the Tikun HaKlali, time after time after time. They only paused to sing songs about Rabbeinu and Uman, and throughout, they were full of infectious happiness and joy. I wasn't used to participating in that sort of group activity, but even though I'd never met them before in my life, I felt as close to them as if they were my best friends.*

# The Stolen Light

*They kept going for two whole hours, from 10am until noon. A short while after that, we paused, because we saw that Yaacov's eyelids were moving, the way they do when a person is having a very intense dream. We all started singing again and clapping our hands together, and then Yaacov fully opened his eyes and looked around him, completely dazed by the sight that greeted him. The room erupted into wild shouts of praise to G-d, as we all thanked Him for the amazing open miracle he'd just done in front of our eyes. All of us started hugging each other, and a few people had tears in their eyes.*

*Just then, a doctor came into the room to see what all the hullabaloo was about, and froze in her tracks in amazement: she simply couldn't believe her eyes. I think part of her wanted to cover it all up, because it was just too hard to swallow the magnitude of the miracle that had just been done. But I said to her, 'the laws of nature are one thing, but the Creator of the world is far above the laws of nature, and He alone decides what is going to happen to whom, and when. He decides everything, and we can either try to ignore what happened, or we can join in and thank G-d for the tremendous open miracle He's just done for Yaacov."*

*So it was that this surreal scene unfolded, where doctors were dancing with yeshiva guys and soldiers, and everyone was just singing and praising G-d. We started singing: 'The whole entire world is a very narrow bridge, and the main thing is to not be afraid,' and it was truly a sight for sore eyes.*

*The ward's head nurse, who was not observant in the slightest, told us: 'You know, I've worked in this hospital day and night for 30 years, and I've never seen anything like this. You guys made us so emotional with your heartfelt prayers and your dedication, that we all started crying. Kol hakavod to you all, for your strong emuna and your love of G-d, and for all your prayers that led to this amazing miracle.'*

*That there had been two such big miracles in the space of two short days was truly nothing less than amazing. It was incredible that Nachman had regained the use of his eyes and his legs; and it was even more unbelievable that Yaacov had literally come back from the dead.*

*Afterwards, Yaacov embarked toward complete recovery from all his injuries. Within a surprisingly short amount of time - just two weeks - he was already walking around unassisted. In the meantime, Nachman had already been discharged from hospital, and I was also supposed to be released soon. Until the big day arrived, I spent a lot of time with Yaacov and found him to be a really sweet, soft-spoken guy. We talked about emuna a lot, and together we read some of the books that Nachman had brought us. For all intents and purposes, we were just like a proper chavruta.*

*We used to meet up in the hospital synagogue every day, and I soon discovered that Yaacov was an extremely gifted student of Gemara. He'd learned Gemara in cheder when he was little, and encouraged me to open a book and join him in Gemara world. We learned some amazing Talmudic stories, or aggadot; and wisdom the likes of which I'd never even heard of before. I can tell you that if we hadn't gotten together via our Torah learning, I would never have had the opportunity to become friendly with someone like Yaacov, who externally was so different from me in just about every way.*

*Nachman really put himself out to come and visit us almost every day, and whenever he came, he'd remind us that Rosh Hashana was only two weeks away. He'd implore us to come with him to the Ukraine, to Uman, and celebrate the New Year there. He also told us that his friends in the kollel had gotten together and raised enough money to completely cover the cost of Yaacov's trip. One day, he showed up in hospital with all his kollel, and they started to really pile the pressure on us to go, pouring out all sorts of quotes and stories and things that Rabbeinu had written in an effort to get us to agree to go with them.*

*Even the head rabbi of the kollel, Rabbi Zushe, showed up and started telling us that in Rabbeinu's books, he'd written a lot about the miniot, the obstacles, which would try to prevent a person coming to him for Rosh Hashana. And it was true that there would be a lot of difficult obstacles in the way, but each of us had to overcome them. We would see that as we kept going regardless, they'd disappear like smoke, and everything would become pleasant and easy. Not only that, we would also merit to rectify everything that needed fixing in the sweetest of ways. After many of these types of discussions, we agreed to join them. The kollel guys told us that they'd sort out all the travel arrangements, and the only thing we'd have to worry about was preparing ourselves mentally for the trip.*

*When I met up with Nachman the following day, he asked me to tell him the story of how I'd gotten injured again, and to give him as many details as I could about the operation. Initially, I wasn't very keen to talk about it, because it was a top secret mission and each detail had to be weighed very carefully. But Nachman kept pressing me to give him more information, until eventually, I cautiously decided that it would be ok to tell him a bit more about what had happened.*

*We'd gotten the first notification about the mission in the middle of July, when we were asked to design a plan to infiltrate a village in South Lebanon. We were given a stack of general intelligence information and then told to come up with an airtight plan of action, involving two special forces teams. Each team was to be made up of a sniper, a sapper, an intelligence officer, and combat soldiers. Everyone involved had to be of the very best stock, because it was a particularly dangerous and challenging mission.*

# The Stolen Light

*The idea was to have two groups infiltrate the village from separate directions, so that if one group was somehow apprehended or attacked, the other group would be able to continue on with the mission. We drilled our mission plan many times over, in locations all over Israel - from Bnei Musa in the south, right up to Tarshicha in the north. Soon, we knew the mission plan inside-out, because all the soldiers were committed professionals and had been recruited from the elite of the IDF.*

*After we'd completed our drills, we waited around for a couple of weeks, still completely clueless as to what we'd be asked to do next. Eventually, we were given more details about our mission. To be honest, we were pretty surprised when they told us what the mission entailed. It was a mission into deeply hostile territory, way behind enemy lines where the terror group Hizbullah held control. As I'd mentioned, the point of the mission was to kidnap one of the leaders of Hizbullah, a man named Dr. Asawiya Mahmoud, who was being guarded by the best guerrillas they had. We understood that the chances of us being able to pull off the mission without alerting his bodyguards was practically zero. But those were the orders we received, and it was up to us to prepare ourselves for all possible outcomes, including the most terrible.*

*Next, they gave us more detailed intelligence about our target and the location. As it became increasingly clear that we could really find ourselves in the middle of a massive mini-war, our superiors emphasized that each one of us had to know exactly what our particular job was and how best to do it, so that we could get in and out as quickly as possible.*

*Now that we had a better idea of what was being asked of us, we drilled entering the Lebanese village of Madj from two separate directions, in the hope that a smaller group of soldiers would draw less attention from the locals and hopefully maximize the chances of successfully completing the mission.*

*We entered enemy territory on the night of August 14<sup>th</sup>. It was a cold night, and we were walking into a chilly wind as we made our way to the village exactly according to plan. Walking quickly, we made our way to the pre-agreed rendezvous point just outside the village perimeter, where we built a camouflaged hideout before dawn had broken. From there, we spied on the village to get more of a feel of what was going on there, and what the enemy forces were doing. We also identified the best route to penetrate the village and the best route out, which would get us back to the Israeli border post-haste.*

*The view all around us was breathtakingly beautiful. We were surrounded by hundreds upon hundreds of cherry trees that protected us from the prying eyes of enemy soldiers, and a carpet of colorful flowers was spread out on the surrounding hills. It was such a peaceful, natural atmosphere that we almost forgot that we were in the middle of a very dangerous mission.*

*But we sobered up very quickly and came back to the reality at hand, namely that we were a few hundred meters away from a bunch of murderous Hizbullah terrorists who would hack us to pieces if they so much as caught a whiff of us being there. The only way we could get away with being right under the terrorists' noses was if we maintained strict radio silence. We also took great care to camouflage our makeshift base as much as possible, so that no one should even glance in our direction until we left to infiltrate the village later that night.*

*We used the time we had until nightfall to carefully monitor what was going on in the village below us, and to try pinpointing the exact locations of the terrorists. I gave the sapper orders to create an area of mines along our path of retreat, which would hopefully slow any enemies down if something happened to go wrong and we needed to make a fast getaway under fire.*

*Planting the mines was the last thing we did before leaving our hideout to enter the village. We knew that Dr. Asawiya was staying in a building that was 10 meters away from Hizbullah headquarters at the furthest end of the village, and that it was going to be extremely difficult to get in and out without endangering the lives of our soldiers.*

*The action was set to start exactly at midnight. At that time, our two squads set off towards the village, one from the north and one from the south. On the way, we encountered a few sleepy sentries, who were quickly and silently dispatched. Three of the soldiers in our unit who spoke fluent Arabic quickly changed into the dead terrorists' clothes and took up their positions as the sentries. Another two soldiers also changed into the enemy uniforms and then made their way into the village, where they took up a position close to Dr. Asawiya's building. The doctor happened to be standing at the entrance, chatting with a couple of other Hizbullah men.*

*Once they'd identified him, the soldiers waited for an opportune moment to gag him, and when it came, they injected him with a prepared syringe full of a heavy tranquilizing drug. While they were waiting for the powerful sedative to take effect, they stuffed him in the storage cupboard under the building's stairs. Of course, Dr. Asawiya tried to fight them off, but that was fine because it just made the drug act all the more quickly. Before long, he was completely unconscious. Once we received the pre-agreed signal that the target had been found and was in our hands, we began the next stage of our plan, which was attempting to exit the village as peacefully as we'd entered it.*

*The plan called for our two soldiers to walk out of the village carrying the unconscious and disguised Dr Asawiya between them, in a sort of fraternal 'hug' from both sides, while the rest of the team hid out behind the village buildings, ready to provide backup if needed. The plan was working like clockwork until suddenly, two jeeps pulled up to the village out of nowhere, and the men in them started shouting the place down. They were trying to alert everyone to news they'd just heard, that the Israeli army was operating somewhere close by.*

*For a couple of seconds, we were all completely stunned by this unexpected turn of events, but then one of the jeeps turned off in the direction of Dr. Asawiya's building, and we realized that we had literally a matter of a few seconds until they discovered what had happened. The electric fence around the perimeter of the village was suddenly lit up by massive floodlights, and loads of Hizbullah terrorists appeared and began combing the area inside and outside the fence.*

*In the ensuing tumult, all the soldiers who'd been directly involved in the kidnapping managed to get out of the village, which was a massive miracle all by itself - because just a few seconds after they'd gotten out and started heading down to the wadi, the Hizbullah commanders gave an order to seal the village shut, and posted guards the whole way around the perimeter fence.*

*We had to get out of there fast. We radioed the second unit that we were heading back to the Israeli border and told them to rendezvous with us. All of a sudden, we heard sounds of uproar from the village, and realized that the Hizbullah fighters had just figured out that Dr. Asawiya was missing. Our whole unit started running like the wind. In the meantime, the terrorists were firing off rounds of bullets indiscriminately into the wadi, without even knowing what or who they were aiming at.*

*Dozens of Hizbullah burst out of the village and ran down the wadi in our direction like madmen, firing as they went. We watched them approach the mines we'd left as a surprise, and sure enough, the mines detonated exactly as planned. The explosions killed quite a few terrorists outright, and injured the rest, neatly taking care of the first Hizbullah onslaught to come after us.*

*But there were still a whole lot more of them to deal with, and they started firing everything they had: hand-propelled rockets, RPGs, mortars, machine guns, you name it. The firepower they unleashed at us was awesome, and the whole landscape lit up from all the explosions. Each time we had to dodge more artillery, we were forced to slow down, until eventually the terrorists started to gain on us.*

*Two of the men in the second unit had been hit and were seriously hurt. We radioed to base for help and to request that airborne artillery strafe the area until we were safely back across the Israeli border. We gave our position coordinates, and were really looking forward to getting a bit of a breather from the unrelenting firepower that was being aimed at us. In the meantime, we could still feel that they were gaining on us.*

*As we continued to move, we set up a 360 degree defense position, which killed and injured many more terrorists. But they just kept coming, and we knew that if the airborne backup didn't get there soon, we were going to be facing some very serious problems. Just as we got to the top of the first mountain that led down to the Israeli border, the terrorists unleashed another round of destruction at us, and this time, Uri the sniper and Yaacov the radio man were both hit and killed.*

*Chaim the machine-gunner saw his two friends cut down in front of him, and went into shock. He stood completely still for a couple of moments, and then it was like some switch was flipped in him, and he started running down the hill at full speed towards the terrorists, all guns a-blazing, mowing down Hizbullah men left, right and center. I think he went out of his mind a little bit with grief and shock; he was shouting, cursing, and firing everything he had at them.*

*I started running after him to try calming him down and getting him back up to the top of the hill where everyone else was headed. A second before I got to him, he was hit by a massive burst of machine gun fire that diagonally strafed him from his stomach to his left shoulder. He was very badly wounded, and he was a big guy who probably weighed twice what I did. But there wasn't time to think about anything, so I just picked him up, put him across my shoulders and then started to run back up the hill with him. I held onto Chaim with one hand, and with the other hand, I was firing back at the terrorists who were still chasing us. I have no idea where I got the strength to be able to do that.*

*A second before I made it to the top of the hill, I noticed that an army helicopter with IDF markings had arrived on the scene, and was raining down fire on the terrorists and across the whole area of the wadi. For a moment, I had a feeling of overwhelming relief that it was game over, and we'd make it home after all. Just then, the terrorists threw a hand grenade at us that landed right next to me. I was standing there with Chaim still on my shoulders frozen to the spot, and everyone else in the platoon was also frozen in place; it was like we all felt that the end had arrived. I put my foot out to kick the grenade away, and at that same instant, it exploded.*

*I was blasted a couple of meters up into the air, and I felt the explosion reverberate throughout my whole leg and body. The next thing I remember, I was surrounded by a bunch of friendly faces who were thanking me profusely and asking me what my name was.*

*When I woke up at the hospital, I couldn't understand how I'd gotten there or where I was. As I'm sure you can appreciate, the whole experience was extremely traumatic. My leg was raised suspended overhead, and I was hooked up to all sorts of different machines which were giving me regular blood transfusions. I started screaming at the top of my lungs: 'What happened to me?! What happened?! Where are my friends?!'*

*A couple of doctors ran over to me, and one injected me with a sedative. I fell unconscious almost immediately, and only woke up the next morning when an army intelligence officer came to visit and debrief me on what had happened during the mission, and how I'd come to be injured. When I asked him what had happened to Chaim the machine-gunner, he told me that he'd survived, but only because I'd dragged him up the hill away from certain death. The officer also told me that I was going to receive the highest commendation you could get in the army, the 'Oz Medal', which was only awarded for extraordinary bravery and courage under fire.*

*I told the officer that I didn't deserve the medal, but that each of my men certainly did. He told me that he'd pass my views up to the army Chief of Staff, because the kidnapping had required a great amount of daring and courage from everyone involved. In the meantime, he told me that Asawiya was being interrogated by the security services, all the injured soldiers had been admitted to hospital and were doing relatively well considering what they'd been through, and the dead soldiers had been buried with full honors and had gone to their eternal rest. Then the officer stood up, and we parted company on good terms.*

*It was clear to me that I'd just had a huge miracle done for me, but I didn't really know how to handle that idea, because it brought up a whole bunch of difficult questions. In the bed next to me was an older guy named Shlomi. We got to talking, and I told him what had happened to me and about all the different emotions that had suddenly bubbled up in me, including the questions about why one should live while one had to die. Shlomi explained to me that the ways of G-d are hidden from us humans, and it wasn't for us to understand everything that occurred in the world. We spoke a little bit about Divine Providence, or hashgacha, and then about Am Yisrael and the unique job G-d had given to the Jews to perform in the world. Shlomi spoke from the heart, and his words flew straight into me.*

*That same day, after I'd woken up and been told about the miracle that had occurred, Nachman showed up, dancing and singing. And that was the real turning point for me, because from that moment on, I realized that I owed my whole life to the Creator of the world. I told Nachman that the conversations we shared had opened up a new way of being and thinking for me, which had helped me to clarify a lot of things - not least just how much I needed to thank G-d simply for being alive.*

*Nachman the chassid thanked me for telling him my story, and praised me very highly for all my acts of heroism. Then, he told me that what I'd experienced was a 'real time' analogy for the spiritual war that we all go through every day, against our yetzer hara. The yetzer is always trying to steal away our time, strength, and emuna - not to mention our happiness - but we have to fight back and go rescue all the things he's kidnapped from us.*

*Nachman continued: 'It sounds like you were an outstanding fighter in the army, but I'm sure that you're going to do an even better job when you join Hashem's army. And we're in desperate need of some brave soldiers like yourself to join Rabbeinu's crack troops, and strengthen the elite units fighting for kedusha. Rabbeinu's initiation ceremony starts on Rosh Hashana in Uman, and Baruch Hashem, you're already signed up for it!'*

*After I agreed to come with Nachman to Uman, that wasn't the end of the story. Even though my career as an active soldier was over, I was still officially enlisted in the army and therefore couldn't leave the country without first getting permission from the army to do so, which was notoriously difficult. I decided to involve Rinat, the official army liaison officer for all the wounded soldiers.*

*I told her that I really wanted to get to Uman for Rosh Hashana, and I also told her the whole story that I just told you, about losing the will to live after the mission, and how Nachman the chassid restored it, and everything that had happened with him and Yaacov. She listened to me intently and agreed to help me apply for the exit visa, which would mean navigating through a whole load of difficult army bureaucracy.*

*The day of my planned flight to Uman loomed ever closer, and Nachman was calling me every day, begging me to start getting organized for it. I explained to him that I still hadn't received permission to travel abroad, and until I did, there was nothing to organize. It could well be that all his persuading would be for naught.*

*Nachman flatly refused to buy into my negative thinking, and asked me to remember what Rabbeinu had said about the enormous obstacles and miniot that always stood in the path of a person who truly wanted to draw close to the tzaddik. In truth, I was having a wobble, and my desire to go to Uman and my emuna itself had begun to waiver. I was starting to tell myself that I wasn't really under any obligation to go to Uman, and I didn't know if I even wanted to do it any more.*

*I think Nachman knew what was going on with me and could see that I was experiencing another big inner struggle. But he wasn't going to let me fall down without a fight, and he came to talk to me again about the importance of getting to Uman for Rosh Hashana. This time around, he brought with him a copy of 'Chayay Moharan[9].*

---

[9] A biography of the life of Rebbe Nachman written by his student, Rabbi Natan

## The Stolen Light

*He started reading a few of the things that Rebbe Nachman had said, such as: 'My Rosh Hashana is bigger than anything!' and 'He told his followers to make a proclamation, that anyone who really believes in Hashem Yitbarach should make sure to be by the Rebbe for Rosh Hashana. No one should be missing, and anyone who was worthy to be with him for Rosh Hashana is entitled to be very, very happy.' and 'Rosh Hashana is the time to be by me, because I can arrange tikunim for people then that would be impossible at any other time. Even those very difficult cases can be rectified on Rosh Hashana, because I can arrange tikunim then that even I can't access at any other time of the year.'*

*When I heard Nachman's words, they warmed my heart and rekindled the fire in me to want to go to Uman. There was so much light in Nachman's eyes as he spoke, and I reached another turning point in my internal battle: I realized it was time to stop sitting on the fence, and to throw myself whole-heartedly into the spiritual world. Once Nachman could see in my face that I was now truly committed to making the trip, he left my bedside a happy man.*

*In the meantime, the officer liaison for injured soldiers had gotten in touch, and left a message that she wanted to meet me to explain what was happening with my request for a permit to leave the country. When I heard that, many different emotions welled up in my heart - one minute, I could already see myself sitting on the plane to Uman; the next minute, the whole thing seemed so far-fetched and unlikely to happen.*

*The liaison officer came and told me that there had been a lot of factors that needed to be considered regarding my request. Firstly, I'd been seriously wounded and was still in the middle of rehab. Secondly, I'd been very recently involved in an extremely sensitive mission, and I knew a lot of highly classified information on matters pertaining to the defense of the State of Israel and its borders. Given these reasons, the army had decided to turn down my request to leave.*

*My heart sank, and I was in so much spiritual pain that I didn't really know what to do with myself. I told the officer that I just had to get permission to make the trip, and I asked her to please reconsider the decision, and to look at the trip as a crucial part of my physical and emotional recovery process.*

*The liaison officer listened, and at the end she told me that she'd just been pulling my leg, and my request had actually been approved! She asked me to say a prayer for her by Rebbe Nachman when I got there.*

*I shouted for joy, not least because I was in shock that she, of all people, should ask me to pray for her at Rebbe Nachman's grave. 'How is it that you are into*

*Rebbe Nachman?' I asked her, while I came as close as a half-crippled person can to jumping for joy. And this is what she told me:*

*'Judging by appearances, I probably look like someone who's completely secular, most obviously because I'm still finding it very hard to start covering my hair, especially here at work. Here, everyone likes to mock anything to do with religion. But you should know that Rebbe Nachman has a very special place in my heart, and I believe in G-d. If you have a bit of time, I'm happy to tell you a story about my sister and Rebbe Nachman, so you'll understand where I'm coming from and why I have such a strong connection to Rebbe Nachman and the other tzaddikim.'*

*Now that I knew I was going, I actually had a million things to do to get ready for the trip - but I was still happy to hear the liaison officer's story. So she began:*

*'My sister Vered, may she be healthy, is 15 years older than me. She'd been married to the love of her life for 25 years already, my brother-in-law Giora, but to their great sorrow, they hadn't been blessed with children. They'd tried everything and gone to every expert. After 22 years of marriage when they were both already 45 years old, they realized there was no way they were ever going to have their own biological children, and decided to try adopting a child instead.*

*They began inquiring into the adoption process, and were told that they were already too old. Apart from their age, the adoption agency also had a bundle of other reasons why they weren't suitable to adopt, even though my sister and brother-in-law are highly educated, warm and loving people with an above-average standard of living. As you might expect, they took the news very hard. They tried to pull a few strings to see if they could get the decision reversed, but nothing worked.*

*My sister felt that she had no choice but to try adopting a child abroad, and then bring him or her back to Israel. So she and her husband flew out to Ukraine to adopt a non-Jewish boy. They'd already taken care of all the paperwork, paid the $20,000 up-front fee, and were now on their way to the orphanage in Kiev to pick out their new son. They were given a choice of three boys, and after deliberating for a couple of days, picked the one which most appealed to them. But, man plans and G-d laughs. It turned out that the boy they'd chosen was terribly ill with pneumonia, and they only realized something was wrong after they'd taken him out of the orphanage and were already on their way back to Israel.*

*Once the airport officials realized how ill the child actually was, they refused to let my sister fly out with him, and told her to send him to the hospital so he could*

# The Stolen Light

*recover and recuperate before boarding the flight. Back in Israel, my sister's house was all ready for their newly adopted son; his room had been decorated and newly furnished and they'd already bought half a toy store for him. He had a whole wardrobe of new clothes waiting, enough for at least ten kids. But as it stood now, they couldn't even get home. They were stuck in a Ukrainian hospital alone, with no friends or family around, waiting for their adopted son to get better.*

*One day, my brother-in-law was on the way to the hospital to relieve my sister who was sitting with their newly adopted son, when a charedi guy came up to him, and asked him if he'd be prepared to help complete a minyan. My brother in-law was surprised that the guy knew he was a Jew, but apparently, you just can't hide that fact, particularly while in chutz l'aretz. My brother-in-law told the chareidi guy that he was just on the way to the hospital, but he wouldn't take no for an answer, and told him that the whole thing would take less than two hours. He said to him: 'in the merit of helping us make a minyan, I'll ask the Rebbi to bless you, and I promise you, after that you won't need the hospital anymore!' My brother-in-law tried to tell him that he didn't even know how to pray, but the chareidi guy wasn't going to be put off so easily. 'So don't pray!' he told him. 'Just be with us.'*

*Giora called my sister and told her what was going on, and she gave him permission to come a bit later. She actually told him that she was fine to wait there for even four hours, it was totally fine. Little did she know that she was accurately predicting the future, because in the end, the whole experience took at least that long...*

*So Giora got into the chareidi guy's car, wondering to himself, 'what's a chareidi guy doing driving a fancy car around Ukraine?' Because obviously, the only money chareidim were meant to have was the cash they were bleeding out of the State.*

*The two started driving out of the city towards the minyan, and while they were travelling, my brother-in-law told the guy why he was in Ukraine. The guy asked him if they were going to convert the kid once they brought him to Israel, and Giora told him that conversion was mandatory under Israeli law. Then, the chareidi guy asked him why he and my sister were going to so much trouble just to adopt a non-Jewish child. He asked, 'wouldn't you prefer to adopt a Jew?' So Giora told him about all the trouble they had had trying to adopt a Jewish child.*

*The chareidi guy barely knew my brother-in-law at this point, but said to him: 'I can find you a Jewish baby to adopt who's kosher l'mehadrin'! He's a four-month-old whose mother recently died from the big 'C', G-d preserve us. The baby's father has 14 other children to look after, and would be very happy to have his baby son adopted into a loving home."*

*My brother-in-law was completely dumbfounded, but the chareidi guy continued, 'Of course, that's only on condition that the boy would be raised as a Torah Jew - he wouldn't eat traif, he wouldn't break Shabbat, he'd go to school at a Talmud Torah, and he wouldn't watch TV at home or any of that sort of thing.'*

*Both my brother-in-law and sister were completely apathetic about religion. They weren't against it, but up until that point, they certainly hadn't been at all interested in leading an observant lifestyle. When Giora realized that the guy was completely serious, he called my sister-in-law to ask her what she thought about it all. My sister was completely shocked, initially. When she recovered her wits a bit, she told my brother-in-law that she didn't think it was a good idea, not least because after two weeks of being in the hospital with the Ukrainian baby day in and day out, she was really starting to develop a connection with him, and felt that he was also starting to warm up to her.*

*While all this was going on, they'd arrived at Rebbe Nachman's Tzion in Uman, which was a 45-minute drive away from the hospital. Eight other men were patiently waiting there for their friend to come back with the missing tenth man, and were so happy to see Giora that they started dancing and singing, and gave him a super warm welcome. Then they got straight into the prayers, because it was almost past the time for Mincha.*

*The chazzan appeared to be the rabbi of the little group, which is maybe why the prayers took a bit longer than usual. Once the service was over, everyone sat down and Giora motioned to the chareidi guy who had brought him there that he absolutely had to get back to the hospital to relieve my sister. The guy signalled him back that they'd leave soon, and then the rabbi started to speak.*

*Afterwards, Giora told me that the rabbi's words had seared their way into his soul, and made such an impression on him that he knew them by heart even many weeks later. Incidentally, Giora is a very smart scientist and has a phenomenal memory, but I don't think that's the only reason he remembered it so well.*

*The rav began: 'at some point in our lives, we all need help. Maybe we're weighed down with a particular problem or issue, but whatever it is, we still have to throw ourselves to G-d's mercy and kindness and ask Him to help us. It makes no difference if we really believe in G-d or if we don't, G-d forbid. G-d will still help us regardless, and as soon as we ask Him for help, He'll turn everything around for the very best.'*

*The rav continued with a parable that he'd heard in the name of the Chafetz Chaim, zt"l. 'Once, there was a poor pauper who was walking along carrying a heavy sack over his shoulders. Suddenly a wealthy man appeared on the road next to him in a fancy carriage that was being pulled by fine, thoroughbred horses. The rich man saw the pauper trudging along completely weighed down by his heavy burden, and felt deep compassion for him. 'Hey, you man!' he called out from the window, 'come and ride with me in my carriage! I'll take you wherever you need to go.'*

*The poor man gratefully climbed up into the carriage and sat down - but continued to hold his heavy sack. When the rich man asked him why he wasn't putting down his heavy burden, the poor man told him in all humility, 'It's enough that you're giving me a lift! I don't want to impose on you even more by having you carry my luggage, too.' The rich man started laughing when he heard this. 'Silly man! Don't you realize that your sack is being carried along by my carriage, regardless of whether you continue to hold it on your own shoulders or not? So put down your bag, and enjoy the ride!'*

*'And that's exactly what's going on with us and Hakadosh Baruch Hu!' Exclaimed the rabbi. 'Whatever is happening in our lives right now, we need to rely on G-d 100% to bring us through it. And if we truly start to let Hashem carry our burdens, we won't be worried or fazed by anything that happens. And that's exactly what the passage means when it says, "Cast your burdens on G-d, and He will support you." Our job, our only job, is to rely on G-d, and He will carry both us and our problems along, solely in order to make His Great Name known in the world. Take the mitzvah of raising children. The whole point of a Jew having children is simply to for them to continue to make G-d's Name known in the world; but Hashem also enables us to benefit from the process, because our own names and memory are also perpetuated by the children we leave behind.'*

*For the second time that day, Giora was in complete shock. How had the rabbi all of a sudden started talking about the mitzvah of having children, of all things? He was absolutely certain that the chareidi guy who'd driven him here hadn't spoken to the rabbi even to say hello. Right then, Giora spoke up and asked the rabbi, 'what happens if a person can't have their own children? Does an adopted child also count, to perpetuate his memory?' The rabbi didn't flinch, and responded: 'Right now, you're in the Tzion of the provider of Am Yisrael. People come here from all over to ask for help with spiritual matters and physical matters; for a good shidduch, for parnassa, for children. Why don't you ask for whatever you need?'*

*Initially, Giora was far too embarrassed to start praying, but the rabbi came over to him and they had a quiet word. 'You know, the Tzaddik has a lot of patience for everyone, and is prepared to listen to our every word and request, and to answer any question we might have. All we have to do is try.'*

*Thus, Giora found himself standing next to the Rebbi's grave, but his heart was still frozen solid. He looked at his watch: two hours had passed since he'd last spoken to Vered. He looked around and saw that his fellow congregants were all busy learning together. He took a step towards the stone marker over Rebbe Nachman's grave, and touched it. His heart was full of questions: 'who am I even supposed to be talking to? I don't even believe anyone is listening to me... I don't even believe in life after death! I'm just making a mockery of myself.'*

*But the moment his hand touched the gravestone, hot tears began streaming from his eyes like an unstoppable spring. He couldn't get a grip on himself, and before he knew it, he was sobbing and sobbing, as all the pain, heartache, and disappointment of 25 childless years came pouring out of him in a torrent of tears and heart-wrenching cries.*

*He stood there sobbing for two whole hours, and at some point in between the crying and the moaning, some words of prayer appeared. Giora had never prayed before in his life, but as with his weeping, it was something he had no control over and he simply couldn't help himself.*

*After two hours he collapsed exhausted onto the floor, which was wet from his tears. The men from the minyan gathered around him as Giora started to recover himself, and each one gave him a big hug and some words of encouragement, and blessings that his prayers should be answered. Giora felt like maybe he'd just died and gone to heaven.*

*The rabbi also came over and told him, 'I have no doubt that your prayers were accepted. Ashreicha, that you had the merit to pray at the Tzion of the Tzaddik, the Foundation of the World, Rabbeinu Nachman.' Then, he gave Giora a Tikun HaKlali to read. Just as he finished saying it, Giora's phone started ringing - it was Vered. He spoke to her for a couple of minutes, then hung up and came back over to the chareidi guy who'd driven him to the grave to ask him if there was still a possibility that they could adopt the 'kosher l'mehadrin' baby after all.*

*What had happened? Well, by some weird 'coincidence', the biological mother of the Russian boy they were trying to adopt had shown up at the hospital together with the manager of the orphanage. Apparently she'd suddenly decided out of the blue that she didn't want to put her son up for adoption after all. She gave Vered back all the money that they'd paid up front - and my sister was left completely broken. Giora told her to find a taxi and come immediately to Rebbe Nachman's Tzion.*

*Initially, Vered refused, but Giora didn't back down, and absolutely insisted that she come - a level of insistence which was unusual for him. An hour later, she showed up at the Tzion, and also came over to the grave and started crying her heart out. She was there sobbing for four hours, and she too had no idea what had come over her. It was like she was being compelled from on high to stand there and weep.*

# The Stolen Light

*Their chareidi friend came over and told them that if they were prepared to raise the child in a Torah-observant home, he was happy to arrange the matter he'd spoken to Giora about. They flew back to Eretz Yisrael, turned their whole lives around a complete 180 degrees, and two months later, adopted my sweet nephew, David. Today, they live in the religious town of Elad, but that's not even the end of the story. A year after they adopted David, they were blessed with twins. So now, you can see why I have such a soft spot for Rebbe Nachman.'*

*As the woman finished telling me her sister's amazing story, I told her that now I was even more excited to get closer to Rabbeinu and to travel to Uman. She told me her name and her mother's name and gave me a 100-shekel note to give to charity in her name, and I promised I'd pray for her. I was new to this whole thing, so I felt a bit strange taking the money from her. After she left, I called Nachman and told him that permission had been given, and I was joining him in Uman this year. As the words left my mouth, I felt the warmest, most amazing sensation throughout my whole body. I felt so calm and excited and happy, even though I really had no idea where I was going or what it entailed. Just the thought of being in Uman gave me an indescribable sense of peace and wellbeing.*

*I talked to Nachman a bit about all the feelings the trip was bringing up for me. It was so incredible to think that me, Zevik, the son of two fierce secular left-wingers and a decorated IDF commando, was going on a journey with a completely new chevra to a place that was going to reconnect me to my ancient roots, and also continue the process that had already begun, of bringing me closer to G-d. The whole notion felt huge, and so wonderfully overwhelming.*

*That night, Nachman came by to pick me up. Yet again, I was starting a mission, but this time I had no idea where I was being taken or what I was supposed to be accomplishing. Nachman told me to just be patient, and that my patience would eventually bear fruit. We left the last suburb of Haifa and continued driving south down the highway towards Jerusalem. We passed the Efrat Winery by the entrance to Beit Zayit and then started ascending up into the Jerusalem forest. The chevra were singing a medley of holy songs, and as we drove further in to the forest, the feelings of camaraderie and joy just got stronger and stronger.*

*My curiosity was piqued, and I asked Nachman what was going on. Why were we driving into a forest in the middle of the night, and what were we going to be doing there? Nachman explained to me that we'd come to the forest to do some hitbodedut - to pray directly to our Maker in our own words. We'd request whatever we needed and pour out our hearts before G-d. Nachman told me that you could talk to G-d exactly as you would a good friend, and that I should tell G-d about anything that was bothering me or upsetting me and get everything out into the open, whether it was a problem with a family member, or friend, or anything else in the world.*

*Nachman explained that after hitbodedut, a person's soul feels light and free, which makes it much harder for the things that might otherwise bother or oppress us spiritually to pull us off track. Hitbodedut would also help me expand my emuna in G-d, because it would start to build my certainty that G-d is there for me and would help me with whatever I needed.*

*That night of nocturnal hitbodedut in the Jerusalem forest was filled with holy light for me; I felt so spiritually exalted. We got out of the car and each of us went off to find our own quiet spot in the forest where we could concentrate on our private dialogue with Hashem. For the first couple of minutes, it was slightly unnerving - I'd never been all alone in a dark forest in the middle of the night before.*

*Once I'd managed to get used to it and feel more comfortable, I began really listening to the sweet silence that enveloped me, and slowly, I said a few quiet words to G-d. Before I knew it, I was wrapped up in my own quiet little bubble where the only thing that interested me was pouring out my heart before Hakadosh Baruch Hu. I just started thanking Him so much for saving my life, and for looking after me through all the incredibly dangerous and difficult situations I'd found myself in when I was in the army. G-d had pulled me back from the brink of death on more than one occasion, and I knew it.*

*Even when I heard Nachman calling me back to the car, I still couldn't stop the flood of words that were pouring out of me like a river; I just couldn't pull myself away from G-d. I'd spoken to Him, and I really felt as though He'd spoken back, and it was something I'll never, ever forget. I made myself a promise that come what may, whatever challenges I'd have to face in the future, from now on I was going to take every opportunity to talk them through with the Creator of the world, and to meet them head on.*

*Once everyone was in the car, we headed back in the direction of Haifa. On the way, we stopped at the freezing natural spring next to Motza Illit, which the chevra wanted to use as a mikveh. It was cold enough to freeze your blood solid, but I hardly noticed because once I plunged in, all I felt was a tremendously joyful sensation that lifted me higher and higher. On the way back to Haifa, I spent some time thanking G-d for connecting me with all these warm, sincere people. They'd taught me the real meaning of respecting others, even when they were very different from you. And they'd also taught me about trying to make others happy and doing your best to help your fellow Jew, just because it was what G-d wanted and not because you were going to get anything tangible out of it. Rebbe Nachman wrote that the depth of the love between himself and his followers would astound the world, and that's exactly how it was.*

# The Stolen Light

*Nachman called me the next morning and told me that we could pick up the tickets for Uman in a couple of days, which gave us plenty of time to arrange all the logistics before we flew out. He needed to arrange buying all the food and drink for the group to take with us and who would take what in their luggage, because we were flying with a charter company which would make you pay through the nose if you went over their baggage allowance of 25 kilos a person.*

*We agreed that we'd drive up to Jerusalem that Tuesday, pick up the tickets from the travel agency, and then continue on to the airport from there. All ten of us squeezed into Shimon's car. As we drove, we were initially busy discussing our stay in Uman, and all the different logistical arrangements that had been made for Rosh Hashana. Slowly though, we left the mundane matters behind and dove in to the spiritually uplifting words of Rabbeinu HaKadosh, which Reb Avraham, our resident scholar, expounded upon.*

*The drive itself seemed to drag on forever, partially because there was a lot of heavy traffic on Route 4, and partially because Shimon's car was pretty old and was finding the whole trip heavy going. It kept overheating, and each time we'd have to pull off to the side and let the engine cool down for a few minutes before we continued. Luckily, Shimon had foreseen the problem and brought a big jerry can of water along, ready for when the cooler needed another topping off. It goes without saying that each time we had to pull over, we all piled out of the car and started dancing around it until we were ready to go again. Nachman said that the car was overheating so much because we were all on fire for Rabbeinu.*

*In some places, the highway shoulder was so narrow that you felt as though you were taking your life into your hands, even if you stayed inside the car. It wouldn't take much for a serious accident to occur because people were driving by at high speeds, often just a few inches from where we were parked. It really bothered me that in this day and age, the State of Israel still hadn't fixed up the country's main highways enough to make them sufficiently safe to use.*

*In my head, I started composing the pointed letters I was going to send to the Highway Agency: they needed to urgently look at widening out the roads and ensuring that each of the main highways had shoulders that were wide enough to be used safely. I told Nachman that it was a real shame that people usually only woke up after something terrible had happened.*

*Anyway, the journey dragged on and on because every few minutes we'd have to stop, and even when we were going, we were inching along at a snail's pace. The only thing that made it bearable and kept our spirits up was the fact that we were all learning Rabbeinu's Torah and thinking about our final destination: Uman. The time was now 1pm, and the heat of the day almost unbearable. Yet again, the car overheated and we had to pull over and get out. Yet again, I started hoping that we wouldn't get caught up in an accident on the too-narrow shoulder, G-d forbid.*

*Another one of the chevra, Avi, started rummaging in the back for the jerry can, but this time we discovered that we were down to the last drop. We stood on the side of the road trying to flag down a passing car that could help us get some water. It took ages until someone actually stopped to help. We told the driver what our problem was, and he opened his truck and gave us two enormous six-packs of bottled water. He explained that just the week before, the same thing had happened to him, except that he'd been on a pretty remote road and was stuck there for hours and hours until he managed to flag down another car to help him. After that, he made a promise to himself that he would do his best to help other people in whichever way he could, whenever he saw someone stuck by the side of the road.*

*Avi filled the car up with water and had just closed the hood when suddenly, a big furniture delivery truck appeared, careening down the highway half in our lane dangerously close to where we were standing. I already had a premonition of what was going to happen next, so I started screaming at everybody to get away from the car. I couldn't really see who'd moved or who'd heard me, but a few seconds later, my fears actualized and the truck smashed into the car, sending it flying. It crashed back down to earth a couple of seconds later, completely smashed to bits and on fire.*

*The driver of the truck got down from his cab looking stunned, no doubt having realized that he was responsible for what just occurred. I made my way back to the smashed, blazing car, terrified about what I was about to discover. I saw that six of my friends had been standing far enough of out the way and were fine, but three people were still missing. Once again, a sick fear clutched my heart, because it appeared that those three must have been inside the car when it was hit, which meant that they were still in the smoking, mangled wreckage.*

*Suddenly, a series of piercing screams broke the heavy silence that had descended on us immediately after the collision. The guys who'd escaped from the accident just stood there frozen to the spot, unsure of what to do next or how to help their injured friends. I guess my army training came in handy, and I automatically stepped into the 'commander' role. The first thing I did was have someone call the police and the ambulance. Next, I got the guys who'd escaped to tackle the fire in the car by dousing it with whatever water we had and smothering it with whatever dirt was available.*

*Once the fire was out, we decided to try and wrench the car doors open and free our friends. I don't know where we found the strength to get those battered doors open, but we started tearing away at them, and before long we'd wedged them open wide enough to get out friends out of the car.*

# The Stolen Light

*In the meantime, tens of cars had stopped next to us, and people were milling about to see if there was anything they could do to help, but most of them just made the whole situation even more stressful. I was still worrying when the first ambulances and police cars showed up, because I knew we'd need to create a sterile area for them to start treating the injured parties on the spot. That's when we got the last and most amazing surprise: no one had been badly hurt by the crash. My friends had a few minor cuts and bruises, but after a quick visit to the hospital, they were released shortly afterwards.*

*The whole chevra was overjoyed, firstly because nobody had been seriously injured, which given the circumstances of the crash was completely miraculous; and secondly, because we'd all made it in time for our flight to Uman after all. We recited the blessing you say when you've experienced an open miracle, and then spent the rest of the trip thanking the Creator of the world and Rabbeinu HaKadosh for all the many, many miracles they'd performed for us all just to get here."*

Zevik concluded his incredibly long story by saying, "This is the fourth time I've been here now, and each time I know it's a massive privilege - and you've also been given that massive privilege, Avi. Anyway, it's long past your bedtime. I wasn't planning to tell you the whole story, but in the end, I felt I kind of had to. We'll speak tomorrow, *tzaddik.* Sleep well."

I went back to the salon and saw that everyone was asleep on the floor in exactly the same spot I'd left them. I looked at the clock: 4am. In another two hours, they'd all be waking up to get to the morning prayers, and I hadn't even managed to go to sleep yet.

I got into bed, but couldn't stop my brain from whirling round and round. It was full of so many different thoughts, so many different scenes from the airport, from the plane, from here in Uman. I tried to shut it all out and force myself to go to sleep, but it didn't work.

I remembered this family of musicians that I'd seen at the airport. It was actually a really great story. I was waiting for the plane together with my brother Motty and his *chevra*, another few thousand *chassidim*, and a bunch of dreadlocked *chilonim*. All told, it was quite a unique group of people and a once-in-(my)-lifetime scene, and the airport workers were scurrying around trying to sort out the arrangements for all these people who were trying to catch their planes to the World to Come, a.k.a. Uman, Rosh Hashana. In every corner of the airport lounge, there were circles of men dancing around and singing at the top of their voices: "Uman! Uman! Rosh Hashana," and it was clear that they were really, really happy to be going.

By contrast, I was standing there more than half bored, dispassionately waiting for them to start letting us onto the plane already. Boarding had already been delayed time after time, always for some security reason, or at least that's what they were telling us. I already knew to expect all this; because Motty had told me that the path to Uman was always stuffed full of *miniot*, obstacles, but that *Rabbeinu* would take care of them all.

After another long wait, they made an announcement that our flight was being delayed again, this time until 10:00 am the next morning. Great! Now we had to spend the night on the floor of the airport, or if we were really lucky, on one of the airport seats. I was so pleased that I wasn't the one paying for my trip, because if I'd had to contribute even a shekel, I would have been complaining all night and trying to get my money back any way possible.

I'd barely slept the whole day. I had left my parent's house at 4am to get to the airport on time for check-in, and now it was 4pm the following day and we still hadn't left for Uman. The time passed idly, punctuated by conversations with the *chevra* about Uman and about the amazing holiday atmosphere in Uman at Rosh Hashana. The more I heard everyone else talk about it, the more I wanted to see it for myself. There was so much time to kill; my brother and his friends murdered it by reading one Rebbe Nachman book after another: Likutey Moharan; Likutey Halachot; Sefer HaMiddot, all these different tales that everyone told me would 'open my eyes and sweeten my soul'. I preferred to listen to the CDs that I'd brought with me.

So I sat there listening to my music and thinking about my parents whom I'd left home alone for the holiday. I think the boredom and inactivity really started to get to me and kind of dragged me down into this really sad state of mind, where I started questioning why I'd ever signed up for this in the first place. Why had I agreed to come, instead of just spending the holiday with my family at home? And who even knew if my whole big plan was going to be at all successful?

Just then, a family appeared in front of me, a mom and dad together with their five kids. They caught my attention because it was obvious that not all of them were planning to fly out to Uman, and I wondered what they were all doing there. So I watched them for a while, and I saw the four smallest kids, aged between five and ten, going from person to person trying to sell them some sort of amateurish CD, and then bringing the money back to their parents who were watching them. Meantime, the eldest boy was standing a little way away from them busking with his guitar. This family of polite, petite, CD salesmen melted the hearts of everyone who saw them. Most people they asked happily opened their wallets and gave them a generous contribution in return for the CD.

You could understand why the kids were generating so much positive feedback - each time after they sold a CD, they'd run back to their mother with the money and she'd give them all a big hug, cover them with kisses, and then send them out with another disk.

I kept watching them and soon enough I started to understand what was going on. The family were doing this whole CD selling thing in order to raise the money for the oldest brother to make the trip to Uman. They wanted to buy him a ticket, but they didn't have enough money to pay for it, which is why they'd decided to enlist the whole family to try collecting the remaining money from the crowd gathered at the airport.

I came a bit closer and tried to get a glimpse of the CD they were selling. It was called '*HaNachmanim*' or 'The Nachmans', and it was a collection of Rebbe Nachman songs sung by the father and the oldest brother. The CD itself looked pretty amateurish, both from its packaging and from the picture that was printed on the front cover, although the music itself sounded nice enough. Once I understood what they were doing, I also came over to buy a disk, and was happy to pay four times the asking price to try and help the family out and speed up the process so they wouldn't have to suffer more than they already were.

Even with my generous contribution, I didn't rate highly their chances to collect all the money they needed, because the CDs were not exactly flying out the door in record-breaking numbers. As the hours ticked by, the children steadily brought in shekel over shekel, but they were still a long way off from having the amount they needed. What's more, their chances of finding a spare seat on a flight was dwindling with each minute – my group and I were now officially flying out on the last plane to Uman!

The announcer had told us that 'Arkia is very sorry for the long delay to our flight, which occurred because of security reasons.' The flight had now been rescheduled again; this time to leave at 2:30am, and that would be the last flight out of Ben Gurion airport bound for Uman.

As the evening wore on, I kept watching the family, and at a certain point a group of the eldest brother's friends showed up at the airport and tried to persuade him to come with them instead. They were going on to Tel Aviv for *Shabbat*, and then spending the rest of the holiday together - and they wanted him to join them. The boy's mother came over to them, and asked them to stop. *Bezrat Hashem*, she said, her son was going to be flying off to Uman today, and had to concentrate on what he was doing so as to earn the remaining money they needed to pay for his ticket.

After they'd gotten that gentle rebuke from his mom, each of the boy's friends picked up a handful of CDs and went around trying to sell them to anyone they could, to help their friend to achieve his goal of celebrating Rosh Hashana by Rebbe Nachman this year.

That scene really stuck in my head, and I remembered everything that my brother Motty had told me about all the tremendous effort that a lot of people made just to get to Rebbe Nachman. Now that I was seeing it in action, I couldn't help but be amazed by it. But the icing on the cake happened when it was finally time to board our plane. I was in line with my boarding pass when I realized that right next to me was the oldest son and the father, both holding their long hoped-for tickets.

I turned to them and told them that I'd been watching them all afternoon. How had they managed to come up with all the money they needed? The father told me, 'After my son's friends showed up and started selling the CDs, the money started piling up, and before long, they'd collected enough money for me to buy a ticket, too. I wasn't intending to go to Uman this year, but once that happened, I understood that *Shamayim* also wanted me to make the trip to Rebbe Nachman ben Faige, *yishtabach shemo la'ad*. My wife, with tremendous self-sacrifice, agreed to me going along with my son, and we bought my ticket at the last possible minute.'

As he finished telling me his story, the man's eyes filled with tears. And as I watched him crying with joy, I realized I was witnessing yet another amazing moment in this journey to Rebbe Nachman, which was packed so full with amazing moments.

## Chapter 12

*Let me finally tell you what actually happened on the 'big day' - the first day of Rosh Hashana - and how it went with my big plan to get rich quick.*

F-I-N-A-L-L-Y, I collapsed into bed. In the background, I could hear the sounds of people starting to wake up and move around. Motty came over to me and tried to wake me up; I barely managed to tell him that I'd come and pray a bit later, before I fell back asleep, completely finished.

The next time I surfaced, it was already midday.

I was shocked to see how late it was, and feared that my whole plan for the morning had just gone out the window. But I didn't let the despair I felt keep me down, or affect my ambitions to leave Uman a rich man. I decided to grab a quick shower, drink a strong cup of coffee, and then make a start on whatever suitcases I could get my hands on in the time that was left to me.

I sat up in the bed and was hit by a huge wave of tiredness; my legs were so heavy I could barely move them. As I sat there pondering this new development, I heard the sound of someone opening and closing suitcases from the neighboring room. I dragged myself out of bed and tiptoed over to the doorway of the other room, and what did I see? Some Ukrainian guy was opening everyone's bags, rummaging through them to find the cash and valuables, and cleaning them out.

The nerve of the guy! Here he was taking everything from everyone, and there wouldn't be anything left for me. This heartless, immoral Ukrainian wasn't taking $10 here and $20 there like I'd planned to; he was taking the whole lot. And if I wasn't mistaken, the suitcase he'd just picked up belonged to none other than Aaron the unwilling realtor.

I was in a quandary: if I hollered, the guy might well just turn around and kill me. I'd heard about how cruel these Ukrainians could be, and for all I knew, this could even be a mafia man on top of being Ukrainian, which was not a fun mix. He might very well chop me into pieces as soon as he caught sight of me and then dump the pieces into a few different trash cans around town, and no one would be the wiser. I'd read a lot of books about the Holocaust, and the Nazis made good use of the Ukrainians' natural homicidal tendencies and penchant for committing the most atrociously cruel acts, *yemach shemam.*

As all these thoughts of what the Ukrainian would do to me if he saw me buzzed through my incredibly tired head, I kind of went into auto-pilot, and without really thinking about what I was doing, I looked around and spotted a thick iron pole propped up against one of the walls. I had no idea what it was doing there, or what it was supposed to be for – later, I remembered that it was part of the bed that had collapsed when everyone jumped on it yesterday afternoon. If that's not Divine Providence, then I don't know what is. Anyway, I picked up the heavy pole and tiptoeing behind the burglar, I smashed the guy in the back of the head as hard as I could.

The guy collapsed face-first on the ground, spread-eagle, and a stream of blood started spurting from his head, which really messed up the parquet flooring.

Frantically, I looked around and found a piece of cloth to use as a makeshift bandage, and tied it round his head very tightly to try and staunch the bleeding. The guy reeked of vodka, and it seemed to me that even his blood was 80 proof. I was busy wrapping the material around his head when the thought hit me that maybe I'd just killed the guy. If I had, things would be very bad. I started to panic and the fear completely paralyzed me.

Thank G-d, I noticed he was still breathing and calmed down a bit. Just to make sure, I said out loud, "*Baruch Hashem*, he's breathing." My brother Motty had once brought a sticker home that said '*Baruch Hashem*, I'm breathing'. Back then, I'd really gone to town on him and his dumb stickers, but now I was starting to see them in a completely different light. Breathing was actually pretty important.

Anyway, at this point you could say that I was rather unnerved. I went outside the apartment to check if he had an accomplice waiting for him, because if he did, things would be much worse. I opened the door, and this *chassid* appeared out of nowhere and said to me, "My brother, I see you haven't yet managed to kill your *yetzer hara.* But there's still time! It's not too late! Kill him now, and come and pray!" And with that, he disappeared, running off down the stairwell. Not for the first time today, I was stunned: why had the guy said that to me? Could it be that he'd seen something, and knew what had just happened?

# The Stolen Light

I quickly put the mystery *chassid* out of my mind, because I had much bigger problems to deal with right now. Thank G-d, there wasn't a *goy* in sight, which meant the thief had been operating alone. I went back into the apartment, and he was still sprawled lifeless on the floor, looking exactly like a corpse. I tried to think through some options of what to do with him.

Looking at him, I noticed that his jacket was stuffed full of green dollar bills. I realized that the guy had already been through quite a few suitcases and apartments, and that we were just the latest place on his rounds. I put my hand in his pocket and it was bursting with bills, many of which had been tightly squashed together. Clearly, he'd already been at it for hours when I found him. I emptied out that pocket and went over to the other - same story, stuffed full of dollar bills. I emptied out that pocket too, and then I searched through the jacket's inner pockets - every pocket was full of dollar bills of every denomination - $1, $10, $50, and even quite a few $100 bills.

"I'm doing a *mitzvah*", I told myself, as I cleaned the guy out. "I'm returning stolen Jewish property." I found a bag to put all the cash in, which I then carefully stowed away in my own suitcase. For some weird reason, I couldn't shake the idea that I really shouldn't be touching the money, because it was *muktzeh*...

Suddenly, the Ukrainian started to mumble something incoherent, and once again, I was frozen to the spot in terror, in case he woke up and realized that I'd just robbed *him*. What on earth was I going to do with him? As my mind raced, I had a moment of crystal clarity, and the word 'Bardogo' floated into my consciousness. Bardogo! He had experience with stuff like this, and could for sure give me some good advice about what to do next. But where was I going to find him, amongst all the other 40,000 people in Uman?

OK, it was time to do the experiment: "G-d! *Abba* in *Shamayim*, I don't know if you're listening to me. I know I'm not a *tzaddik*, but I'm really in a lot of trouble right now. At the end of the day, I just wanted to stop this thief from stealing everyone's money, and OK, I had plans to steal some of their money myself, but certainly not on the same scale as this guy, who took everything and didn't plan to leave them even a cent..."

As I was trying to verbalize my first official prayer, my eyes came to rest on the suitcase that the Ukrainian crook had just picked up. As I thought, it belonged to Aaron, the unwilling realtor. Unbelievably, the guy hadn't even made a move on it yet. I opened up the suitcase, and just like Aaron had said, I saw that it was full of bundles of $100 notes. If I told you that I wasn't tempted to take a couple of bundles for myself, I'd really be lying... but I didn't take any. Now, my priorities had changed somewhat. I continued asking G-d to help me track down Bardogo for a couple of minutes more, and then decided to go out and look for him.

I washed all the blood off my hands and ran off in the direction of the *Tzion,* because from what I could remember, I believe he'd said he was planning to pray there. The street was completely packed with people, and everywhere you looked, there was another *minyan* happening. Some of the crowd - the guys with the towels - were trying to get to the *mikveh,* or were just coming back from there. Suddenly I spotted him: Bardogo, my angel of mercy, just a few short feet away.

"Bardogo!" I yelled out his name the way a small, lost kid might, who'd just been reunited with his father.

"Avi, *tzaddik!* What's going on? Did your *neshama* finally wake up?"

"Bardogo, you have to help me. I am in a massive amount of trouble."

Bardogo could see that there was something especially amiss. He took me over to the side and asked me, "What happened?"

"Some *goy* broke into our apartment and started rummaging through all the suitcases," I told him. "I heard him moving around just as I'd woken up, and I wasn't really thinking so clearly, so I found some iron p-p-p-pole and I b-b-b-bashed his head in." I was so nervous, I was stuttering.

"*Ashreicha, tzaddik.* What self-sacrifice!" Bardogo smiled a big smile at me, and I felt instantly calmer, although still petrified.

"Enough with the congratulations and the *tzaddik* stuff, the guy is still out cold in the middle of our dining room, and is bleeding all over the floor. I don't know what to do with him. Bardogo, you have to help me - what do I do now?"

As I figured, Bardogo didn't lose his cool for a second, and started to weave through the crowd, heading back in the direction of our apartment. He told me, "I was intending to go for a quick dunk in the *mikveh* before *Mussaf,* but you're allowed to even break *Shabbat* in order to save another Jew's life, so certainly you're allowed to miss *mikveh* and *Mussaf.*"

We got to the building, climbed the stairs to the apartment, and there was the Ukrainian, still out cold on the floor. Bardogo grabbed his jacket and expertly flipped him onto his back. "He's still alive," he told me, then sat down on the nearest bed to think.

"While we decide what to do with him, start cleaning all the blood off the floor," he told me. "I have a feeling this guy belongs to one of the Russian mafias that operates around here."

That did the opposite of relaxing me. If he was just some regular local thief, then it would be much easier to hush everything up and get rid of him somehow. But if he belonged to the local mafia, they would be after me for sure. I gulped. "Bardogo, I'm really finished, aren't I?"

"You're finished? I don't think so. Right now, he's the one that's finished."

"But what are we going to do with him?" I felt that any second now, I was going to burst into tears. In my head, I could already picture the scene: I'd be trying to run away from Uman, followed by hundreds of crazy Ukrainian Mafioso who wanted to tear me to pieces.

"The first thing we need to do is to dance a little dance to sweeten all the harsh judgements; after that, we need to go and talk to a rav to see what's permitted and what isn't in these particular circumstances. Once we've got his input, then we'll have a better idea of what we can do with him."

"Do a dance?!" When I heard that, I really thought I was going to faint. Right now, doing a dance was the absolutely last thing that I felt like doing, but Bardogo didn't exactly give me much choice. He grabbed both my hands and started dancing with me, saying, "When you dance and clap your hands, you cancel all the *dinim*." If someone would have peeked in then and seen what was going on, they would have thought they were witnessing a scene from some absurd *filme noir*.

Just when we finished dancing and clapping our hands, Aaron the unwilling realtor showed up at the apartment. He looked at us, the dancing duo, then saw the flattened Ukrainian mafia guy, still bleeding all over the floor.

"What's going on here?" he asked us, suspiciously. "Who's the unconscious guy who looks like he's dead?"

"You really owe Avi a huge thank you. That Russian guy was seconds away from stealing all of your money. Avi stopped him by hitting him with an iron bar."

"Is he dead?" Aaron asked, apparently nonplussed.

"He's not dead, but I've nearly died from fear about ten times already," I told him.

"Wow, I can't believe it. I simply can't believe it. I'm really in shock," Aaron started muttering. He sat down heavily on the nearest bed and burst into tears. It was hard to say if he was crying from joy, or crying from the shock he'd just received.

"Do you know why I came back to the apartment just now?" he asked us. "I don't know why, but in the middle of my praying - and I was really enjoying the prayers this year, much more than usual - I suddenly got all antsy, like a small child. This idea suddenly popped into my head that maybe I'd been a bit dumb to leave all the money like that in my suitcase. I tried to get the thought out of my head; I told myself that no one would be looking for my money, because no one would expect anyone in their right mind to leave a sum like that lying around unprotected in their luggage. But then you, Avi, came to mind, and I suspected that maybe you were going to try and steal it... And all the time, you were trying to help me. What terrible ingratitude I've shown you! What a horrible evil eye I've got..."

Of course, he was much nearer to the truth than he could possibly have known - not that I was going to take everything, you understand - but it's really amazing just how intuitive a Jew can be. Of course, I didn't tell him any of this. I didn't want to spoil his image of me as a heroic *tzaddik*; and I didn't want to ruin it for Bardogo either, or if the truth really be told, for myself. I was really enjoying the feeling of being the hero *tzaddik* good guy, for a change.

"I forgive you for suspecting me of wanting to rob you," I told Aaron. "In the meantime, what are we going to do, Bardogo? I'm waiting for you to have a stroke of genius here."

Bardogo went over to the Ukrainian and started shouting at him: "Sergei, Sergei!" while shaking his shoulders, trying to wake him up.

"What are you doing?" I yelled at him.

Bardogo continued trying to shake the thief awake. "To leave him here on the floor, unconscious, would not be a good idea," he explained. "In another two hours, we're supposed to be having our festive meal. If we tried to smuggle him out of the flat, even if we dressed him up like one of us, that would arouse a lot of suspicion and potentially cause a lot of problems. Eventually when the Ukrainians found him, they could make a really big deal out of it. If we tried to take him down to the medical center here, the local guards would notice us. Some of them work for the mafia and would probably recognize our friend here, so that wouldn't work. If we threw him out of the window, he'd definitely die from falling from the ninth floor, and then there'd be a big investigation into why he was in our apartment in the first place. Then, they'd autopsy him and see that he had a big dent in his skull before he even landed - and would come accusing us of all sorts of things. All these options could make things very uncomfortable for us and everyone in Uman, so I believe that the simplest thing to do would be

## The Stolen Light

try waking him up and getting him to leave of his own accord - and that's the end of the problem. Sergei! Sergei!" He continued to shake the unconscious man.

"In the meantime, you two should pray that he wakes up and walks out of here without causing us any more fuss."

Aaron had been trying to get his suitcase straightened out, and he asked us what he should do with the money now.

"Just shove it under the bed," I told him, then I continued saying prayers, and reciting verses from Psalms that Bardogo's plan should be successful, for all our sakes.

"The money is *muktzeh*," he said. "It's forbidden to touch it."

I looked at him like he was from a different planet. We were talking about $250,000 here, and he was worried about *muktzeh*! I went over to his luggage, lifted it, and stowed it under one of the beds. Aaron tried to stop me.

"No! Don't touch it! It's just as forbidden for you to move it as it is for me. You're not my *Shabbos goy!*" Just as Aaron was trying to prevent me from touching his bag, Sergei woke up. I don't know if 'Sergei' was his real name, but Bardogo had decided to call him that, and in my opinion, it suited him fine. Sergei sat up, touched his head, winced from pain, and tried to say a few words in Ukrainian that none of us understood.

Bardogo started asking him in English what he was doing in our apartment, and what had happened to him. Why was he bleeding all over the place? Sergei stuttered back in Pidgin English that he had a head wound, and that he had no idea how he'd gotten it. Bardogo explained to him that maybe the iron pole that we'd found right next to him had somehow dropped on him from the ceiling. Sergei was clearly not a big thinker (although in fairness, after the blow he'd got to the head he was very lucky to still be thinking at all) - and he swallowed Bardogo's explanation, hook, line and sinker.

Bardogo asked him again what he was doing in our apartment in the first place, and how he'd gotten in.

Sergei was clearly finding that line of questioning rather stress-inducing. He babbled some more in Ukrainian, then quickly heaved himself up off the floor and headed out the door. Bardogo followed him out, yelling a couple of the Russian words he knew, like 'Politzia' (police). Sergei tore down the stairs, while Bardogo continued shouting 'Politzia! Politzia!' at him. A minute later, I saw him leave our building and start running up the road like he was trying to win a gold medal for the 200m dash – not bad for a guy with a bashed head.

I felt an amazing, deep happiness well up inside of me. I thanked Bardogo for all his help, but he told me, "Don't thank me; thank *Hashem* that it ended this way. All too easily, things could have been very different, and you could have found yourself in a Ukrainian jail, G-d forbid. And *Hashem* only knows when they might have let you out, if ever."

**Chapter 13**

*I'm going to tell you about my first trip to the mikveh, and about Zechariah the Yemenite's meeting with a millionaire who also had a small problem with the Russian mafia.*

Bardogo told us that he to fly like the wind now to get to the *mikveh* and then to Mussaf on time, and Aaron said that he had to do the same. I told them that I'd just get the apartment straightened out and then I'd join them. I spent a few minutes cleaning the bloodstains off the floor in the salon, and then I decided that at least for today, I was going to put all my plans of stealing more money on hold. My experience with the Russian had been more than enough excitement for one day.

I finished tidying up, then locked up the apartment and headed off in the direction of the *Tzion*.

Even though I was definitely feeling calmer than before the Ukrainian had gotten up and ran away, I was still battling some strong feelings of paranoia. I had a picture of the guy's fractured, bleeding head engraved on my brain, and every few seconds I felt compelled to look around, half expecting him to jump out of a bush, together with a couple of his gangster buddies.

I was scared he was going to try to kidnap and murder me. Alternatively, I was scared that Sergei was going to turn me in to the police, and I pictured the Ukrainian prison cell that I'd have to call home for the next 50 years, and all the different ways the other prisoners would try to torture me. Then, I got scared that I was going to be the target of some massive police witch hunt, and saw myself running down different Ukrainian streets being chased by a baying mob of Ukrainian policemen. Wherever I went, there were big 'wanted' pictures of me - the incredibly dangerous, violent criminal - posted up on the walls. It was just a matter of time until the hundreds of police caught up with me... and of course, none of my friends or family would ever have any idea about what had happened to me, because everyone else would have already made it back safely to *Eretz Yisrael*...

As you can probably tell, I'd gone completely paranoid.

As I was walking down the street, I happened to bump into Bardogo, and gave him a hug and thanked him again for all his help. He said to me, "If you really want to feel like a new person, you should go dip in the *mikveh*, and then afterwards come pray Mussaf. I'll keep you a seat next to me, and I promise you, you won't regret it."

I told him that I was happy to do as he suggested (not because I really wanted to, you understand, but just because I wanted to do something nice for him after everything he'd done for me. The guy had helped me out of really tight spot, and it wouldn't be polite to throw it back in his face). But I seriously could not fathom how dunking in a pool of dirty water was going to help me in the slightest.

So against my will, my legs took me off in the direction of the *mikveh*. There was a funny smell when I entered that didn't bode well, but my legs kind of ignored it, and continued walking ahead into a massive room that was full of big wooden benches. Without any exaggeration, there must have been at least 200 men in there.

My gut reaction was to make a fast U-turn and get the heck out of there, but right then, my brother Motty showed up. He'd just been in the *mikveh* and was now climbing out - which meant that now it was my turn to go for a swim.

"Motty! Don't ask me what just happened right now, because even if I told you, you wouldn't believe me."

My brother moved fast, and was already almost dressed when he told me, "It's forbidden to talk in the *mikveh*. I'm running to catch Mussaf now, so let's talk afterwards. Come to the *Tzion* - I'm sitting next to Bardogo, and there's a seat there that I've been saving for you." It was a classic pincer move: one got me to go to the *mikveh*, and the other one made sure I was going to come and pray.

I found the whole idea of using the *mikveh* pretty revolting, but nevertheless, something compelled me to go in anyway. Initially, I felt rather uncomfortable, not least because I'd forgotten to bring a towel with me. The water was warm, but not scalding hot, and I tried to find a spot over to one side. I was pleasantly surprised to find that despite the four million people who'd already used it, the water was actually still relatively clean. A couple of the guys closest to me were talking about 'the incredible delight' of using the *mikveh*, and one of them explained to the other that the Ukrainian workers were changing the water here every two hours. The two guys were talking so enthusiastically about the *mikveh*, I figured they must be pretty new recruits to *Hashem's* army.

I inhaled deeply, and took my first dip under the water. My poor, exhausted body, which had been completely battered by lack of sleep, the horribly uncomfortable bed, and the insane, earth-shaking experience I'd just been through, felt completely healed - and a wonderful sensation started flowing throughout my body.

I dunked again. The second time under, I felt like I didn't want to leave this place. I closed my eyes, and I went under another few dozen times. I think I was in the water for around half an hour, and words don't really exist to properly explain to you what happened to me during that time.

The first amazing thing was that my brain got wiped clean from the whole incident with Sergei; it's almost like it had never happened. The paranoia completely disappeared, and the paralyzing sense of fear just dissolved. So the first present I got from the *mikveh* was that I started to feel secure in myself, and in the world generally, like I had someone to rely on. Who I had to rely on, I still didn't know, but the important thing was that I felt safe again.

I had a flashback to a scene from my childhood with Motty, when we'd gotten up to one of our usual escapades together. As I remembered it, I was suddenly flushed with a profound sense of love for my brother. After the four or five years of cold war between us where we'd become disconnected from each other, I realized just how much I missed my brother. I forgave him for betraying me by getting *frum*, and even more than that, I decided it was time to admire him for making such radical changes to his life, in the name of truth.

I climbed out of the *mikveh* and headed off to the benches. I can't even begin to describe how calm and relaxed I felt. I had an inner calm that I hadn't felt for the longest time. I got dressed and left the *mikveh* beaming and feeling amazing. I was even looking forward to sitting in the seat my brother and Bardogo had saved for me at the Tzion.

Suddenly, this older guy popped up out of nowhere and asked me, "Have you made *Kiddush* yet?" I told him that no, I hadn't, and he persuaded me to join him for his *Kiddush*. We sat down next to a table that was right by the *mikveh*, and he told me, "There's a G-dly light shining out of you. Tell me, what have you done to get that?"

A G-dly light? I was about the furthest thing you could get from being a holy light bulb, and I didn't have the first clue about all the spiritual 'lights' everyone kept going off about around here. But I answered the man simply and honestly: "I just went to the *mikveh* for the first time in my life."

He gave me a big smile. "*Ashrecha!* I give you a *bracha* that you should have the merit to use the *mikveh* every single day of your life!"

With that, he filled his cup full of grape juice and asked me if I could make the *Kiddush.* I told him that I'd never made *Kiddush* in my life, and had no idea how to do it. He took out his *siddur*, opened it up to the right page, and showed me which parts to read. So I made *Kiddush* - stammering a little at parts, from embarrassment - but I made it through in one piece. We drank the grape juice, ate a cookie together, and then he asked me, "What brings you to Uman?" I gave him the basic version of how my brother had brought me along with him, because it's not like I had any real 'story' myself. And then of course, I had to return the favor, and ask him what *his* story was.

"Do you have a bit of time?" he asked me. I said yes, and then he launched into his tale. By the way, the guy's name was Zechariah, and he told me that despite the fact he was as pale as a ghost, he was actually Yemenite. Anyway, here's his story:

*"As I'm sure you know, each and every Jew is considered to be a whole world in and of himself. Hashem arranges the circumstances of each person's life specifically in order to help that person achieve his tikun, according to his soul's eternal requirements.*

*"Let me tell you something: all my life, I kept Torah and mitzvot. I was born into a traditional home, and while we weren't chareidi, we kept the basic things that every Jewish home should keep, like Shabbat, tefillin, trying to pray three times a day with a minyan, and so forth. I was okay doing these things, but I never managed to really learn Torah - partly because I'm just not cut out for book learning, and partly because I work very hard and I'm always pressed for time. Baruch Hashem, I have eight children, and we've already married off five of them. All my life, I've worked like a dog - working two jobs sometimes just so that I could afford to give my children the basic things they needed to have. Even so, I still found myself in a whole lot of debt.*

*I live on a moshav near the city of Beit Shemesh. One day, a young rabbi showed up to our moshav and said he was going to teach a class about Rebbe Nachman's works right after the Ma'ariv evening prayers. Usually, I just go straight home to eat my dinner, watch the news, and spend a bit of time talking to my wife and kids before I fall into bed to gather my strength for another day of hard work. But that particular day, my wife had taken the children out to buy shoes, and I knew they wouldn't be back for at least another hour. There was no food waiting*

*for me at home, so I decided to stay for the class instead - or to be more precise,*
*I decided to stay for the class so I could grab some winks, instead.*

*The rabbi started to speak, though I really didn't understand most of what he was*
*saying, because he was talking about very lofty ideas. But one thing he*
*mentioned still struck me: he said that Rebbe Nachman had made a promise that*
*if someone brought their son to him before the age of seven, and if the son would*
*say the Tikun Haklali by his grave, Rebbe Nachman would guarantee that the*
*boy would stand under his chuppah free from sin, and in particular, free from*
*any sins related to kedusha - personal holiness.*

*You're still a young man, so you have no idea just how painful it is for a parent*
*to watch their child go down the wrong path in life. To my great sorrow, three of*
*my kids had already left the path of Torah and mitzvot. To my even greater*
*sorrow, my oldest boy had immigrated to Scandinavia and married some goya*
*there. Once an Israeli has no Torah and no mitzvot to ground them, anything's*
*possible. My son saw a relatively easy, nice place to live where he could find*
*work that interested him, and where he could have a gentile wife that*
*'apparently' loved him. You'll see why I said 'apparently' in a minute.*

*He was earning good money, and thought he was living a good life. In the*
*meantime, all his 'good' completely broke my heart, and my wife's heart. We*
*tried to persuade him to leave it all behind and come back to Israel, but there*
*was no one to talk to. In the meantime, we had another son who had been a*
*Torah genius in his younger years, and who would come back from yeshiva with*
*one commendation after another. That boy joined the army, and there he met a*
*completely secular kibbutznik girl whom he ended up marrying. Today he's the*
*head of a kibbutz, but completely far away from Torah and mitzvot.*

*But Baruch Hashem, I still had three children left at home under the age of*
*seven: Naor, who was already six and a half, Tirtza, who was five years old, and*
*Shaltiel, the child of my old age, who was three. I said to myself that Shamayim*
*arranged for me to be sitting in this synagogue today listening to this Torah*
*class, and it was not a coincidence. G-d arranged all this for a reason. And there*
*and then, I decided I was going to take my son Naor to Uman before he turned*
*seven years old.*

*I got the telephone number of the avreich who'd given the Torah class, and then I*
*came home and told my wife what I'd decided to do. On one hand, she was happy*
*that I wanted to go, but on the other, she was very worried about what it would*
*mean for us, because we were already drowning in debt. She wanted to know*
*where we would find the $1500 it was going to take to pay for the trip, when we*
*already owed the bank and our friends and relatives over $40,000. What would*
*we say to them? How could look them in the eye? I told her that she had a good*

*point, and that I'd look into the matter to see how we could solve this big problem.*

*When I got to work the next day, I told one of my religious friends there about my plan and about my problem of how to pay for it, and he told me straight out that I should fly to America to collect money for the trip - and to pay off all my debts. He told me that I'd come back with a hefty sum. As you can appreciate, I wasn't so keen on the idea of collecting donations, but my friend kept trying to convince me. 'Listen; there are multimillionaires and billionaires there who are more than happy to help out their fellow Jew. More than the calf wants to suckle, the mother wants to nurse. You're actually doing them a favor!'*

*His words made a big impression on me; I was just hoping that they'd make a big impression on my wife, too. I'm very fortunate that my wife is one of those women who likes to make their husbands happy. She agreed to me making the trip, and two weeks later, I was already on the plane out to the USA. I had some addresses with me of people I could stay with. One of them, my wife's non-religious cousin, invited me to stay with him the whole time I was there collecting, and with Hashem's help, I got everything arranged and sorted out very quickly and conveniently.*

*I got to America and settled in to the house of Yochanan, the cousin. Happily for me, he helped me very much the whole time I was there, and even came out collecting with me. He even drove me everywhere I needed to go in his luxury car. The following month, Yochanan was to be marrying the daughter of a multimillionaire who owned close to 30 hotels, as well as a popular chain of restaurants that you could find all over America.*

*Yochanan drove me from place to place, from one address to another. Here they gave me $10; there they gave me $50; occasionally, I'd get $100. Most of the people gave me $18 - 'chai'. I'd been collecting for a week and a half already, and had only two days left before my return flight to Israel. So far, I'd managed to collect just under $3,000, but once you took off the cost of the plane ticket to the USA, I was left with around $1,800. It was exactly the amount I needed to cover the trip to Uman for Naor and me. The problem was, my sister-in-law had heard about my trip and was expecting me to pay off the money I owed her from the windfall I was supposed to bring back home with me. I called my wife and told her about the situation, and what happened next really just shows you that a woman's emuna can really move mountains. She said to me, 'You still have two days left! G-d is going to send you a massive miracle!' She had no idea just how right she was.*

*The next day in the morning, Yochanan and I drove off to see a rich man that someone had told us about; if he took a liking to us, he'd have no problem writing out a check for $500. Before we got there, I addressed a silent prayer to* *the Creator of the world that the wealthy man should look favorably at us, and we were shown in to see him. I told him all about my debts and about the two jobs I worked so hard at just to support my family - and it seemed like my prayers might just have worked, because he took out his checkbook and wrote me a check for the princely sum of $500.*

*I was so happy, I started thanking him profusely for his generosity, and without really paying attention to what I was saying, I let it slip as I was walking out the door that I'd pray for him when I got to Uman.*

*The second he heard the word 'Uman' he stopped me from leaving, and asked me: 'What did you just say?' Oy va voy! It seemed to me that the guy was probably anti-Rebbe Nachman. I'd heard a few stories about the anti-Breslev people, and was sure that now the guy was going to ask for his check back. What a stupid slip of the tongue, though I really did mean it in all sincerity.*

*He told me that if I was really going to Uman, I should come and sit with him a while longer and he'd tell me the most amazing story. I was torn; on the one hand, I hadn't flown all the way to America to hear stories, especially when every minute I spent listening to his tale was going to cost me $18. On the other hand, it wouldn't be very polite to just take his money and run, particularly when he'd given me such a handsome donation...*

*So Yochanan and I went back inside his spacious house with him, and were shown through to the salon. He rang through for tea and cookies to be brought to us, and then started telling us his story:*

*'As you may or may not already know, my main line of business is in oil drilling. My company controls around 70% of the oil exploration in the US and Mexico. Around 10 years ago, I was approached by some Ukrainian investors about the possibility of expanding my drilling operations into Ukraine. We were talking about a massive business deal that was potentially worth billions of dollars. After a comprehensive background check, I agreed to meet them and to take the project on, even though it was going to require my being away from home for at least two months, which ordinarily I'm very loathe to do. But when there's that much money on the table, sometimes you make an exception.*

*In any case, I flew out to Kiev with a bag containing $2 million, which was the initial amount of money I needed to hand over to the Ukrainian partners. I met with the project's main architect and manager, and they took me to see the location where we were supposed to start drilling. In the meantime, they told me that they'd already installed some infrastructure on the site, such as offices, some basic accommodation units, a restaurant and a security station. They'd basically built a little village, because we were planning to bring in hundreds of workers once the project really got underway.*

*We were driving out to the village discussing the latest progress on the project, when suddenly a Russian police car appeared out of nowhere and pulled us over. Four policeman got out, and the project manager, who already knew what was going on, took four crisp $100 dollar bills out of his wallet, ready to hand over to them. Except this time, Hashem had a different plan: the policemen ejected the project manager and the architect out of the car, and four policemen squeezed in and we started driving off, destination undeclared.*

*I asked them what was going on and where were they taking me. They were completely indifferent. Not one of them bothered to answer me, and we just kept driving along. We were all squashed together in the car and everyone was smoking like a chimney. I'm allergic to cigarette smoke, and even the driver was puffing away on a cigar, which was really starting to kill my lungs.*

*After an hour of this - and I was still convinced at this point that they really were policemen - we suddenly turned off the road and drove into some deserted forest, which is when I started to panic, because that's when I realized they weren't policemen. They actually were the infamous Ukrainian mafia, who are known the world over for their cruelty. Even now, I have no idea how they knew exactly where I was going to be and when. It could be that one of the investors was a mafia spy, or maybe someone just tipped them off from the Kiev airport.*

*The car came to a halt, and they bundled me out and tied me to one of the nearby trees. It goes without saying that they took my bag with the money, my cell phone and laptop - and then disappeared into a little log hut. They left one person behind to guard me, who just stood there drinking one beer after another. I realized that everyone here was apparently stoned and / or drunk; I also understood that this was probably my best - and maybe only - opportunity to try and escape.*

*I tried bribing the guard with money. I promised him $20,000 if he let me go - no response. So I kept raising the amount, until I got to $100,000. Nothing. Then, I tried to get him to have mercy on me, by telling him that I had a wife and children waiting for me at home, but again nothing worked. In stilted English, he told me that they were obliged to kill me, because that was their rule for every person they kidnapped. They didn't want the person to go to the police after they were released and make trouble, so the easiest thing was just to kill them and be done with it. He asked me how I'd prefer to die: they could shoot me, strangle me or slit my throat. What did I want?*

*I nearly died from shock. I turned to G-d, and started crying out to Him from the bottom of my heart: 'G-d, I know I'm not a complete tzaddik; I know I'm not even half a tzaddik, but even so, G-d, all my life I've still kept Shabbat. I still learned in yeshiva, I still set fixed times to learn Torah, I still donated large amounts of money to many yeshivas, and supported many poor families. G-d, what have I done to deserve such a terrible fate? If they kill me here in this horrible forest, I'm not even going to merit having a Jewish burial, and who knows what the wild animals are going to do to me after I'm dead? G-d! Please have mercy on me! If not for my sake, then for the sake of my wife and children, who are going to miss me terribly and who will have no idea what even happened to me...'*

*I was crying like that for a good few minutes, until the others came back out of the log hut. They were talking to each other in Ukrainian, and then the ringleader came over to me and said in an incredibly cold voice, 'I'm sorry mister, but it's time for you to leave this world now.' He took a pistol out of his pocket, aimed it at my head, and then asked me, 'Do you have any last requests?'*

*Believe me, my mind was whirring around at the speed of light. What on earth could I say to him to buy my life? I told him I was prepared to pay him $10 million if he'd let me go unharmed; I told him I'd arrange for him to move to America, and I'd buy him his own big mansion there; I told him I'd make him my deputy in the business... whatever the guy wanted! Just let me live! He responded very coolly: 'I'm one of the richest men in Ukraine. I don't need your money. Last request, mister.'*

*Suddenly, I heard this voice that wasn't really mine start talking from my mouth, making my last request: 'I want to go to the grave of Rebbe Nachman.' I have no idea where that voice came from. To be completely honest with you, I had no plans to go to Uman at any point throughout the two months I was supposed to be staying in the Ukraine. But be that as it may, this was the request that came out of my mouth in the last few seconds I had left to live. And it worked like magic. As soon as the gorilla with the gun heard me say 'Uman', a complete change came over him, and he immediately shoved his pistol back into his pocket.*

*'You want to go to Uman?' he asked me.*

*'Yes, I want to go to Uman,' I told him. 'I'm a follower of Rebbe Nachman, and the main reason I came to Ukraine was just to go to his grave.'*

*The gorilla freed me from the ropes that had been tying me to the tree. The guard had tied the ropes so tightly that my hands were a very dark purple and felt completely numb. The gorilla told me to follow him into the log hut, and then he kicked out all his comrades and told me to sit down. He asked me if I wanted to eat or drink something. I told him that all I wanted to do was to get to the tomb of Rebbe Nachman, and then go back to America, to my wife and children. He told me that very soon, I'd get everything I was asking for, but before that happened, he wanted to tell me why he'd just freed me.*

# Chapter 13

*I thought: 'I'm free? They aren't going to kill me?!' I was beyond shocked. Then the mobster started telling me his story. It turned out that his father had been a complete anti-Semite who'd hated Jews with every fiber of his being. It was like a family minhag that had been passed down from father to son for generations. The mobster told me that around 40 years ago, the governor in Uman had also been a murderous anti-Semite, and that man would stop at nothing to try and exterminate any Jew that came anywhere near him or Uman.*

*The Jews who were still trying to visit Uman at that time had no idea that their trip was putting them in mortal danger. But after a couple hundred Jews got cruelly murdered in Uman, the Jews in the area realized that if anyone wanted to get to Uman, the only chance they had of making it out alive was if they went in disguise.*

*The man explained: 'The governor had given my father the job of keeping watch on Rebbe Nachman's gravesite, because he knew that the only people who would actually try to stop at that site to pray had to be Jews. My father's job had been to spy on the grave, and as soon as he saw someone try to pray there, he was to run to the official Jew-killer who was on duty that day, and tell him that he had another customer. Our house was right opposite the grave, and my father spent most of his time sitting next to the window with a glass of beer or vodka in his hand. He caused the death of dozens of Jews.*

*One day, after a couple of quiet months when not a single Jew had ventured anywhere near the grave, my father thought he'd spotted a Jew quietly trying to enter. He was very happy to have another opportunity to do his job, but before he made the call to have him murdered, he just wanted to check that he was right. He ran over to the gravesite, went inside, and saw that indeed there was a Jew there, prostrated on the grave. He turned around ready to sprint off to inform the official Jew-killer, when he suddenly came face-to-face with another Jew, who looked very threatening.*

*This Jew told my father: 'Right now, I could burn you to a crisp and scatter your ashes all over the world, without leaving so much as a fingernail.' My father was so terrified, he was rooted to the spot. You should know that my father was a powerfully built, cruel man who terrorized the whole of Uman; he certainly wasn't a coward. To this day, I still have scars on my body from the blows he gave me when I was growing up. He used to beat me a lot, and only stopped when once I fought back and dealt him a blow that he never recovered from.*

*Anyway, so this scary looking Jew glanced to the side at a tree that happened to be close by, and my father followed his gaze and watched in amazement as the tree shot up a meter, and then shrank back to the ground. This strange phenomenon happened a few times, and my father knew he was not imagining it, even though he was a big drinker. My father understood that he was dealing with someone who could control the forces of nature, and that he didn't have a hope in hell of overcoming him.*

*But that didn't stop him from trying. He pulled his arm back, ready to try to punch the Jew that was standing in his way - and he ended up punching himself in the face. He literally started beating himself up, and when he tried to stop, he simply couldn't. The Jew then said to him, 'You are childless; I promise you that if you look after the Jews that come to my grave to pray, that I will bless you with a long life, and with a son who will grow up to become one of the richest men in the Ukraine. But from now on, if you, your son, or you grandchildren hurt even a hair on a single Jew's head, the very second you touch them, you yourselves will die.' After the Jew had spoken, he disappeared.*

*'My father was so terrified, he was shaking like a leaf. The Jew had left him with a feeling of dread that he'd never before experienced in his whole life. And so from that moment on, he started protecting the Jews that came to Rebbe Nachman's tomb. Of course, he had to pretend he still wanted them dead for the governor, but he was just playing the part now, and no more Jews came to any harm because of him.*

*'I was born a year later, when my parents had already been married for 35 years without having any children. When they had me, my father was 70 years old and my mother was 65. It was so unusual, my birth made headlines all over the Ukraine, and a parade of journalists came to interview my parents. My picture was everywhere - even from the day I was born, I was famous. Before he died at the ripe old age of 105, my father told me everything that had happened to him, and that it had all happened exactly as that Jew had told him it would. He warned me that I too needed to protect any Jew that came to pray at the grave of Rebbe Nachman. So take your money, and we'll take you to pray at your grave, and then we'll take you back to the airport. And I hope you aren't going to make any trouble for us.'*

*The mafia boss concluded his story, and his men returned my briefcase with all the money, right down to the last cent. They drove me off to the Tzion and didn't even smoke so much as one cigarette next to me. Every time someone wanted a smoke, they'd stop the car and he'd go smoke outside, so we were stopping and starting every five minutes. We got to the Tzion, and I threw myself down on the grave and cried like a baby for an hour, thanking Rebbe Nachman with all my heart for saving my life. And since then, I've had a soft spot for anyone travelling to Uman to be by Rabbeinu.'*

*The rich donor finished, and I said to him, 'What an amazing story! You have to tell that story to as many people as possible. It's so incredible, it's almost hard to believe!'*

*'You can believe it happened, because it happened in Uman,' he replied. 'While we're talking, how much more money are you hoping to collect here before you go home?'*

*I told him that I needed to collect somewhere in the region of $40,000 to pay off all my debts. He didn't even blink; he simply took out his checkbook and wrote me out a check for the entire amount. He just asked that my son and I pray for him when we got to Uman. I was in complete shock. I was not prepared for the enormous miracle that had just been done for me. Yochanan was even more shocked than I was, and we both left the mansion overwhelmed with gratitude and joy.*

*I called my wife and told her about the massive miracle that had just occurred – and if that wasn't enough, another massive miracle occurred: the rich man's story seemed to have ignited some sort of feeling of teshuva in Yochanan, and he decided to fly out to Uman together with my son and me.*

*All this happened just over a year ago, a little bit before Rosh Hashana. These days, Yochanan is already a fully-fledged serious baal teshuva and learns at yeshiva in Jerusalem. He's also here this year. He still married his non-Jewish Caroline, but only after she decided to convert. Unfortunately, her father wasn't thrilled about that, and he completely disowned her. Caroline is an only child, so you understand that we're talking about tens of millions of dollars here. But they both believe it was completely worthwhile, because Yochanan got so lit up with a burning passion for Judaism that after he came with us to Uman, he passed that fire on to Rivka (formerly Caroline). If you saw her today, you'd be amazed. She looks like such a tzaddeket, and they are happily living on a shoestring budget, despite the fact that she's spent all of her life in the lap of luxury.*

*You should have seen Yochanan the first time he came to Rebbe Nachman's grave last Rosh Hashana. He was standing there with a Tikun HaKlali in his hand, and initially looked so cold and unmoved by all the holiness around him, mamash like a statue. I persuaded him to recite the Tikun HaKlali together with my son, and five minutes later, Yochanan was crying his heart out on the grave. He spent three whole hours crying out the Tikun HaKlali. I tried to go over to him, but he couldn't see me or anyone else for that matter, because a river of tears was streaming from his eyes, Baruch Hashem.*

*But this isn't where the story ends. As I mentioned, my eldest son Reuven was living with a Scandinavian goya at the time. After Yochanan made teshuva, he found the whole idea of my son intermarrying so painful that he declared that he wasn't going to move from the Tzion until heaven had accepted his prayers that my son should divorce his non-Jewish wife. In my heart, I felt rather cynical at this, because my son was happily married with two children, lived in a big beautiful house, and had a well-paying job he really liked. I had no idea where*

# The Stolen Light

*Yochanan got the emuna to believe that his prayers could really change what was happening with my son, not least because his mother and I had cried over him for years already...*

*After the Chag, we still had a couple of days until our flight home, so my son and I went to visit the graves of Rabbi Natan in Breslev and the Baal Shem Tov in Medzhibuzh. We set out at 10am on Sunday morning and came back to Uman at around noon the next day, physically depleted but spiritually replenished. We found Yochanan at the Tzion in exactly the same place we'd left him. He was still standing there, crying and praying. I had no idea where he was getting the strength to keep going.*

*Our flight was supposed to be at 7pm that evening, which meant that we had to leave Uman at around 1pm to get to the airport on time. I went over to Yochanan and whispered in his ear that we were running out of time, and had to get the suitcases organized and stowed back on the bus. He stopped praying for a moment, but only to tell me, 'I'm not moving from here until I know that Reuven is leaving his goyish wife. You can go without me, I'll manage here somehow.' As he spoke, my phone suddenly started ringing.*

*Before I tell you the next part, you should probably sit down, because it's a real shocker. I picked up, and it was my wife, and she was finding it very hard to speak coherently. 'Reuven just came home,' she told me, 'and he's planning to stay in Israel now.'*

*'What, he came back to live in Israel with his shiksa?!' I asked her.*

*'No!' she practically shouted at me. 'She left him! She met some other man and moved out. She took the kids and just disappeared! He sold everything he owned, and now he's back in Israel for good!'*

*Stunned, I handed the phone over to Yochanan, so he could hear this bombshell for himself. Then I draped myself over the Tzion and started crying my heart out, I was so full of joy. I thanked the Creator of the world for sending us such a faithful messenger like Rabbeinu, and for all of Yochanan's prayers. With that, we packed up and left.*

*Today, my son is managing our farm on the moshav, and very soon, he's going to marry a local religious girl, yishtabach shemo la'ad. Praise be the King of Kings, who has never forgotten, and who never will forget, His holy people."*

In high spirits, I parted from Zechariah the nice Yemenite who'd invited me to join his *Kiddush* and told me his amazing story.

One of the most interesting and unique things about Uman was the profound sense of camaraderie there. You literally felt like you were friends with everyone around you, and that they really loved you.

Back home in Israel, I could meet hundreds of people and not relate to them in any way, even if I'd been living alongside them for years. On a good day, you'd exchange a quick *'shalom'*, or a polite 'good morning', and that would be that for another six months. Without exaggerating, I'd spoken to more than 100 people since setting out for Uman, and with every single one of them, it was like talking to my best friend. No one was pretending anything or wearing a mask, no one was trying to one-up the other person or manipulate anyone for their own gains. We were all just being ourselves.

At this stage, I still wasn't considering making *teshuva*, but I did have my eyes and my heart, and I had to admit that more earth-shaking things had happened to me over the last three days than had occurred in all the 25 years of my life put together.

# The Stolen Light

**Chapter 14**

*Let me tell you about the dance with the Ukrainian soldier, and why sometimes it's better to sing than to speak.*

With a happy heart and a skip in my step, I headed off in the direction of the *Tzion*, where I hoped that they'd still be praying the *Mussaf* service. I had no idea how long all the praying was supposed to take, but I thought they'd probably be nearly done by now, judging by how long the evening service had taken - which I thought had to be the longest *davening* of all time. I hoped that no one else was going to stop me en route to tell me their story - not because I didn't like listening to them, because I really did - but I just wanted to go in and join my brother and Bardogo already.

I entered the *Tzion* which was completely jam-packed full of people, and then with great difficulty, tried finding my brother. I stood on one of the benches to try to get a better look, which is when Bardogo noticed me and motioned me over to them. It took me around 10 minutes to get there, and when I finally arrived, Bardogo and Motty gave me a big group hug. Motty had already heard what happened with the mafia *goy* that morning, and he told me that I had to recite *birkat hagomel*, the prayer said when one just came through a life-threatening situation. Then he started singing my praises for the daring actions I'd taken that morning in helping my fellow Jews.

I felt like I was a holy *Moshe Rabbeinu* or something, the way people were praising me so highly, and somewhere deep down, I actually started to believe it a bit myself. I'd completely forgotten that the whole point of me coming to Uman had been to get rich quick, at the expense of all the poor *chassidim*.

I sat myself down and became a little apprehensive. The memory of yesterday night's prayers were still fresh in my head, and I was worried I was going to get bored out of my skull again. For that reason, I took a seat on the outside of the congregation, right next to the emergency exit. On my right, there was a

224

Ukrainian soldier, one of the many that were guarding the site. Every ten meters or so, there was another soldier with a cold, impassive look on his face and his gun at the ready. Their eyes were so dead and lifeless that they barely looked alive, and seemed they could be capable of anything. You could see why they'd gotten a reputation for being the Nazis' henchmen, *yemach shemam.*

My father was a Holocaust survivor, and he'd gone through the horror of the death camps as a child. He obviously had a deep lifelong hatred for the Nazis, and in particular, the Ukrainians. My father had seen both his parents cruelly murdered in front of his eyes by a Ukrainian soldier, who'd ordered them off the transport that had brought them to the death camp. My grandparents were very weak after a week of travelling in the most horrendously overcrowded conditions, and they had almost no water left to drink. The Ukrainian soldier who ordered them off the train was infuriated by how long it was taking them to move, so he shot them both on the spot, as my physically weak, emotionally broken father looked on. Some time later, my father tracked down that soldier and avenged his parents' blood by killing him, before escaping from the camp.

Anyway, I was sitting there with a *siddur* in my hand trying to figure out how and what to pray, when a *chassid* suddenly started singing, *"Ha Kadosh Baruch Hu,* we really love you..." Some of the congregants tried to shush him, but it was too late: the song swept through the gathering like a fire through a field of dry thorns, and thousands of people started singing along. I thought to myself, 'here we go; they'll be singing this now for at least the next 45 minutes.' Stranger than fiction, the rhythm of the song seemed to have a life of its own, and the singing just went higher and higher, and deeper and deeper, penetrating to the very depth of your consciousness. Some people were using the garbage pails in the *Tzion* like makeshift drums, some people were clapping their hands together, and everyone without a single exception was loudly and enthusiastically singing along.

After half an hour, the song morphed into the Uman anthem: *"Ashreinu, ashreinu, she'zachinu le'hitkarev le Rabbeinu, Uman, Uman, Rosh Hashana."* That song was guaranteed to catapult the whole crowd up to the higher spheres. You could already see that most of them had already left this lowly world; they had those big, star-struck eyes, and were completely absorbed in the song. Every now and then, one of the congregants would stand up on a bench or try to climb up one of the supporting pillars, and start swinging and waving a towel or something around his head like some sort of actual Rebbe Nachman fan.

Initially, I didn't join in with the song, because I didn't really feel so connected to all the words. I glanced over at the Russian soldier, and saw that after half an hour of listening to all the singing, his face looked a bit less serious than before, and his gun had gone from being at the ready, to being relaxed and hanging from his body.

# The Stolen Light

This moved me somehow, and I smiled and started clapping along with the beat. Then, I closed my eyes so I wouldn't feel too self-conscious, and started singing along with everyone else. I sat like that for ten minutes as I found myself really getting quite swept up by the simple tune, which is when I opened my eyes again to see if anyone was looking at me. But everyone else was still in a state of ecstatic *dvekut* with *Hashem*, which appeared to be growing and deepening with each passing second.

I shot another glance at the soldier, and he was already starting to move around to the song's beat. His gun was now slung over his back, and it looked like he was saying something. I went a bit closer to him to hear what he was saying, and he was singing in his thick Russian accent, "Hu-man, Hu-man, Rosh Hashana, Hu-man, Hu-man, Rosh Hashana.' Delighted at this, I closed my eyes again, and just then, the crowd switched to another song, which took me a couple of minutes to pick up: "*Uv'chain tzaddikim yiru v'yismachu v'yesharim ya'alozu, v'chassidim b'rina yagilu.*"[10]

Something about that song just caught me, and like everyone else, I started to melt into the melody, and my body began to sway with the rhythm. Gradually, I started singing along, albeit a few seconds after everyone else as I was still learning the words, and I got such a kick out of singing along with everyone. And then in the most natural way without anyone arranging it or organizing it, the whole room split up into groups and started dancing around in a big circle. I had no idea how it happened really, because there wasn't even room in the place to swing a cat, but we were all way past caring about the impossible logistics, and I was dancing and singing along with the best of them.

Not that I was thinking about making *teshuva*, you understand, or anything close to that. It's just that I really love to sing, so why not? I was holding the hand of the guy in front of me, while my other hand was behind me, holding the hand of the next guy along, and we were all dancing and swaying together. The guy behind me was swinging my arm around a bit too enthusiastically, so I turned around to see who it was - and I was stunned to find myself holding hands with the Ukrainian soldier. He'd stowed his gun away completely, and now was dancing along with everyone else in the room. Apparently, the guy didn't give a care who saw him, nor the possible consequences if one of his colleagues or a superior caught him dancing around instead of standing guard like he was supposed to be doing.

Anyway, we were happily singing and dancing around like that for two hours solid. The singing changed again, to these words: "*Tihay ha'sha'a hazot sha'at*

---

[10] "And then the tzaddikim will be overjoyed and awed, and then the honest people will also be happy, and the *chassidim* will be ecstatic with their song."

*rachamim v'ait ratzon milfanecha*[11]. Everyone was standing up and hugging their neighbor, and then they started dancing around again, each man's hand on the next man's shoulder. Everyone had those big, beautiful, star-struck eyes and everyone, including the Ukrainian soldier, had tears in their eyes.

What can I tell you? It was more than I could stand, and without any warning, I suddenly exploded into loud sobs. I started maneuvering my way through the crowd to get to Rebbe Nachman's grave, and miraculously, the crowd parted and I found myself right there. I bent over the gravestone, and the words just started tumbling out of me. I have no idea how long I was talking for, and I have no idea what was going on around me. It's like I was in my own little silent bubble, and I just stood there and cried like I hadn't done since I was a small child. I told the Creator of the world, and Rebbe Nachman, everything that I'd gone through from the earliest times I could remember, right up until the present. Why had I needed to go through all that suffering, I wanted to know?

At some point during this, when I was talking to G-d and *Rabbeinu*, I felt what I can only describe as a glowing hand that came out of the grave, felt around in my chest where my heart was, removed what seemed like a big black ball, and took it back inside the grave. I opened up my eyes a crack, to see if I was imagining the whole thing, or if it really was happening. I just felt like something so profound was occurring, something that I couldn't put into words; it was like I didn't have a body anymore, and was just standing there -100% soul.

When I came back down to Earth, the *Tzion* had cleared out substantially. My brother was still there, quietly standing next to me reading Psalms and patiently waiting for whatever spiritual awakening I was having to run its course. He smiled an angelic smile at me, gave me a hug, and said: 'Welcome home, my dear brother! I've been waiting for you for so long. I have missed you so very much.' I was speechless. I felt amazingly filled up with spiritual warmth, but also completely and utterly exhausted.

I kissed the gravestone and we left the *Tzion* in silence. We went back to the apartment, and the rest of the *chevra* were already there, enjoying their festive meal.

When I came into the room, Bardogo started to sing, and everyone joined in with him. They gave me such a warm welcome, like I was a big respected rav from out of town or something. They danced around me, they hugged me, they kissed me, and then blessed me that I'd merit to get married within the year, and that I'd have a year of tremendous good health, and *parnassa*, and everything else possible for a good year.

---

[11] "May this hour be a time of mercy and may this be a favorable time before You."

## The Stolen Light

We all sat back down to eat, and Aaron the unwilling realtor told everyone the story of what had occurred in the apartment that morning, albeit with a few extra details that made me sound even more brave, courageous and noble - I really felt like I'd found my Garden of Eden.

## Chapter 15

*Let me tell you about the singer and actor, who one night found himself playing a life-saving role.*

Sitting there at the meal, I realized that there was another guy there who wasn't with us the previous night. I recognized him instantly, because he was a pretty well known singer and actor who frequently appeared in the Israeli media. He asked me not to give his name in this memoir, because he's still associated with the arts scene in Israel and preferred to stay anonymous. Nachman the *chassid,* who went around collecting people for *Rabbeinu* all over the place back home in Israel, had also lit this guy's soul up, via one of the Torah classes that Nachman regularly gave in Tel Aviv.

The meal turned out great - the food was delicious and the atmosphere was really nice. Nachman told us a few short *divrei Torah*, and this time I actually paid more attention to what he was saying - and even liked it. What can I tell you? Rebbe Nachman was a very wise dude who understood human psychology inside and out. His advice just seemed to penetrate right down to the very depth of your *neshama*, and you just had to admit that there was something to him and his understandings. If not, how else could he have managed to attract all these thousands of different people into his camp?

Nachman, the leader of our group, talked about how the first man and pinnacle of creation, Adam, had been created on Rosh Hashana, and so each Rosh Hashana, it was as though each of us was being re-created afresh. And as a result of this, the glory of *Hashem Yitbarach* was being magnified throughout the world, which directly influenced all the bounty pouring down from the Upper Worlds...

I actually really connected to what he was saying, because I, for one, truly felt like I'd just been re-created as a completely different person. In fact, I liked what he was saying so much that I'll record it here verbatim, so you can experience it for yourselves:

# The Stolen Light

"All the pleasures and the loves of this world, they are all just pale imitations of the real pleasure that exists in the Upper Worlds. Our true *tzaddikim*, who don't take anything at all from the pleasures and enjoyments of this lowly world, work very hard to break their physical lusts and their worldly desires, and elevate these things back to their holy root in the Upper Worlds.

"It creates so much glory for *Hashem* and his *tzaddikim* when human beings choose to overcome their own lusts and desires. On our level, we have to eat, drink, etc, because that is the way of the world. But the test for us is to not get too attached to all the bitter-sweetness that is this lowly world, and to try to sanctify ourselves by keeping the Torah and elevate all the goodness of this world back to its holy roots in the Upper Worlds. Indeed, all the physical beauty and the wisdom of the world were all created by the Creator of the world. If He created it, what can be more beautiful than Him? Who can be wiser than the Creator?

"The real test for us is to make sure that we don't exchange the whole point of being alive for the unimportant 'fluff' that can distract us and confuse us so much. How do we do this? How can we live in this world, and look at this world, and not get completely confused by it all? There's only one way: prayer."

I could really dig what Nachman was saying. Today, for the first time ever in my life, I'd experienced a little of what it meant to pray. The words that had poured out of me at Rebbe Nachman's grave had been my first ever real prayer. I'd had such an amazing sense of connection with G-d when I was talking straight to Him, and really, I hadn't wanted the experience to end. Not that I was making *teshuva*, you understand, or keeping *Shabbat*; I couldn't make any big promises like that. But I knew for sure that from then on, I was definitely going to continue talking to Him.

I was inspired to start singing: "The whole world is a very narrow bridge, and the main thing is not to be afraid" - and the whole table to the last man joined in with me.

Nachman turned to the singer who'd joined us at the table, and I realized that it really added something to our gathering that a famous person was sitting there with us; I guess because it gave us a certain element of *chizzuk*. Anyway, Nachman asked the singer to tell us how he'd gotten close to Rebbe Nachman. Initially he refused, I think because he was a bit embarrassed. But after everyone encouraged him, he started telling us all about his process of *teshuva*, and how it had brought him close to *Rabbeinu* and the Creator of the world.

*"I don't really know where to start... I'm not usually the type that gets scared when I have to talk in front of a crowd of people. When I'm up on stage, I usually*

*have enough confidence for two, but right now, I'm feeling like a little kid again. But Nachman asked me to tell my story, and if it gives chizzuk to even one person, and if it helps them in their own avodat Hashem in whatever small way, then it's all worth it.*

*First off, let me introduce myself: Like many of the people here in Uman, I was born into a completely secular family. To give you an idea, I don't remember us ever making Kiddush on a Friday night, and I don't recall ever seeing my father putting on tefillin. Occasionally, my dad would go to the synagogue for a couple of minutes when it was a Jewish holiday, just to show his face and carry on the family tradition.*

*My Saba, my father's father, used to pretend he was religious to the outside world, because he had a business that was somehow connected to supplying things to the religious community, and he didn't want to lose his customers. So he'd pretend to be a believer, but at home there were no pretenses; he'd eat traif, break Shabbat, and do whatever he could secretly get away with.*

*My father carried on the minhag by occasionally showing up to shul, and during my childhood, he used to take me with him - and believe me, even the minute or two we used to spend there dragged on forever and felt like a life sentence.*

*Before my bar mitzvah, the only genuinely religious Jewish experience I had happened in the middle of the first Lebanon War, when Israel was in the middle of some very hard fighting and was suffering heavy casualties. The local rabbi went around trying to bribe as many children as possible to come to shul to say some Psalms. He was offering Bamba, Bissli, and soda, and at the end we'd also get a book as a present to take home. The book was the clincher for my friends and me, so we left the playground to follow him into the synagogue, where we stayed for a good half hour.*

*We really did try to say some Psalms, but kept cracking up every few lines because we had no idea what the words actually meant and they sounded so weird. For a kid who'd built his vocabulary from watching TV and movies, the archaic language of the Psalms seemed really odd, and none of us could connect to the holiness hidden in the words. And that was it – that was my only real childhood experience of Yiddishkeit. My family, my cousins, my entire extended clan - we were all completely secular, so apart from that one time in shul, I didn't have any other Jewishly connected experiences growing up.*

*My next religious experience happened when I had to learn for the mandatory high school Tanach and Judaism courses. Most of the time, we were just learning passages from the Prophets or looking at the same eight paragraphs from the Rambam, so as you might expect, I skipped most of the Torah classes, just like I cut my history and geography classes too. I simply wasn't interested in the stuff they were trying to teach me, and I couldn't see what the American agricultural industry, the Austro-Hungarian war, or the Rambam had to do with my life.*

*I was a social, funny teenager who was the life of the party, and I was also an outstanding basketball player whom everyone thought was going to go professional. By the age of 14, I was already playing for an adult team in the Israeli National League, so I really did have a good chance of hitting the big time. Unfortunately, my basketball career got cut short prematurely by two knee operations, which although relatively minor, were enough to put to rest any hopes I had of playing pro for the NBA. They must have decreed in Shamayim that my life was meant to go in a completely different direction.*

*My artistic career started completely by accident. Until it actually happened, I'd had no plans to go into music or drama. One day, I was sitting in class in high school, trying to answer some bagrut exam questions that looked like they were written in Chinese. I was getting very frustrated, so I started trying to talk G-d in code, if that makes sense. I asked Him if He could help me pass the exam, because I really couldn't understand a word of it.*

*Apparently, my little conversation with G-d started bothering some of the other students, and even though we'd shared a lot of laughs together, they still complained about me to the teacher, who promptly ejected me from the classroom and told me that I couldn't come back until I'd calmed down a bit. I left in fine spirits and headed off in the direction of the school kiosk to buy a snack. Just then, I spotted the headmaster roaming the corridors, and I knew that if he caught me outside the classroom, I'd get a KGB-style interrogation as to why. My headmaster was a tough educator who expected excellence and diligence from all of his students. Needless to say, he was widely feared.*

*So when I saw him coming towards me I didn't think twice; I opened the door of the nearest classroom and scooted inside. I had no idea what class I'd just stumbled into, and I didn't really care, just as long as it got me away from the prying eyes of the headmaster. It took me a couple of seconds to get my bearings, but then I realized that in front of me was the school's music teacher, Chaim Zalman, a Russian immigrant. He sat behind a desk with a big accordion in his hands, and there were a handful of students patiently sitting off to the side. I was standing there awkwardly, not quite sure what I'd just got myself into, when Chaim Zalman said to me, 'So, what are you performing for us today?'*

*'What am I performing?' I tried to wing it, because I obviously hadn't prepared anything. But because I was something of a natural performer anyway, I said to him, 'Tell me what you want, and I'll do it.' Again, I had no idea why I said that, but the words just popped out of my mouth. Chaim Zalman asked me if I knew the famous song from Fiddler on the Roof, 'If I was a rich man'. It just so*

*happened that a few months earlier, the school had taken us to see that play, so I actually still remembered most of the words. 'Sure!' I told him, and he started playing the tune on his accordion as I sang.*

*One of the students came over and gave me a sheet of paper with the words, and after I'd sung the chorus and a couple of verses, Chaim Zalman flashed me a big grin and said, 'You have a great voice, and your sense of rhythm is spot on. From my point of view, I think we've just found our lead. What we need to do now is to send you off to the play director to check your acting skills. If he thinks that you're up to it, then you'll play Tevye, the lead in our forthcoming production of 'Fiddler on the Roof'.'*

*It turned out that there was a theater track in our high school that I didn't even know about, which put on a different play each year - and this year they were doing 'Fiddler on the Roof'. Well, already in it this far, I told Chaim that I was happy to try out for the director, Yonatan Becker, and a little while later, I was doing just that. After a couple of minutes, he was giving me an even bigger smile than Chaim Zalman, and said to me, 'Where have you been hiding until now? You are our Tevye!' It turned out that they'd been auditioning loads of students for a month already, and until I'd accidentally turned up, nobody else had fit the bill.*

*What can I tell you? I was now living the dream of every middle schooler, inasmuch as I got out of going to class for the next three months straight. We started daily rehearsals within a week of my accidental audition, and the school administration took care of my exams without any further ado, because the annual play was one of the things that gave the school its national reputation for excellence. It was like someone had gotten me out of exam prison, and not only that; I went from being just another student to being the star of the school.*

*Yonatan lauded my acting abilities, Chaim loved my musical talents, and my parents were over the moon about my exam results, because Ronit Solomon, the class genius, was given the responsibility for making sure I passed in whatever way it had to happen. To sum it all up, everything was going great!*

*We performed the play nearly 20 times and got rave reviews, the best the school had ever received for a production. That's when I started to get famous. In the town where I grew up, people started pointing me out to their friends, and a few journalists wrote stories about me. As part of the whole 'international culture swap' scene, they sent my play on tour to Germany. We got rave reviews there, too, even though I hated every second because all the Germans looked like Nazis to me.*

*Once time, some friends from the play and I took a ride on the German subway, and we were talking rather loudly like Israeli teenagers often do. An old German*

# The Stolen Light

*couple were sitting next to us, and I overhead the man saying to his wife, 'what a shame we didn't finish them all off in the camps.' My parents used to speak Yiddish at home, so I understood exactly what he was saying. I went over to them, put myself right up in the man's face, and said to him, 'I'm going to kill you.' He and his wife both looked like they were going to have a heart-attack; they immediately stood up and walked right to the other end of the car, and I followed them. I came over to them again, and I told them in English: 'I'm going to kill you.' They got off at the next stop, just to get away from me.*

*I stood in the train doorway making throat-cutting motions so they'd know I was still going to get them. I felt really good that in some small way, I'd just made those Nazis pay. I decided I was going to get back at the hated Germans in any way I could.*

*A short while after that subway incident we had another German performance, and halfway through I spontaneously changed the words from 'If I was a rich man', to 'If I had a machine gun, (diddle diddle diddle diddle diddle diddle diddle dum), all day long I'd chase the Nazis down, because I am a vengeful man. Yes, I'd really start to work hard, (diddle diddle diddle diddle diddle diddle diddle dum) I'd kill them, beat them, shove them in the ground, because I am a vengeful man.' The crowd was enthusiastically clapping along to the chorus, while the stage director was going mental down in the pit, signalling me to stop this immediately. But I didn't care; even if it was going to get me into a lot of trouble, I was still going to pay those Nazis back.*

*My last three years of high school were very pleasant. I continued on in the theater track, which meant that I didn't have to worry very much about the rest of the subjects. After high school, I naturally progressed on to the army's entertainment unit, and from there to acting school, and from there, to a flourishing stage and musical career.*

*I was 27 years old, and professionally, I was at the top of my game. I wasn't a conventional actor, so I'd decided to found my own theater group - which became successful beyond my wildest dreams. I was swimming in money, and all the A-list actors were lining up for their chance to perform with my theater group. I had proposals pouring in all the time, asking me to direct a play or look over a script, and I was also appearing in at least two productions a day. I had four or five different theater crews working with me, and each one was staging a production in a different part of the country.*

*At around the same time I decided to settle down, which was a pretty unusual decision to make for most people in my line of work - where promiscuity and casual relationships are the norm. But the party lifestyle didn't really interest me very much, and I was looking for something more solid, so I got married. In the meantime, everything I touched turned to gold. Every venture I undertook in theater or music bore fruit - but there was one area of my life that remained completely barren, namely my marriage.*

*My wife had been trying to get pregnant for two years, and nothing was happening. After two years, it was really starting to trouble her deeply, but I wasn't too bothered back then. What did I need children for right now? I'd seen a few of my friends have children, I'd seen how their lives had changed as a result, and I was in no rush to copy them. But my wife's happiness did matter to me, and she wanted us to start making more of an effort to get things moving.*

*So I went along with her to a series of different tests, which is when we found out that my wife had some serious fertility problem, which might hopefully be resolved by an operation. She had the operation, which seemed successful - but still nothing happened. The doctors advised her to have another operation, which I was against, but my wife was already 30 years old and feeling the pressure, so she agreed to do it. Once again, the doctors told us that it had apparently been successful, but still – nothing.*

*After that, we started IVF treatment, which also turned no results. After every couple of failed attempts, we'd switch doctors and go to another specialist. After the last attempt, the doctor took us into his office, fixed on his most serious doctor's face, and told us that in his opinion, we had no chance of getting pregnant, no matter how many more cycles of IVF we went through. According to all the x-rays and all the information they'd gathered from our previous attempts, there was no chance of the IVF ever succeeding; or to be more optimistic, there was one chance in a million that we'd come out with a healthy baby. In his opinion, our best course of action now would be to try adopting a child. He told us that he'd help us in whatever way he could, and that he'd put a good word in for us with the people at the adoption agency.*

*Receiving that news, my wife collapsed into heart-breaking sobs, and I too was broken and flooded with despair. We'd gone from doctor to doctor, always believing that one of them would be able to help us, and now not only had they not helped us - they'd completely destroyed any hope we had of having children. The doctor's words, more than the failed treatments themselves, cast me into the deepest pit of despair. More than 200 hundred years ago, Rabbeinu foresaw all this, and warned his followers to keep away from doctors as much as possible because they are agents of the angel of death.*

*In any case, my wife begged the doctor to let us try one more round of IVF. He wasn't very keen on the idea, but he couldn't talk her out of it, so eventually he agreed to arrange one last cycle, to start at the beginning of the month. That gave my wife and I a week and a half to prepare for our next and last IVF nightmare. I said to my wife, 'Let's go away for a short break somewhere, where we can detox from all the stress and the upset we've been through. We'll leave all the bad stuff behind us, and we'll come back relaxed and ready for our last try.'*

We decided to travel out to the desert, in hopes that the profound calm and tranquillity there would somehow percolate into us. The whole time we'd been undergoing fertility treatment, the doctors had been warning us against smoking. No regular cigarettes, and definitely no 'special' roll-ups, because smoking would destroy our chances of the treatment working. But after we'd received that harsh news, my wife and I started smoking like chimneys, to try and help us deal with it all.

Before we set out for the desert, I went over to my bookcase and started looking for a good book to take along to help pass some of the time. There were hundreds of books on the shelf, but by some strange chance, my eye landed on a copy of Likutey Moharan, which I'd gotten as a wedding present from one of my friends who'd made teshuva. He probably gave it to me thinking that if this book didn't get me interested in Judaism, nothing would... But until that moment, I hadn't even opened it. After I'd gotten it, the book had just sat there on the shelf next to my copy of Nietzsche, all but forgotten. But now, it seemed like the perfect book to take along for a week in the desert.

I spent most of the week in the shade, because I wasn't used to the hot desert sun - and even in the shade, I was still getting a bit sunburned - but the Likutey Moharan didn't leave my side. I didn't fully understand the concepts of what I was reading, but I still couldn't stop myself from going back to it and reading more. I'd try to explain to my wife some of the profound stuff I was reading about. My wife was really enjoying the week away and being out in the sun. Every now and then, she'd go for a dip in the pool to cool off, and then we'd enjoy one of our roll-up cigarettes.

At the end of the book, I read that the writings of Rebbe Nachman were a segula for curing infertility, and told this to my wife. She didn't seem that excited by it, but I couldn't shake the idea that maybe, just maybe, the book would really work for us.

We came back to Tel Aviv and went straight into an IVF cycle that was officially our 'last chance' of having biological children. We went to see the doctor, and once again sat through all the explanations of when and how to give the IVF injections and everything else. I didn't plan to do it, but in the middle of his shpiel I suddenly blurted out: 'Before we start this, I just want you to give my wife a pregnancy test.'

The doctor was incredulous. Why waste everyone's time? If we took the time to do that test, it would delay everything, and we may well end up having to postpone the cycle of treatment for another month. But I was stubborn, and wouldn't let anyone put me off, including my wife, who also thought I was being *ridiculous. After all, according to the doctors, there was zero chance of us getting pregnant naturally... But once I'd decided on a course of action, it was very difficult to get me to budge, so the pregnancy test went ahead. For the next four days, I was pins and needles. I was praying the whole time, even though I didn't really know whom I was talking to, or where the miracle I was asking for was supposed to come from. During those four days, my wife refused to speak to me, and the atmosphere at home was tense and hostile. Every now and then, I'd hear my wife talking to her mother or a friend on the phone, and pouring out her heart about how hard and cruel it was to have to wait another whole month.*

*On the fourth day, I was doing a show in Ma'aleh Adumim when I got a phone call from my wife, who was sobbing so hard she was finding it hard to breathe. She told me that the doctor had called her and told her that the pregnancy test had come back positive: it appeared that she was pregnant! The doctor wanted us to come back immediately to do a follow-up test to confirm that my wife really was pregnant. I ran out of the theater and drove straight home to take my wife to the test that would prove to the pessimistic medical experts once and for all that she really was pregnant.*

*I'd be lying if I told you that I made teshuva after that miracle, or that I even thought about making teshuva. Of course, I was deliriously happy about what had happened. For days already, I'd been denounced as the cruel, heartless, crazy husband to everyone my wife spoke to, and now, I was being lauded as the most amazing, wonderful husband who'd ever walked the face of the earth. I didn't take either the insults or the compliments too seriously, because it's a woman's way to talk. A lot. They say that when G-d created speech, ten measures descended to the world and the women took nine of them, which is why they always have to have something to talk about. It could be the weather, it could be the view, but their favorite topic of all is their husband, and Be'ezrat Hashem, they should only say good things about us.*

*Over the next nine months, my wife and I kept buying things for our unborn baby. My wife had to know if we were having a boy or a girl, and once she found out it was a boy, she started buying all sorts of furniture and clothes. She bought so many clothes for him that he'd be able to wear five different outfits every single day and we'd still have enough left over to dress a couple of kindergartens. She bought so many toys for him that his room looked like a branch of Toys R Us. I let her get on with it, because I understood that all the shopping was just an external expression of her inner joy and happiness. Chazal definitely didn't say this, but I learned it out as a kal v'chomer that ten measures of shopping descended to the world, and the women bought all of them on sale.*

*One day, my wife decided that she wanted to go to the Ramat Gan mall, because that was the only place she could find the particular socks that matched the particular trousers that she'd already bought, despite the fact that she was still only three months pregnant. I went along with her as her taxi driver, and*

# The Stolen Light

*dropped her off at the mall. She asked me to come shopping with her, but from previous experience I knew that we were talking about two or three hours spent comparing baby socks, and that was one test I definitely wouldn't stand up well to. And the socks wouldn't be the end of the story either, because from there she'd almost certainly gravitate over to the toy store, and after that, she'd just want to 'pop in' to a few hundred more stores... I knew that I'd be looking at three or four hours of complete and utter boredom, so I told her to call her shopaholic sister and ask her to be the driver instead.*

*In the meantime, I decided to go visit Oded, my actor friend from the theater, who lived pretty close to the mall and who I didn't get to see very much because my wife wasn't so taken with him. This isn't an unusual phenomenon; it's very common that the wife doesn't like the husband's old friends, and it's not just old friends, it's anyone who might take the husband's attention away from the wife.*

*So I drove down there and knocked on Oded's door. No answer, so I tried the door and it opened, and I popped my head in. I was completely stunned by the sight that greeted me: Oded was standing in the middle of his salon completely wrapped up in his tallit, with a pair of tefillin on his head, and waving himself around like a lulav. He had no idea that I'd just let myself into his house. I sat down for a few minutes and waited for him to finish his prayers, but I still felt completely shocked, because I had no idea that he had any connection to religion, and certainly not the devotional attachment that I'd just witnessed. It clearly wasn't Oded's first time praying like that.*

*Once he finished and caught site of me patiently waiting in the corner, he got a very pensive look on his face, and started stuttering out an apology and hastily putting his tefillin back in their boxes. Embarrassed, he quickly tried to change the subject by steering the conversation away from what he'd just been doing. But I didn't let him. I immediately asked him, 'What's the story with the tefillin?'*

*'What's the story with the tefillin?' he replied, a bit incredulously. "I've been laying tefillin every day since I had my bar mitzvah.'*

*I was astonished. 'How come you never told me?'*

*'What's to tell?' he retorted. 'Do you tell me everything you eat for breakfast, or what movie you watched last night? It's just a normal part of my life that I keep to myself because I know that most of the performing arts chevra holds religion in contempt, and I don't feel like having to defend myself all the time.'*

*I asked him if he would help me try on the tefillin. Initially, he thought I was pulling his leg, but I told him I was serious, and he happily agreed to show me how to lay tefillin.*

*I'd be lying if I told you that I felt anything particularly special or out of the ordinary at that moment, but it was nice, nonetheless. I told him about the big miracle that had happened to us and asked him to keep the news secret, because my wife was very nervous about attracting the evil eye. He told me in all seriousness that he knew for a fact that the miracle had happened in the merit of Rebbe Nachman, and in the merit of his holy book, the Likutey Moharan. It surprised me that he believed that; I was even more surprised when he told me that this year, he'd be going to Uman for Rosh Hashana, to be by the grave of Rebbe Nachman, and that he'd pray there that my wife should have an easy delivery and a healthy baby.*

*We sat, talked, and learned some more of Rebbe Nachman's Torah for another couple of hours, until my wife called me to come get her. As I suspected, she'd been in the mall for almost four and a half hours, and now was content but completely exhausted. As we drove home, she was happily telling me about the seven pairs of socks she'd bought, and the 'big miracle' that had happened for her, namely that these amazingly cute matching pants and shirt sets had shown up just as she was in the store, and she'd bought four pants and five shirts... I was sort of jealous of this child, my firstborn, who was being brought into the world with more clothes than I think I'd ever owned in my life. But who cared about all the money we were spending on his wardrobe, if it made my wife happy, content and relaxed?*

*Around six months later, my wife gave birth to our son. I was so giddy with happiness; I was like a small child. I called my parents and told them the good news, then I contacted our close friends who knew what we'd been through to get to this point, and everyone was overjoyed for us. That night, I came home from the hospital completely pumped up with adrenalin, and couldn't seem to calm myself down. A little before midnight, Oded called me and asked if he could come by and visit with a couple of his friends. I told him I'd be very happy to see him, and that he could bring along whomever he wanted.*

*A little while later, Oded showed up at my door with his two hard-core baal teshuva friends, who were dressed in long black coats and had side-curls down to their shoulders and big white kippas on their heads. They came in dancing, and singing 'Siman tov u'mazal tov, u'mazal tov u'siman tov'. We all sat down and talked as though we were old friends.*

*After a while, one of the chareidi guys turned to me and said, 'Do you know that when you have good news like this, it's important to also thank Hashem, and to talk to him? You know, He really did a massive, massive miracle for you, and it's really important to tell other people about it. The most important thing of all is to thank Him, and to talk to Him, and to include Him in your simcha.' I heard him and nodded my head to tell him I understood, and would consider doing what he said - and I left it at that. We continued talking for another while, and after they left I tried to relax enough to go to sleep, but it just wasn't happening.*

*I lay on the bed tossing and turning for a couple of hours, and then I gave up and went to smoke a cigarette in the salon. I couldn't get to sleep, but I didn't have the energy to read or to do anything else. So what else was there to do, except to try talking to G-d? Then all the questions started bubbling up: how, exactly, do you talk to G-d? Who are you actually trying to talk to, anyway? It all seemed like such a big mystery to me, but I decided to try, regardless (I apologize if what I'm about to tell you sounds disrespectful, but that's where I was holding back then).*

*I started the conversation, and it went something like this, 'Ok, well I don't know who I'm talking to, or if anyone is even listening to this. But I talk to myself plenty of times when I'm rehearsing my lines, so I'm happy to try and talk to You...but I have to tell You the truth, that I didn't grow up with You in my life in any way at all, and I wasn't raised to have any G-d-awareness, so I'm telling You up front that I don't know anything about You, apart from the massive miracle You did for my wife and me.*

*'Although sometimes big miracles like that do happen here and there, maybe what happened to us was just some big, unusual, coincidence? I don't pretend to be some wise or righteous, but I am a truth seeker, and all my life I've tried to keep far away from lies and hypocrisy. In any case, if You really are listening to me, and if You really were behind the miracle of my son's birth, then thank You. I thank You from the bottom of my heart. All the heartache, all the painful experiences we went through along the way, it was all worth it to hold my beautiful son in my arms. I think he even smiled at me today, although the nurse told me it was just a reflex. But a father's heart knows the truth, and I know that my son smiled at me. You know, it's actually been really nice talking to You. It's not like talking to another human being, who doesn't give you the space to really talk and is always cutting across your sentences before you've finished saying them. It's been really weird talking like this, but also really great... '*

*I was talking to G-d along those lines for around half an hour, and the conversation began to flow out of me as though I'd been used to talking to the Creator all my life. I don't even really remember what I spoke about, but I do know that from that day on, I decided I was going to make talking to Hashem a regular part of my day. That's not to say that I made teshuva, but I started talking to G-d about all the things I was finding hard in my life, and often, I felt like I was sent some amazing answers.*

*As you can probably guess, I kept my newfound communication with G-d a strict secret from my wife. One day as I was talking to G-d, I decided to start laying tefillin on a regular basis. I called up my mom and I asked her to send me the tefillin that they'd bought me for my bar mitzvah, which were still sitting in pristine condition up in their attic.*

*My mother's Hebrew isn't so fluent, so she misheard me: 'What Teflon?' she asked me.*

*'Te-fi-llin,' I spelled it out for her, 'not Teflon.'*

*A pause. 'You're not going crazy and trying to make teshuva on me are you, chas v'shalom?'*

*'No, mom, I'm not making teshuva,' I told her. 'I just need them for a play I'm putting on about religious people, that's all.' I hadn't planned on lying, and I didn't like having to lie, but I also didn't want her to stress it too much.*

*The tefillin arrived after a couple of days, and I hid them away in my desk drawer because my wife never usually looks in there. Then I waited for my first opportunity to use them.*

*A month and a half passed, and I was completely consumed by work. My career was going from strength to strength, to the point that all the success seemed to be deadening my spiritual renaissance. Then came a day when I was travelling down to the Dead Sea by bus for one of my shows, when I suddenly got this urge to start reciting the Traveller's Prayer. The driver happened to have a siddur, and it goes without saying that once they knew what I was doing, the whole bus started laughing at me and catcalling.*

*Someone called out, 'What, do you really think saying a couple of words from a book is going to protect you?' Others started muttering about how unbecoming it was for a successful A-lister like myself to fall for all the rubbish put out by the 'parasitic chareidi missionaries', and there were other nasty comments like that. But I'm pretty thick-skinned, so I just ignored them and continued praying.*

*Just when I finished saying the prayer, the coach suddenly squealed to an emergency stop, and we heard a massive bang. Very soon after, we heard police and ambulance sirens. A bridge had just collapsed on top of the two cars ahead of us - another couple of seconds, and our bus would also have been buried in the rubble from the collapsed bridge. For once, the crew didn't have anything to say. Amazing coincidence or not, it had still been very close to home and pretty frightening.*

*On the way back from the Dead Sea, the coach pulled over at the rest stop at Shaar HaGai to fill up on gas and to let us stretch our legs. I looked exactly like what I was: a secular actor, with my group of other secular actors. Just then, a chareidi guy appeared, and came over to me. He took me off to the side, and then started scribbling different sentences down on a piece of paper, which he gave me together with a big hug. As he turned to leave, he told me, 'If you want to get your life in order, you need tefillin and Rebbe Nachman.' And then he disappeared as fast as he'd popped up.*

*I was pretty shaken up by the way these two things had happened on the same day, and came back home with a renewed desire to start laying tefillin. I decided that come what may, I was going to use my tefillin for the first time the next morning. The next day, I woke up at 4am, went down to my study, and turned on the light. Then, I crept back upstairs to make sure that my wife and the baby were still both sleeping soundly, so that there was no chance she'd catch me red-handed. Thankfully, she was in a deep sleep, and our beautiful baby was also still fast asleep. I gave the baby a quick kiss on his head, and then on his nose, and then on his hand, and then on his foot, and then I went back to my study and carefully removed the tefillin from the cupboard where I'd been hiding them.*

*I heard a creak upstairs, and became antsy. At times like that, you really start to understand just how important it is for you and your wife to be on the same page about the important things in life. I held my breath to see if my wife was waking up, but she was just tossing around in her sleep, and seemed to settle back down. The experiment could continue. I took the arm tefillin out of its box and started tying it around my left bicep. Just then, I heard a terrible shrieking noise, which really put the fear of G-d into me. Where had the noise come from? What was going on?*

*This was around the same time that Tel Aviv had experienced a couple of bad terrorist attacks, and everyone was feeling more tense and scared than usual. I started worrying that maybe there was a terrorist on the prowl outside, looking for victims to attack. I opened the window shutter and stuck my head out for a few seconds to see if I could hear anything unusual. Nothing. I could hear a couple of dogs barking off in the distance, and that was all. I started to think that maybe I'd just imagined the blood-curdling scream.*

*I sat back down, placed the tefillin back on my arm, and just as I started to wind the straps tightly around, I heard the same horrible scream as before, again completely shattering the peaceful calm of the Tel Aviv dawn (Of course, Tel Aviv's 'peaceful calm' is never that peaceful, but it's all relative). I realized something was going on.*

*My wife still hadn't woken up, so I crept over to the front door, and opened it a crack to peer outside: all was quiet. I stuck my head out and looked around, then immediately pulled it back in, like I was on some kind of urban combat army mission. Not that I'd ever actually done that myself, but in my army days they'd shown us a film about how to take control of a dangerous area, and I still vividly remembered it. Once I was back inside my house, I pressed my ear up to the door and listened: nothing.*

*When I heard the shriek for the third time, even though I was absolutely petrified of what might be out there, I realized that I could never live with myself if I let my fear stop me from helping another human being who was probably in big trouble.*

*After a few seconds of trying to convince myself that I really was a brave, courageous person, I grabbed a knife from the kitchen (just to be on the safe side), switched on the porch light, and headed back outside. Once again, I heard the scream, and determined that it must be coming from the building right next to my house. I ran over there, and once inside the stairwell, I fumbled for the switch to turn on the lights and waited for any would-be attackers to try to make their escape.*

*There was no attacker, thank G-d, so I started climbing the stairs to the second floor. As I got up there, I made out the shape of a young man, one of my neighbors, lying prone on the floor. I didn't know him very well, but we'd exchanged a few 'good mornings' a number of times. He was lying there on the floor severely spasming, and with his last bit of strength, he let out another heart-rending cry.*

*One of my friends lived in the apartment to the right, so I immediately started pounding on his door and yelling at him to open up because there was an emergency. My friend was panic stricken; he'd had no idea what was going on in the corridor because he hadn't been able to see his neighbor writhing around on the floor through the peephole in his door.*

*As soon as he opened up, I started barking orders at him: 'Bring me a cup of water right now, and mix 10 teaspoons of sugar into it,' I had no idea where this was all coming from. 'And then call an ambulance immediately.' He ran to do what I'd asked, and in the meantime, I knelt down to get a better look at the young guy on the floor. I lifted his head so that he wouldn't swallow his tongue and choke to death while he was spasming, G-d forbid. I tried to talk to him to find out what had happened, but I could see that his eyes were rolling around furiously in their sockets, and that he was in very bad shape. I started screaming at my friend to hurry up with the sugar water. As soon as he handed it to me, I forced the guy's mouth open, and started pouring the liquid down his throat. Some of it went in, and the rest spilled all over the floor.*

*'Why are you doing that?' my neighbor asked me.*

*'Really, I don't know,' I told him, as I continued to pour the sugar water into the guy's mouth. 'Did you call the ambulance?'*

*'Yes, it's on its way. Maybe he's not meant to have any sugar, and what you're doing is just going to make things worse?' my friend questioned me.*

*'I hope you're wrong,' I said. 'Bring me another cup of sugar water, because most of it spilled on the floor.'*

*I saw that the young man's eyes were starting to focus, and that they didn't seem to be rolling all over the place the way they had been. By the time the ambulance showed up, the patient was already sitting on a chair, and telling us, with some difficulty, that he'd forgotten to give himself his insulin injection that day. He asked me how I'd known that he was a diabetic, because he went to great lengths to hide his condition, even from his closest friends.*

*I told him that I'd had no idea he was diabetic, and that even if I had known, I still wouldn't have had the first clue about what to do to help a diabetic who was experiencing an insulin shock. Even today, I have no idea where I got the idea to give him that sugar water. I think a voice must have come out of heaven and put the idea into my mind.*

*Of course, he thanked me profusely for saving his life. The paramedic also told me that if I hadn't gotten that sugar water into him when I had, he'd likely have ended up dead. Anyway, they took him off to the hospital to check him out, and I came back to my house feeling completely overwhelmed by my emotions. After all, it's not every day that you get to save someone's life.*

*I was stunned by the series of major 'coincidences' that had taken place in the last few hours. It was only yesterday that I'd met the chareidi guy at the gas station, and it was only yesterday that I'd also been saved from death when the bridge collapsed on the two cars ahead of us, crushing them. My tefillin had been in my desk cupboard for two months already, and I hadn't even touched them. Then this morning, I'd finally decided to get up at 4am to try putting them on, and then came the incident with the diabetic. Today, I know that according to the halacha, you're only supposed to put on your tefillin after a certain point in the morning, but I didn't know the halacha then - because if I had, I wouldn't have been awake to save my neighbor's life.*

*I suddenly understood that there was a Heavenly hand guiding every little detail down here on our small planet. I had to hold myself back from waking my wife up right away to tell her about all the amazing things that had just happened to me. I decided I'd tell her over breakfast instead, and in the meantime I would try again to put on the tefillin. I had no idea what to say, but I remembered that people said Shema Yisrael with one hand covering their eyes. We didn't even have a siddur in the house, so after I'd said Shema, I went and got my copy of*

*Likutey Moharan, which was the only holy book I had in the house, and I opened it up randomly and read the passage in front of me:*

*"And the rule is that it's forbidden to cause yourself to fall into despair, because even a simple man who doesn't even know how to learn Torah or a person who finds himself in a place where it's impossible to learn Torah, even so, a person like this is still obliged to simply strengthen himself with the fear of Heaven, and with whatever holy things he is able to accomplish, and then even he will be able to receive his vitality from the Torah...*

*"And even if, chas v'shalom, someone is on the lowest spiritual level imaginable, Hashem should have mercy on us; even if someone finds himself in the lowest pit of hell, even so, he still shouldn't fall into despair. Rather, he should cry out from the belly of hell itself, and strengthen himself with whatever vitality he can receive from the Torah. And the main thing is to strengthen himself in any way that he possibly can, because there is no such thing as despair...*

*"And we all need to ask Hashem Yitbarach repeatedly to help us have the merit of coming close to the True Tzaddik, because fortunate is the person who has the merit of coming close to the True Tzaddik while he is still alive. Praiseworthy is he, and fortunate is his lot, because after his death, it is much, much harder to come close, which is why we need to increase our prayers and our supplications that we should merit while we are still alive to draw close to the True Tzaddikim. Because the Evil One is paying a lot of attention to this matter now in order to confuse the world, as the people of Israel are now very close to the end, and thus the people of Israel are now experiencing a great longing and a great yearning for Hashem Yitbarach that didn't exist in previous generations."*

*I felt as though these words had been personally written for me, and it was absolutely clear to me that I needed to get closer to the Tzaddik who'd written this amazing book. I called up Oded and asked him for the phone numbers of the two chassidim he'd brought to visit me the day my son was born; I told him that I wanted them to show me how to get closer to their Tzaddik. Oded gave me their information, and then I apologized for waking him up so early with the phone call. He told me not to worry, because he hadn't actually been sleeping; he was off shortly to say selichot at his local synagogue, and he'd just been on his way out the door when I called.*

*He invited me to join him, and I agreed, even though I had no idea what 'selichot' was. It was yet another experience that I'd never had in my life, part of a whole, vibrant other world that I simply didn't know existed, despite the fact that it was there all the time, right under my nose. On that particular morning, dozens of old men had gotten out of bed at 4:30am to come to shul to pray and to ask G-d to forgive them for all of their sins - and they were planning on doing that for a whole month. It was truly amazing to me: these people lived in one of the most secular cities in the whole world, but they weren't embarrassed by anything or anyone, they just did what their heart and soul told them to do, in utter simplicity and purity.*

*I hummed along with all the tunes for the selichot service, and my heart was skipping wildly all over the place. I was thinking about the Creator of the world, and about the fact that we all have to give an accounting of ourselves and our lives when we get to heaven, and I asked: 'G-d, where have You been all my life? Why didn't anyone tell me that I had to give You an account of how I'm spending my time down here?' That same day, I bought a ticket to Uman, and two weeks later, I flew out to meet the True Tzaddik for the first time ever in my life.*

*And since then, every single year, bli neder and b'ezrat Hashem, I come to Uman for Rosh Hashana, because once someone has tasted the Hungarian wine[12] of Rabbeinu, you can't satisfy them with any other type of wine."*

The singer / actor concluded his fascinating and well-delivered tale. The *chevra* gave him no shortage of adulations for standing up to all the anti-religious pressure and for not conforming to the Bohemian norm of his surroundings, and by the time they were done, it was already the end of the meal.

---

[12] An allusion to one of Rebbe Nachman's parables, comparing his teachings and Breslev chassidut to the finest Hungarian wine, that simply can't be matched by cheap imitations.

## Chapter 16

*Let me tell you about Tashlich, and the story of the son of the king and the son of the slave who got switched around, and of the son and daughter of the King, who got married thanks to a shidduch that was completely out of this world.*

We finished the Rosh Hashana meal, and part of the group went to rest while the other sat down to learn. They told me that soon, there was going to be another prayer session called *'Mincha'*, and that after that there would be a very special event that only happened once a year, called *'Tashlich'*. Usually, you had to do tashlich next to the sea or a river or something, but if there wasn't anything like that nearby, you could go somewhere where a sea or a lake was visible. Then, you pantomimed throwing all your sins into the water. I have to say, the whole thing sounded a bit strange to me.

I sat for a while with Nadav, and it was really nice to talk with him, because I felt that we'd both been through some fresh, ground-shaking changes in our life. My brother and most of the rest of the *chevra* were already quite a bit further along in their process, whereas Nadav had only had his 'big awakening' yesterday, and I'd only really woken up four hours ago... I asked him if he wanted to go for a walk together, and he agreed, so we left the apartment and headed off in the direction of the lake. The two of us were still on an amazing spiritual high, so we went for a dunk in one of the local streams that was full of green plants and leaves. We didn't indulge ourselves too much in the water, and just stuck to dunking under a couple of times, to try to add to the purity and *kedusha* we were both already feeling.

Afterwards, we walked around and talked for a bit, and then we just sat down somewhere and quietly contemplated the world for a couple of minutes. Part of me still wanted to talk, but part of me was feeling that right now, words were completely unnecessary. I started to understand how so many of the different experiences I'd had in my life were actually connected. At the time, I'd had no idea what was really happening, or why I'd had to go through what I went through, but now I was really starting to see everything as being part of a much bigger picture. A lot of apparently random things acquired new depth and meaning, and I started to see how it just couldn't really have been any other way, and that everything that had happened had been perfectly tailored to fit me.

I broke the silence, saying: "So, they were telling us lies the whole time?"

Nadav responded, "I don't know if they were telling us lies on purpose - our parents were told the same lies, don't forget. You know, I have no idea where the problem really started, but *Baruch Hashem*, at least it has an end. The thing that really scares me the most, is that I could have kept on wearing those blinders all my life, and been telling myself that all these religious people were the blind ones."

I asked him, "What's going to happen when we get back to Israel? Maybe, whatever experience we had here is going to fade, and we'll go back to being exactly the way we were? Maybe we're only like this here, in Uman?"

"It could happen," he said. "Although right now, I'm feeling so strongly that G-d is the only reality in the world, and this is so clear to me that I think it would take another supernatural event to even begin to convince me otherwise. Right now, I can feel 100% that there is only G-d. Do you understand what I'm telling you? He is everything and everything is Him! *Ein Od Milvado*. It's not just some empty theory or philosophical fad, it's the only reality that exists."

I understood exactly what he was telling me: G-d was constantly communicating to us via all of creation; He wasn't just hidden inside every detail of our lives and environment - everything actually *was* Him.

"But I don't get how it's all supposed to work," I said. "How can it be that G-d really is everything, but that He still gave people the option of thinking that He doesn't even exist? It's a big mystery, no? How is He managing to hide Himself away so effectively, and why is He even doing that in the first place? What's the point of Him hiding like that, when all it does is just confuse people like us, who were groping around in the darkest of dark places until just a few short hours ago? And why did He happen to open *our* eyes, when there are loads of people out there who are much smarter, and nicer, and more successful than we are, but He's not helping those people to see what's really going on?"

"I'm sorry for interrupting your conversation, but when I overheard what you were saying, it went straight to my heart." Initially, I thought one of the trees was talking to me (I guess anything's possible in Uman…) but after a couple of seconds, a *chassid* dressed all in white stepped out of the forest, and identified himself as the owner of the voice. He had short *payot*, a very spiritual air about him, and an infectious smile. "Your conversation reminded me of my own musings and yearnings and questions, back when I started my journey towards G-d and *Rabbeinu*. You were saying exactly the same sorts of things I used to say, the first couple of months after I made *teshuva*. Do you mind if I sit with you a bit?"

"With pleasure," I told him. "Be our guest," added Nadav.

"You can find the answer to your question in *Rabbeinu's* story of the exchanged children, about the son of the king and the son of the slave woman. Do you know that story?" Neither of us had ever heard of it, so our new friend launched into the tale.

"This story is so amazingly holy that even Rebbe Nachman himself said that it was a true wonder. It's a story about a king who had a slave woman in his household. On exactly the same day that a son was born to the king, a son was also born to this slave woman. The attending midwife decided to switch the babies around, just to see what would happen in the future. Of course, initially she didn't tell anybody about what she'd done, but some time later, she told someone about the exchange, and the rumor made the rounds until it even reached the ears of the king himself - who at this point, was the birth son of the slave woman.

The slave woman's son, who'd grown up in the palace as the prince, was very upset by the rumors, and fearing for his throne, he banished the true prince (who'd grown up as the slave woman's son) from his kingdom. After that, the true prince's situation continued to deteriorate, until he found himself in some of the lowest places a person can be, places that were completely unsuitable for a person of royal blood like himself. He fell into all sorts of illicit desires and bad habits, until he himself really started to believe that he must truly be the son of the slave woman. The story has all sorts of twists and turns, but eventually, the king's true son managed to regain his kingdom, and once again understood and believed that he really was the true prince and ruler all along....

"This story is one of the principal chassidic tales of the Breslever *chassidim*, and it's the secret behind the whole exile of *Am Yisrael*, who were kicked out of their country and lost their place in the world. The man who was kicked out of his home and his true position is us - and now we have to wander, scattered, amongst all the nations of the world. Today, because of our many sins, these foreign nations rule, and we are subservient to them as though we are the children of slaves and maidservants, and all of this only came about because of that initial exchange...

"And this is the secret why the nation of Israel, and each one of us individually, are still in exile - and it also explains what is happening to us, both nationally and personally. The main feature of this soul exile is that we are all mixed up with the *goyim*; we dress like them, we copy their culture, and it really seems to us as though they are the true nobility, and we need to imitate them in every way. And this is how we get further and further away from our Father in *Shamayim*.

"All this came about as a result of the sin of *Adam HaRishon*, who ate from the tree of the knowledge of good and evil - because in truth, *Am Yisrael* is really the only nation fit to govern, as each one of us is a child of the King. And the rule is this: the main aspect of slavery comes from the body, and the main aspect of freedom comes from the soul. Each of us was created to overturn his animal nature by subduing the body and making it serve the soul. And each time the body gets overcome by a physical desire or lust, our job is to break the body's desire and to force it to do the soul's bidding - and *ashrei* to whoever manages to do that! But even then, he's still in the category of being a slave, because his *avodat Hashem* still feels like hard work to him.

"But the person who succeeds in completely subjugating his body to his soul to the point that the body simply doesn't have any other desire or lust other than to serve G-d and do His will, *that* person is then accorded the title of 'Son of the King'. Why? Because he is truly doing G-d's will out of love for Him.

"And that's your situation right now. Over the last couple of days, G-d has given you a tremendous present, for free. At some point in the future, G-d is going to take away that amazing, wonderful spiritual light, and then you're going to have to work really hard to get it back, as me and few million other good people have done before you. I'm not telling you this to bring you down, G-d forbid; I just want to make sure that you're prepared for when you have to start doing the real work that's waiting for you. Welcome to the world of *Rabbeinu*!"

He was sitting between Nadav and me (remember, he'd known us a whole five minutes) and had both of his arms around our shoulders in an affectionate hug. I felt like all of us were feeling the same strong sense of unity and friendship, and a deep sense of peace that I'd never before felt in my life. Nadav took the opportunity to ask our new friend the question of questions: "How did you find out about the Creator of the world, and about *Rabbeinu*?"

*"How did I get close to Rabbeinu, and the Creator of the world? It's quite a story, and it started around six years ago. I come from a very wealthy family, and I really do mean wealthy, far beyond what most people could even imagine. My parents had three children - my brother and me, and my sister. My brother is two years older than me, and he's our company director. My sister is five years younger than me, and she's the company's marketing manager, and me? I liked to do the work 'on the ground'.*

*My family is in the construction business, and we've built properties all over Europe. Our company is behind around 15% of all European construction, so we're really talking about billions of dollars of business being done a year.*

*I started working for the family business when I was 22; by the age of 25, I already had my own expensive penthouse apartment in one of Tel Aviv's most exclusive residential buildings. By the time I was 27, I also owned expensive apartments in London, Hamburg and Paris. In that world, I was a very big success story, although clearly a lot of the credit has to go to my father, who let me take a lot of risks with the company's money.*

*The story really starts when my father decided that he wanted to start making some serious inroads into the construction business in Russia and Poland. He gave me the job of conquering Eastern Europe, and I was finding the going pretty tough. I threw myself into the task, and for a whole year solid, I lived, worked, and slept on the job. As you might expect, I made it as easy on myself as I could by buying a luxurious villa in Poland and another one in Russia, and I shuttled between the two for a whole year. At this point, I was 44 years old and still unmarried, and that was really starting to bother me.*

*Everyone around me thought I was having a great time; after all, I could do whatever I wanted without having to get anyone else's permission. I was jetting all over the world and living the 'good life' to the max - except that really, I was sunken into such excruciating mental torture that it's impossible to describe. I'm not talking about feeling embarrassed or ashamed, or even about any pressure I was getting from my family to settle down. My brother was already married with two kids, and my sister was married and had three daughters. And me? I was lonely, empty, and broken.*

*It's not that I didn't want to get married, but I spent nearly all of my time out of Israel apart from two weeks in the summer and two weeks for Pesach, and the only women I was meeting were non-Jews. Even when I was in Israel, I spent nearly all the time relaxing and trying to catch up with family and friends. When I was abroad, I naturally found myself hanging out exclusively with goyim, and I'd nearly gotten married three times already, only to call the whole thing off at the last minute. Why? Because I'd always get this suffocating feeling that I couldn't have children who'd be goyim - and I didn't even understand why!*

*Apart from the fact that it says that I'm a Jew on my teudat zehut, I didn't have any other connection to Yiddishkeit, and I really mean ZERO connection. But despite that, my heart simply wouldn't agree to me marrying out of the tribe, so I was stuck in the most difficult, agonizing position. I couldn't even bring myself to talk about what was going on, because I didn't think anyone would understand me, and they'd just tell me that I was being too picky.*

# The Stolen Light

*From their point of view, I was being offered the cream of the crop: beautiful women who came from incredibly wealthy families with the best social pedigrees in the world. But none of those things carried any weight with me, and before each wedding, I'd toss and turn on my bed endlessly, until eventually I made the decision to call it off. As a result, I'd gotten a bad reputation for being a rascal and a womanizer, but it really wasn't like that.*

*In the meantime, our business interests in Poland and Russia started to burgeon, and we won contracts to build four big complexes in Poland, plus another three projects in the Ukraine. Right from the beginning, I'd invested my heart and soul (not to mention most of my own money) into our expansion in Poland and Russia, and now that investment looked like it was going to pay off handsomely. When all was said and done, I was due to receive somewhere in the realm of two billion euros, which would quadruple my existing fortune of around 500 million. I was set to really hit the big time.*

*On one of my regular trips between Warsaw and Kiev, I was driving in my custom-built 3 million euro Mercedes, when my chauffeur suddenly asked if he could have a small break from driving. He needed to relax for a bit and drink some vodka, and then afterwards he'd be reenergized and able to continue.*

*I agreed to his request, and he pulled into the closest town. I was trying to decide whether to bother getting out of the car or not, when I caught sight of some Yemenite looking Jew with long payot who was just standing there, stroking his beard. I did a double-take: what on earth was a Yemenite chassid doing here? Not that I even knew where 'here' was in the first place. I wound down the window and I bade him hello. He enlightened me that my driver had decided to take his break in Uman.*

*"Uman? What's Uman? Where is Uman?" The Yemenite chassid informed me that there were around 1,000 Jews in Uman at the moment. It was Tu B'Shvat, the 'New Year' of the trees, and these Jews had come to Uman to pray and say the Tikun HaKlali by the grave of Rebbe Nachman of Breslev - which was the first time I'd ever even heard that name.*

*I didn't know why, but I immediately felt drawn to this Yemenite Jew, and asked him if he could take me with him to the Tzion to say the Tikun HaKlali. He was very happy to bring me with him, and on the way he told me a bit more about who Rebbe Nachman was and why people travelled from all over the world to visit his grave, and also about the Tikun HaKlali. To tell you the truth, I didn't find what he was telling me particularly interesting, but I felt like I also needed a break, however small, from all the pressure and stress of work.*

*While we were talking, he asked me if he could catch a ride with me afterwards to Kiev, because he had a flight in six hours, and didn't think he was going to make it on time if he had to wait for the bus. I happily agreed, why not? By this time we'd arrived at the grave, and both went inside and started saying the Tikun HaKlali. I didn't feel anything in particular until I got to the sentence: 'If I forget you, O Jerusalem, then let me forget my right arm, and may my tongue cleave to my palate.' It seemed to just jump out at me, and I had some vague notion that people usually said this at Jewish weddings. Yes, I could definitely remember at least one wedding where the officiating rabbi (who'd seemed like a nice guy), had said those words in a very moving way.*

*I stopped reciting for a moment, and started talking to Rebbe Nachman about helping me find a shidduch. I came straight out and asked him why wasn't I married, already. What did they want from me? 'Rebbe Nachman, you can help me! Please put a good word in for me.' I closed my eyes for a second, and then suddenly this incredibly bright light started shining straight at me, apparently coming from the direction of Rebbe Nachman's grave.*

*Right after that, I had a kind of vision, and while I knew it wasn't actually happening, felt like the most real thing I'd ever experienced in my life. I saw myself under my chuppah; I saw my bride; I saw the rabbi who was officiating at the wedding; I saw my parents, my wife's parents... I was the happiest guest at my own wedding for a good few minutes.*

*After a little while, it suddenly dawned at me that people were looking at me funny, like they thought I'd just gone mad or something. I'd come to the Tzion wearing an expensive designer suit and looking like a serious and seriously wealthy businessman, which is in fact what I was. But then, during the time of my 'vision' (this is what they told me afterwards) I'd apparently taken off my suit jacket and taken one of the prayer shawls off the chair nearby, wrapping myself up in it. Then, I'd started yelling out all the sentences that in my vision, the officiating rabbi told me to say, and then I started shaking hands with everyone that was standing next to me at the grave and wishing them mazal tov, please G-d by you, soon! Then I'd danced with them, and by this point, everyone standing close to me was convinced I was a madman.*

*The Yemenite chassid told me later that after all that, he'd been reconsidering taking a ride with me to Kiev. After all, there was no shortage of crazy lunatics in the world, and he was now convinced that I was one of them.*

*In any case, we left the Tzion together and went to my car, and on the way he invited another Yemenite chassid to join us. We started driving, and I asked them what they'd felt when they were praying by the gravesite. They told me that they just prayed, made a few heartfelt requests, learned some Torah, ate a bit, drank a bit, felt happy - and that was that. I was completely shocked, because I was sure that everyone that went to the grave was given their own personal vision, like I'd experienced.*

# The Stolen Light

*I asked them again, and this time they exchanged a long look between them. Why? Because they'd already determined that I was most likely a crazy lunatic, and here I was proving their thesis by apparently asking the same question over and over. They were clearly starting to feel uncomfortable that I was discounting everything they'd just told me, so I started to tell them about the vision I'd had by the grave.*

*After he heard me out, the Yemenite chassid told me that the vision had been nothing less than miraculous, and very unusual - and if it had happened like that, he could promise me that I was going to get married within the year. The second Yemenite guy yelled out 'Amen!', and we all exchanged phone numbers and parted as good friends.*

*I stayed on in Kiev for another two months, until Pesach rolled around and I decided to go back to Israel as I usually did to celebrate the Seder with my parents. Of course, I'm not talking about a traditional Jewish Seder, or anything even close to it. It was just an opportunity for my family to sit down around a table together. And instead of eating matza and maror, we usually ate bread and all sorts of unkosher meat, and drank champagne.*

*On one of the days of Pesach, I suddenly got the idea in my head to go visit the Kotel. I didn't have anything else particularly pressing to do, and I just fancied the idea of taking a drive down to the Western Wall. As you might expect, I had a regular chauffeur for all the places I went, and depending on my mood I'd either rent a really fancy car, or just borrow something from my parents. This time, I went for the limousine that I usually used when I was home in Israel, and I asked the chauffeur to come and pick me up at 8pm.*

*He told me that he couldn't make it then, but that he'd send a replacement driver to bring me to Jerusalem, and then would meet me there and drive me back home. As long as we got to where I needed to go, I didn't really mind who was driving.*

*At exactly 8pm, the limousine was waiting for me outside my parents' villa in Kfar Shemaryahu. I climbed in and made myself comfortable, and then realized that instead of a man in the driver's seat, there was a women, who turned out to be the sister of my regular chauffeur. She somehow looked very familiar to me, and I was racking my brains trying to remember where I might know her from. I asked her a couple of questions to see if that would jog my memory - which is when the penny dropped: my driver looked exactly like the girl that I'd married in my vision in Uman...*

*I was in complete shock; I didn't know if maybe I was dreaming it all or having another unexpected vision. We drove for a quarter of an hour in complete silence. I was completely overwhelmed by my feelings, and I could see that she was also experiencing something very strange. When we drove past the airport, I couldn't keep quiet any more, and I started to tell her everything that had happened to me in Uman. I also told her a bit about myself, and what had been going on in my life up until that point - my whole life. I'd never been as frank and honest with another human being as I was with her then. I couldn't stop talking and telling her everything about myself, even if I wanted to. It's like something else had taken over, and was operating me by remote control.*

*I spoke to her for half an hour non-stop, and when I finally stopped talking, mostly from sheer exhaustion, she pulled the car over to the side of the road, and then said to me:*

*'You probably aren't going to believe this, but last night, I dreamt that my Saba, who died around ten years ago and was a big tzaddik, came to visit me. In my dream, he told me that tomorrow, I was going to meet my husband. I asked him how I would know who he was, and he told me it would be the man who told me a story about Rebbe Nachman from Uman. He said that the man who did this would be the husband that G-d had designated for me from the beginning of time.'*

*Both of us started sobbing, and we continued crying the whole rest of the way to Jerusalem. We got to the house of her brother, the original driver. Instead of him taking over as planned, we got out of the car and I asked him if he'd be prepared to take me to his parents' home, to discuss the plans for our forthcoming wedding. He started yelling at me, because he knew of my bad reputation. Every time I needed a driver when I was back in Israel, I called him, so he was well aware of my three broken engagements.*

*After the initial shock had worn off, he calmed down and asked me to promise that I wasn't going to mess with his sister. She was very, very dear to him, and she was a sensitive, spiritual soul. Despite the fact that she was 30 years old, she'd never been married before, or even close - she hadn't even had a boyfriend before. I promised him that I was completely serious, and only after I managed to convince him, did he agree for me to meet his parents.*

*He drove us down to his parents' very modest home in Jerusalem's Bucharim Quarter, and we went inside. His parents were a religious couple, getting on in age. We sat down, my future wife and I, and told them that we wanted to get married. Her father asked me if I was intending to keep Shabbat, and also if I was going to keep the laws of family purity. I told him that I'd do whatever my wife decided. The father nodded his head in agreement, and his wife let out a few piercing 'yela-yelas', before she broke the traditional plate on the floor and then brought out some wine and cookies. We were officially engaged!*

# The Stolen Light

*My parents reacted somewhat differently. I called them to let them know that in another hour or so, I was bringing my fiancée home to meet them. When we turned up, they didn't break a plate on the floor, and instead I got the distinct impression that they wanted to smash a plate over my head. They were completely against the wedding, even after I'd told them the whole, amazing story that clearly showed that everything had been orchestrated by Divine Providence. But with their typical coolness and cynicism, they rejected everything I said, and told me they weren't going to help me to pay for anything. I couldn't help but find that amusing, because they'd obviously forgotten that my recent deals in Poland and Russia had set me on track to become the richest member of my family.*

*In short - we got married, of course. Today, we have twin boys, Nachman and Natan, aged two years old, and we are living such a good life in every sense of the word. By the time we got to the brit, my parents had decided to make up with us and to accept us for who we are. I'm still working hard and still earning a lot of money, Baruch Hashem, and the only thing I'm lacking is some of the amazing insight and inspiration I got at the beginning of my journey - but when I was listening to your conversation, I got it back again, at least for a second.*

*"Ashreichem, Am Yisrael, ashreichem, that you had the merit to come close to the True Tzaddik, Rebbe Nachman."*

You know, out of all the Rebbe Nachman stories I was told, this one touched me the most. I kind of felt like the story I'd just heard was a modern-day twist on the story of the exchanged children. We continued to sit there, silently thoughtful, for another few minutes.

We left the forest as the sun was already starting to sink down in the sky and headed back towards the lake. There, we were met by a sight that you couldn't do justice to with mere words. An enormous number of *chassidim* were gathered around the lake; tens of thousands of holy princes were standing there, crying out to *Hashem* and trying to throw their sins away. I watched them for a moment, and then got the urge to go and join them.

Exactly then, my brother Motty appeared out of nowhere and gave me a big hug.

"Where are you, my brother, where are you?" he asked me.

"I'm in heaven, my brother," I replied. "I'm in *Gan Eden*."

"Sure enough, it is *Gan Eden* here right now," he agreed. "But the question is, how do we take it back with us to Israel? How do we hold onto this when we're back in our routine and back in the daily grind of trying to make a living, educating the children, and pointlessly hating other people?"

"Someone needs to organize free trips to Uman for every single Jew, so that every single person has the merit of experiencing this at least once in their lifetime. They should make it a law."

"We are trying to bring *Rabbeinu* into every Jew's hearts by writing books about him, and singing songs about him, and teaching classes about him, because once a person gets even the smallest taste of the sweetness that is *Rabbeinu*, he automatically starts wanting to come visit him. That's what happened to all of us here, no?"

We left it at that, and went to join the other thousands of Jews who were busy throwing their sins away. I yelled out all the words to the *Tashlich* prayer, and Nadav too was all lit up with spiritual light, and glowing like a full moon.

We started dancing, and then just kept on dancing for a whole hour, as different people came to join us; some were '*frum* from birth', some were *baal teshuvas*, just like us. Who can even begin to describe the tremendous feeling of unity and *achdut* that hung over us all, and bound us all together? From the other side of the circle of dancing men, Nadav was yelling out to me:

"Only *Rabbeinu*…only *Rabbeinu* could do this…"

And I had to agree with him. Everything that was happening around us here was completely supernatural; here, all thought was clear, and all hearts were one.

## Epilogue

So you probably already guessed that my big plan to leave Uman a millionaire didn't exactly work out. But having said that, I still had quite a lot of money that I'd taken from the pockets of Sergei (or whatever his name was) while he was passed out on the floor of my apartment.

I understood that *Shamayim* was giving me a big test with that money now. I told the *chevra* the story, and I asked them to help me figure out what to do with it.

Of course, I didn't tell them *everything* - that I'd been planning to rip everyone off myself. I decided to keep that part of the story strictly between me and G-d. Although now that I write that, it seems that *Rabbeinu* must also have known about it somehow, and maybe even had a hand in arranging how everything turned out. What do you think, was Rebbe Nachman mixed up in the whole story, one way or another?

My friends advised me that after the *Chag* was finished, I should try to do the mitzvah of *hashavat aveda*, or 'returning lost things', and honestly, I was happy to try and get the money back to its owners, for a few different reasons which I'll try to explain:

Firstly, I was really happy that I'd managed to stand up to what was an enormous test for me. In the not-too-distant past, it wouldn't even have crossed my mind to try and find the people the money really belonged to, especially as it hadn't even been me that had stolen it from them, but Sergei. I felt that maybe my heart was a tiny bit more pure than it had been before.

Secondly, I'd met quite a few of the people here (as you now know), and I'd realized that not everyone was rolling in money, and in fact, quite the opposite. Most of the people here had gone to a lot of effort to try and scrape the money together that they needed to make the trip.

On top of all this, I'd also had this very deep realization pop into my head - that all my life was mapped out and planned right down to the very last detail. As such, every shekel had its right place and right purpose. I had to give the money back to its rightful owners so that they could do everything G-d had intended for them to do with it. When I told Motty this, he started guffawing, and told me that newbie or not, I was already discovering some very deep things. Then he launched into this lengthy explanation of how everything we own is just a vessel, and that we need to use that vessel in a way that will rectify both it and us.

In any event, I decided to give the money back. Once the holiday was over, I went to talk to the heads of the committee that oversees everything in Uman for Rosh Hashana, and I gave them the wad of cash. They made an announcement over the loudspeaker telling the whole *kehilla* that if anyone discovered their money had been stolen, they should report to them and reclaim it. They also asked everyone to check their wallets carefully to ensure nothing had been taken.

A few hours later, thirty or forty *chassidim* had shown up to reclaim the money that had been stolen from them - but I was still left with $25,000! It wasn't clear to me how that had happened. I thought that maybe, people had understated how much had been stolen from them just to be on the safe side, or that people didn't want to claim the money just in case it wasn't the same money that had actually been taken from them. Things like that happen in Uman.

One of the big rabbis present ruled that I should keep the remaining money, and that I should try to use it for something that would be for the good of the community. In other words, I should use it to pay for something that would help a lot of people, and not just me. That way, the money would somehow bring some benefit back to the people who'd lost it, either directly, or via the people they were close to.

So I sat and thought for ages about what to do with the money, when suddenly this light bulb went off in my head. I realized that it was no coincidence that I'd had such a bizarre experience in Uman. Similarly, it was no coincidence that I'd hooked up with such an amazing group of people, or heard so many out-of-this-world stories about how they'd found Rebbe Nachman. I no longer had any doubt that Rebbe Nachman had played a big part in arranging things, right down to sending me all this money. So I decided that in his merit, I was going to take the time to write down everything that had happened to me, and all the stories I'd been told, and that I was going to get it printed up to give to other people.

So that's what I did, and in the greater scheme of things, it really didn't take very long to do at all. And now, you've almost finished reading it. Parts of it might be a little mixed up, but I promise you that it all actually happened, and it's just how I remembered it or experienced it. I might have added in a word or two here or there just to make things a bit clearer, because as I'm sure you know, saying something is not the same as writing it. But I wrote all the stories out exactly as they were told to me, and exactly the way they'd be told to you by the people involved, if you took the time to track them down and talk to them yourself.

I'm sure you're sitting on the edge of your seat, wanting to know the answer to the $200,000 question: did I make *teshuva* in the end, or not? Did I also turn into a flaming Breslev *baal teshuva?*

Well, let me tell you the truth, in all sincerity and with all due respect: I'm still shell-shocked by everything that happened to me, and everything that I heard and saw. One thing I can tell you for sure is that I'm definitely not the same person that I was before Rosh Hashana.

I'm not trying to run away from the whole new world I was shown in Uman, and I think I'm going to be doing lots more new things now and in the future, but who knows how it's all going to turn out, or how I'm really going to end up?

I really don't know if I'm going to go 'all the way', but what I can tell you is that the idea scares me much less than it used to.

Sincerely yours,

Avi Neuman

*The End*

# The Stolen Light
Glossary

**Abba:** Father, dad

**Achdut:** Unity

**Adam HaRishon:** Adam, the first man

**Ahavat Yisrael:** The love of the people of Israel

**Al netilat yedayim:** The mitzvah of ritually washing the hands upon waking, or before eating bread.

**Aliya:** Going up, both to the Torah and to the land of Israel.

**Am Yisrael:** The Nation of Israel

**Amen sela:** *Colloquially:* 'Amen until the end of time'

**Amah/Amot:** A biblical measurement, usually translated as a cubit

**Arba Minim:** The Four Species, used on the festival of Sukkot

**Ashkenazim:** Jews of German / European descent

**Ashrey:** 'Happy is'

**Avodat Hashem:** The service of G-d

**Avreich:** A serious student of Torah, usually a full-time learner.

**Baal teshuva:** *Literally:* A master of repentance. Someone who comes back to G-d

**Bagrut:** Israeli high school equivalent of the SATs

**Bar Mitzvah:** The ceremony when a Jewish male reaches the age of 13 and can be called up to the Torah for the first time

**Baruch Hashem:** Thank G-d

**Bat kol:** A voice emanating from Heaven

**Beis Yaacov:** A strictly orthodox network of high schools for girls, based on the philosophy of founder, Sara Schnirer

**Beit HaMikdash:** The Temple

**Beit Midrash:** Study hall

**Bezrat Hashem:** With Hashem's help

**Birkat Hamazon:** The blessing after food

**Bitul:** Self-nullification

**Bli neder:** 'Without making a vow'

**Bracha:** A blessing

**Chabadnik:** A follower of Chabad chassidut

**Chag:** A Jewish festival

**Chareidi:** A person very strict in keeping Torah laws, who usually wears a black suit and white shirt

**Chas V'shalom:** G-d forbid

**Chassid; plural, chassidim:** An orthodox religious Jew who adheres to tenements of the Chassidic movement originating in Eastern Europe, 18$^{th}$ century

**Chaval al ha zman:** Untranslatable! A cross between 'wow', 'oy', and 'that's amazing'

**Chavruta:** A study partner; usually refers to Torah study.

**Chazal:** Our sages

**Chazzan:** Leader of the prayer service

**Cheder:** Religious pre-school

## The Stolen Light

**Chevra:** The group. Refers to a social group, gathering of friends

**Chiddush:** An original Torah idea.

**Chik-chak:** Israeli slang expression, 'in the blink of an eye'

**Chiloni:** Secular person

**Chizzuk:** Strengthening, spiritual encouragement

**Chumash:** The five books of the Torah

**Chuppah:** The marriage canopy used in Jewish weddings

**Chutz l'aretz:** 'Outside the land', refers to anywhere outside of Israel

**Chutzpadik:** Brazen, shameless, cheeky

**Dafka:** On purpose

**Davening:** Praying

**Dvar Torah; plural, divrei Torah:** Words of Torah

**Dvekut:** Complete attachment, merged in G-d's Oneness

**Ein Od Milvado:** There is nothing other than Him (G-d)

**Emuna:** Faith, particularly faith in G-d

**Eretz Yisrael:** The Land of Israel

**Erev:** The eve of

**Erev Rav:** *Literally:* 'mixed multitude'; refers to people who externally appear to be Jews, but who are not actually pure of soul.

**Etrog:** A yellow citrus fruit, one of the Four Species used on Sukkot

**Frum:** An orthodox, religious Jew

**Gabbai:** Person responsible for arranging and managing the service in a synagogue

**Galut:** Exile

**Gan Eden:** The Garden of Eden

**Gedolei HaDor:** The spiritual leaders of the generation

**Gehinnom:** Purgatory

**Gemach:** A free loan fund for money or items

**Gemara:** The Talmud

**Gematria:** Numerology of the Hebrew letters

**Geula:** Redemption

**Glatt:** Usually used in reference to food that is kosher according to the most stringent standards

**Goy: plural, goyim:** Gentile

**Hakadosh Baruch Hu:** Literally: 'The Holy One, blessed be He'; another term
for G-d

**Halacha:** The Jewish code of law

**Har Sinai:** Mount Sinai

**Hashem:** *Literally:* 'The Name'; another term for G-d

**Hashem Yitbarach:** G-d, may He be blessed

**Hashgacha Pratit:** Divine Providence

**Hishtadlut:** *Literally:* 'Effort'. Used in relation to how much effort a person should put in versus how much they believe G-d is really doing everything

# The Stolen Light

**Hitbodedut:** Personal prayer. The practice of pouring our one's heart to G-d in one's own words

**Ilui neshama:** *Literally:* 'raising of the soul'; refers to elevating the soul of a dead person, usually by doing a good deed in their name

**Imma:** Mother, mom

**Kaddish:** The prayer said for the soul of a dead person

**Kal v'chomer:** A logical argument in the Talmud where a principal can be derived from a 'serious' matter to a 'lighter' matter

**Kappara:** Atonement

**Kedusha:** Holiness

**Kehilla:** Community

**Kever:** Grave

**Kibud Horim:** Honoring one's parents

**Kiddush:** The blessing made over grape juice or wine at the beginning of a holiday or Shabbat meal

**Kippa; plural, kippot:** Skullcap

**Kivrei Tzaddikim:** Graves of holy people

**Klipot:** *Literally:* 'Husks or shells'; a kabbalistic term referring to the realm of evil

**Kloiz:** The main synagogue in Uman, originally built by Rabbi Natan to accommodate the growing number of visitors on Rosh Hashana

**Kollel:** Similar to a yeshiva, except the students are normally married with families

**Kupat Uman:** A cash box for savings to pay for a ticket to Uman

**Le'shem Shamayim:** *Literally:* 'For the name of Heaven'; something that's done altruistically

**Litvak:** *Literally:* 'Lithuanian'; refers to one of the distinct groups within Judaism

**L'mehadrin:** An expression meaning 'strictly kosher'; often applied to food products, but also religious practices

**Lulav:** A young palm branch, one of the Four Species used on Sukkot

**Maariv:** The evening prayer service

**Mamash:** Literally, actually, seriously

**Mazal tov:** a term of celebration, congratulation and good wishes

**Massechet:** Tractate

**Mikveh:** A Jewish ritual pool of water. Immersing in a mikveh cleanses a person from their spiritual impurity

**Mikveh Kelim:** A Jewish ritual pool of water used for cutlery, plates and other items that require ritual immersion before they can be used

**Mincha:** The regular afternoon prayer service

**Minhag:** Custom

**Miniot:** *Literally:* 'obstacles'; refers to all the apparently real, but actually imaginary problems and difficulties that usually occur when a person wants to travel to Uman

**Minyan:** A quorum of at least 10 adult males, the minimum required for prayers to be considered as coming from a congregation

**Mishna, plural: Mishnayot:** The Oral Law

**Misrad Hapnim:** Israeli Ministry of the Interior

**Mitzva de'oraita:** A deed or obligation derived directly from the written Torah itself

# The Stolen Light

**Mitzvah, plural mitzvot:** A good deed, a Torah obligation

**Mochin d'Gadlut:** A kabbalistic term referring to a state of expanded consciousness.

**Moranu:** *Literally:* 'Our teacher'; often used in Breslev circles to refer to Rebbe Nachman and also Rabbi Natan

**Moshav:** A socialist, agricultural settlement, similar to a Kibbutz

**Moshiach:** Messiah

**Muktzeh:** Any item that cannot be used by a Jew on Shabbat

**Na-Nach:** A distinct sub-group of Breslev chassidim known for their white kippot and penchant for dancing in public. Connected to Rabbi Israel Ber Odessa, 'The Saba'

**Nachas:** Enjoyment

**Nachat Ruach:** peaceful spirit, or soul; peace of mind.

**Neshama:** Soul

**Netz:** Sunrise, dawn

**Niggun:** A chassidic melody without words

**Nu:** 'So?'

**Off the derech:** *Literally:* 'Off the path'; refers to a Jew who has left or lessened their religious observance

**Olam chesed yibaneh:** A famous biblical phrase: 'A world of kindness He will build'.

**Parnassa:** Livelihood

**Payot:** Side-curls

**Pintele Yid:** Yiddish expression; refers to the inextinguishable spark of holiness that's present in every Jewish soul

**Posek:** An halachic decisor, usually a rabbi of senior standing

**Rabbeinu:** *Literally:* 'Our Rebbe'; used in Breslev circles to refer to Rebbe Nachman

**Rabbeinu Hakadosh:** *Literally:* 'Our holy Rebbe'; used in Breslev circles to refer to Rebbe Nachman.

**Rachmana Litzlan:** *Literally:* 'The Merciful One should save us'.

**Rashbi:** Acronym for the Tzaddik **R**abbi **Sh**imon **B**ar **Y**ochai, who lived around 2,000 years ago

**Rasha:** a wicked person

**Ribono shel olam:** Master of the World; another term for G-d.

**Rosh Chodesh:** The beginning of the new Jewish month, based on the lunar cycle

**Ruach Hakodesh:** *Literally:* 'The holy spirit'; denotes tremendous spiritual insight and knowledge.

**Saba:** Grandfather, grandpa.

**Seder:** The festive meal that occurs on the first night of the Passover festival (and outside of Israel, also on the following night)

**Sefirot:** A kabbalistic term connected to the 10 spheres of creation

**Segula:** A religious practice designed to bring about a specific end, e.g., a segula for making a good living or for having an easy birth

**Selichot:** Special prayers of repentance that are said in Elul, the month preceding Rosh Hashana, either for several days, or throughout the whole month

**Sephardim:** Jews of Spanish or North African descent

**Shabbat:** The Jewish Sabbath

**Shabbat shalom:** The traditional greeting between Jews on the Sabbath

# The Stolen Light

**Shabbos goy:** A non-Jew who helps their Jewish neighbors to
kindle fires etc, on the Sabbath, and other work forbidden for Jews to do

**Shacharit:** The morning prayer service

**Shalom bayit:** Tranquil home

**Shamash:** Attendant

**Shas:** The written compilation of the Oral Law

**Shechina:** The aspect of Hashem's presence here in this world

**Shema Yisrael:** The opening line of a prayer said in the morning and
evening,
and one of the main expressions of faith for Jews

**Shamayim:** Heavens

**Sheva brachot:** The seven blessings given to a bride and groom

**Shidduch:** Marriage partner; eligible prospect for marriage

**Shiksa:** Pejorative term for a non-Jewish woman

**Shinui:** Performing an act that's usually forbidden on Shabbat or a
Jewish festival in an unusual way, to minimize any transgression of the
halacha

**Shlep:** To drag

**Shomer Shabbat:** Shabbat observant

**Shnorrer:** Beggar

**Shpilkes:** Yiddish term, referring to a state of high anxiety and anticipation

**Shtieblach:** The plural of 'shtiebl', a Yiddish term referring to an
informal synagogue or place of learning

**Shul:** Yiddish slang term for synagogue

**Siddur:** The standard daily prayer book

**Simanim:** *Literally:* 'symbols'. Symbolic foods that are eaten at the start of the evening meal on both nights of Rosh Hashana

**Simcha:** Happiness; can also refer to a happy occasion like a wedding

**Simchat Torah:** A religious festival celebrating the Torah

**Sitra Achra:** *Literally,* 'The Other Side'; the dark side, evil

**Tallit:** Four-cornered prayer shawl

**Talmid Chacham:** A learned Torah scholar

**Talmud:** The Oral Law

**Talmud Torah:** Network of religious boys schools

**Tanach:** The first letters of: 'Torah, Naviim and Ketuvim', *literally*: Torah, the Prophets and the Writings

**Tefillin:** Phylacteries; black boxes containing holy texts that are worn on the arm and forehead

**Teshuva:** *Literally:* 'Returning', as in 'returning to G-d'

**Teudat Zehut:** Israeli ID card

**Tikun Chatzot:** *Literally:* 'The Midnight Rectification'; prayers said at midnight

**Tikun HaKlali:** *Literally:* 'The General Rectification'; Ten Psalms (16, 32, 41, 42, 59, 77, 90, 105, 137, 150) prescribed by Rebbe Nachman as the spiritual remedy for every problem

**Tikun; plural, tikunim:** Spiritual rectification

**Tizku l'mitzvot:** 'may you merit more mitzvot'

# The Stolen Light

**Toivel:** To immerse in a mikveh

**Traif:** Non-kosher food

**Tzaddik:** A saintly person; a very holy person

**Tzedaka:** Charity

**Tzion:** The area around Rebbe Nachman's grave

**Yemach shemam:** *Literally:* 'May their names be obliterated'

**Yeshiva Katana:** Religious equivalent of elementary school for boys in Israel

**Yeshiva Gedola:** Religious equivalent of high school for boys in Israel

**Yetzer Hara:** 'The Evil Inclination'

**Yishtabach shemo:** 'May His Name be praised'

**Yishtabach shemo la'ad:** 'May His Name be praised forever'

**Yom Kippur:** A fast day and day of atonement; the holiest Jewish festival of the year

**Yom Tov:** *Literally:* 'A good day'; term used for Jewish religious festival days

**Zchut:** Merit

**Z"l: Zichrono Levracha:** 'May his memory be for a blessing'

**Zimun:** A quorum of at least three men required in order to recite the opening section in the grace after meals

**Z"tl: Zecher Tzaddik Levracha:** 'May the Tzaddik's memory be for a blessing'

To Find Out
About Group Trips to Uman
And For More Breslev Teachings
or Products

Visit Our Website

www.NaNachNation.org

www.ingramcontent.com/pod-product-compliance
Lightning Source LLC
LaVergne TN
LVHW011910080426
835508LV00007BA/332